Pimping God's Word

The Rise and Fall of Pastor N.O. Goode

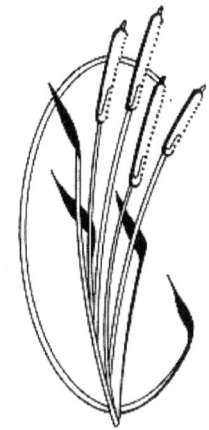

Pimping God's Word

The Rise and Fall of Pastor N.O. Goode

by
Brother James

Editor
Ray Glandon

Senior Publisher
Steven Lawrence Hill Sr.

Awarded Publishing House
ASA Publishing Company
Established Since 2005

A Publisher Trademark Cover page

ASA Publishing Company
Nominated for the 2012 BBB Torch Award
105 E. Front St., Suite 201A, Monroe, Michigan 48161
United States of America
www.asapublishingcompany.com

All Rights Reserved. No part of this publication may be reproduced, stored in a retrieval system or transmitted in any form or by any means electronic, mechanical, photocopying, recording, taping, web distribution, information storage, or otherwise, without the prior written permission of the publisher. Author/writer rights to "Freedom of Speech" protected by and with the "1st Amendment" of the Constitution of the United States of America. This novel is a work of fiction. With this title page, the reader is notified that this novel is in Christian humor form, and the publisher does not assume, and expressly disclaims any obligation to obtain and/or include any other information other than that provided by the author. Any belief system, promotional motivations, including but not limited to the use of non-fiction characters and/or characteristics of this book, are within the boundaries of the author's own creativity and/or testimony in order to reflect the nature and concept of the book.

Any and all vending sales and distribution not permitted without full book cover and this title page.

Copyrights©2012 Henry James (Brother James), All Rights Reserved
Book: Pimping God's Word *"The Rise and Fall of Pastor N.O. Goode"*

Date Published: 11.12.12
Edition: 1 *Trade Paperback*
Book ASAPCID: 2380604
ISBN: 978-1-886528-48-2
Library of Congress Cataloging-in-Publication Data

This book was published in the United States of America.
State of Michigan

A Publisher Trademark Title page

Dedication

I dedicate this work to the faithful and righteous men and women of God who DID NOT use and ARE NOT using the Word of God and the pulpit to enhance their socio-economic status and their material conditions in life. I dedicate this book to those true under-shepherds of God who never aspired to lead a "Mega Church" but were content like the Apostle Paul, no matter their situation ... whether well fed or hungry; whether they were poor or with financial means to make their primary living through their own labor and not from the labor of their congregations. It has often been said that the African American Preacher is the only man, and now woman, who in many instances does not depend upon the larger society (in the vernacular of the street "THE MAN") to earn a living.

I truly and sincerely dedicate this work to Pastors who are nothing like the one featured in this work of fiction.

I dedicate this book to men like my late father, the Reverend Robert Walter (RW) James.

b

Acknowledgements

I would like to thank the following people who in some way helped me to become the writer I am today.

First and foremost, I thank Almighty God for allowing me to emanate from the family which raised and shaped my world view. This world view was shaped by all the people I got to know and all the spiritual, emotional and geographic boundaries I dwelled and survived in, in this, my long and arduous Christian walk.

Secondly, I would like to thank my mother, Mrs. Juanita James (Ms. James), whose undying love for her children drove us to seek higher education. My mother refused to believe the Louisville, Kentucky Public School System's assessment of me, although I had failed the Standard IQ test miserably in the first grade. My mother, along with my first grade teacher, Mrs. Webbie, refused to allow me to be cast in "Group Four," a group at that time established to mainstream those students with learning disabilities. So, I thank God for my mother and Mrs. Webbie.

I thank my father, whom I have previously mentioned for imbuing me with a sense of propriety and a tremendous work ethic.

I also must acknowledge all the public school teachers I had in the Louisville School System and the various educational institutions I attended. They were all true to their profession and helped me develop a voracious appetite for learning, reading and writing. There is one teacher, however, who will forever stand out in my mind, and she was my sixth grade teacher, Mrs. Gilmore. She was, in my most learned opinion, the Marva Collins of the Louisville, Kentucky Public School system. She guided her students so diligently that most of us were reading and writing at the sophomore college level while again we were only in the sixth grade. She was truly a master teacher.

I also want to thank my dear friend, Terry Herron, for taking the time to proof read and make suggestions to my works. Her assistance in this project was invaluable.

My list of people I must thank also includes my editor Ray Glandon. Ray, if this novel achieves any critical acclaim, you will have played a tremendous role in its success. Your skills as an editor are nonpareil. I sincerely thank you for your patience and outstanding expertise.

There is one other person I need to thank, and that is Pastor Jake Gaines, of Synagogue Baptist Church in Detroit. Pastor Gaines, your encouragement and assistance in directing me to an editor and publisher was invaluable. I will never forget your assistance.

I would also like to thank you, the reader, and hopefully a purchaser of this work of fiction.

Finally, I thank God for all the people I encountered in my entire life who were either an asset, a friend, a confidante and a joy to me, or intentional adversaries and backbiters (haters), who were envious of my God given gifts. I learned much from both groups. I pray that those whom I may have offended along this winding and sometimes difficult-to-navigate river called "LIFE" will forgive me if my offenses to them were a result of being naive, inexperienced, or just plain dumb! I have grown in grace and know that I have not always done the right thing.

So again, I sincerely pray for forgiveness and as the old saying goes,

"We all make mistakes!" I have tried to live by the adage of the venerable philosopher, Confucius, when he said, "If you make a mistake, and you do not correct that mistake, then you have made yet another mistake!"

Preface

Let me say from the outset that this is truly a pure work of fiction. My purpose in creating this work is not to denigrate or cast negative aspersions upon the African American Church or its leadership. In other words, I am not trying to give the modern African American Church a black eye. Rather, my intent is to point out to many of the African American church congregants the signs of false teachers and false preachers who have for too long preyed upon those of us who tried to gain a better understanding of God's Word. If your pastor can not break down the Word of God where you clearly understand it for yourself, then your pastor is suspect. If after leaving church one Sunday you encounter a friend who asks you what your pastor's sermon was about, and your response is, "I don't know, but he sure did preach," then you and your pastor are suspect. What do I mean by "suspect"? I mean to state categorically that neither you nor your pastor is following God's command to "Study to show thyself approved." If you do not study the word of God at home, attend Sunday School or Bible Study on a regular basis and have no obstacle prohibiting your attendance, then you are "Suspect"! You are a nominal Christian, and that is diametrically opposed to the teachings in the Word of God. We are to study and then insure that what is being espoused across the pulpit is truly the Word of God and not some words of a man or woman whose only intent is to enrich themselves.

The Apostle Paul addressed the coming of these false teachers, preachers and prophets when he wrote in II Corinthians 11: 13-15: "For such men are false apostles, deceitful workmen, disguising themselves as apostles of Christ. And no wonder, for even Satan disguises himself as an angel of light. So it is no surprise if his servants also disguise themselves as servants of righteousness. Their end will correspond to their deeds."

Too many "Christians" chose to be spoon-fed, meaning the only time they pick up their Bible is on Sunday and the only scriptures they read are those they are directed to by their pastor. It is my contention that if people are to be spiritual and love the Lord, they must "check" what their pastor says from the pulpit and at Bible Study. Any pastor who does not want his or her congregants to study the Word of God but to rely solely on him or her is a false teacher. Just my opinion! We must be like the Bereans of old who, as it is written in Acts 17:11; "Now the Bereans were of more noble character than the Thessalonians, for they received the message with great eagerness and examined the Scriptures **every day** to see if what Paul said was true."

We must have some tools to build that better understanding of God's Word. The King James Version of the Bible is beautifully written. Its prose and rhythm are beyond compare, but no one talks that way today. So I highly recommend that you invest in the following "tools" to enhance your study of God's Word. First, you will need a Study Bible whose modern translation was derived from the King James Version. One such translation is the New International Version or the Life Application Study Bible. Second, you will need a good Bible Dictionary. Third, you will need a good Bible Commentary. Fourth, you will want to have an exhaustive Concordance of the Bible, and fifth, you might want to purchase a Bible Handbook. All of these "tools" are readily available in your major bookstores, and if you are fortunate to have a Bible Book Store in your community, you might get a better deal there.

There is a simple litmus test for all serious, faithful and true preachers, and this litmus test states, "This is a true saying, if a man desires the office of a bishop (Pastor, Apostle, Elder, etc., whatever your spiritual leader calls him or herself), he desireth a good work." A bishop then must be blameless, the husband of one wife (not a polygamous man or an adulterer, or as we say these days, not "a playa." This dictate would not preclude a decent single man from being a pastor), vigilant, sober, of good behavior, given to hospitality, apt to teach; Not given to wine, no striker, not greedy of filthy lucre; but patient, not a brawler, not covetous; One that ruleth well his own house, having his children in subjection with all gravity; (For if a man know not how to rule his own house, how shall he take care of the church of God?) Not a novice, lest being lifted up with pride he fall into the condemnation of the devil. Moreover, he must have a good report of them which are without; lest he fall into reproach and the snare of the devil." (1 Timothy 3:1-7)

So, given the litmus test above, you may ask why I wrote this fictional work if my intent was not to disparage the African American Church and its leadership? Are not all Church Leaders righteous and faithful to their flock? Unfortunately, my response is, NO! While my intent and motivation for writing this book is pure, I hope to show how we sometimes make god's and goddesses of our pastors, and they in turn govern themselves accordingly. But when you read this work, just maybe some truth about a church you have heard about (because I am sure nothing like what I have written here has or is happening in your church or a church in your community- WINK – WINK!) may resonate with you. Just maybe some of what appears here, especially those traits manifested in my fictionalized characterizations, will give you cause to pause and think about those whom we have entrusted our eternal reward. Just maybe while riding in a taxi cab talking to the cabdriver about the latest church news in that community, or reading a newspaper, or watching the news, or simply talking to a friend who is disgruntled with their church, just maybe the things I hear serves as my inspiration for what follows. My father used to say that Jesus and the Apostles were the "model preachers." What palaces did they live in? How many servants did they have? How blessed financially and materially were they? I have heard stories that have distressed me because men and women who purport themselves as being sincere men and women of God reside in mansions, drive extremely expensive cars, wear outfits, the cost of which would take some of their congregants months to make enough money to purchase just one of these outfits, and some even have their own personal jet airplanes to transport them hither and yon while their church sits like the Taj Mahal in the midst of a community that is devastated by abject poverty, illiteracy, teenage pregnancy, overwhelming unemployment and underemployment. We, the congregants, seem to derive some type of vicarious enjoyment out of seeing our religious leader living the "Life Style of the Rich and Famous" while we are just getting by! My intent here is to makes us aware that the Revelation of Jesus Christ warns us about the Anti-Christ, the false teachers/preachers and the churches whose focus will be on teaching false doctrines and the accumulation of money. I pray that I shed light on these truths.

Finally, there is an old saying that, "If you throw a rock into a pack of dogs, only the dog that gets hit yelps." Just something for my critics to think about, should I have any… critics that is!

j

Disclaimer

This is a pure work of **FICTION!** Any resemblance to any character in this work of fiction to anyone living or deceased is purely coincidental. This is a work of fiction that was spawned by the numerous dreams and conversations I have had about the ills of the African American Church and the false preachers and teachers therein. It is also inspired by the writings of the Apostles, especially Apostle Paul and Apostle John who wrote and spoke numerous times about the ills of the first century A.D. church. I sincerely pray that no one is offended in any way should they assume incorrectly that I am targeting them or think they were the inspiration for my characters.

Brother James

Pimping God's Word

The Rise and Fall of Pastor N.O. Goode

by
Brother James

In the Beginning
Many will follow their shameful ways and will bring the way of truth into disrepute. In their greed these teachers will exploit you with stories they have made up. Their condemnation has long been hanging over them, and their destruction has not been sleeping.

II Peter 2:2:3 NIV

In the New Testament era there were preachers who enriched themselves by distorting the word of God and teaching doctrines that were designed to enrich these false preachers and their families.

These false preachers were a constant source of irritation and a major distraction to Paul and the other Apostles. In essence, these false preachers were Pimping the Word of God!

While the form of these "Pimps" has changed, their essence over the centuries remains the same! **Brother James**

ASA Publishing Company

County Court House, 10:12AM Two Weeks Ago Today:

"All Rise! The 24th District Court is now in session, the Honorable Martina Justus presiding!" The bailiff shouts as everyone in the overcrowded courtroom QUICKLY rises to their feet.

"Please be seated," Judge Martina Justus says as she gracefully moves her LONG robe aside so she might sit in a ladylike fashion.

Sighing deeply, Judge Justus says, "I see all counsel are present so we might proceed. It is my understanding that Pastor Nathan Obadiah Goode has decided to enter a guilty plea and let the court render the applicable punishment. Pastor Goode is that your desire?"

Pastor N. O. Goode, a tall, sixty-ish, almond colored black man slowly rises from his seat. He rises slowly as if he is struggling to get up because his girth has him stuck in his chair. He has the build of a football lineman. He is impeccably dressed in a lavender three piece suit with a tie that really accents his suit. He is also wearing a pair of alligator shoes that perfectly match the color of his suit. His attorney and co-counsel simultaneously rise to face the judge, each rubbing shoulders with him.

"Hmm! He looks real nervous," whispers an elderly black woman whose cheap coal black wig sits slightly crooked atop her head, a few silver hairs from her real hair appearing at the temples. She and her great granddaughter are sitting two rows directly behind the defense table.

"You are right, Big Momma! He does look very nervous, and he just ought to be - the crook!" the young girl responded empathically.

"Pastor Goode, it is the court's understanding that you want to plead guilty to all charges to avoid a lengthy trial. Is that correct?" Judge Justus asks.

"Yes, Your Honor. I am ashamed and embarrassed and I just want this whole ordeal over with! I want to end the pain and mental anguish I have inflicted upon my family!"

"Your family!" Judge Justus interrupts sarcastically. Her voice rising.

"What about all the members of your church and others in this community that you have hurt through your deception and scheming. Using the word of God to enrich yourself, in my mind, is one of the most egregious of all offenses. Sir, I ask you what about those who trusted you, leaned on you and now you want to talk about sparing your FAMILY from Mental Anguish! Let me stop!" Judge Justus says emphatically waving her hands in the air as she simultaneously and vigorously shakes her head from side to side. "Pastor Goode, I ask you again! Do you want to plead guilty to all charges brought against you and face the appropriate punishment as prescribed by law?"

"Yes Your Honor," Pastor N. O. Goode says meekly looking down at his reflection in the well polished surface of the defense table.

"You have read the prosecutor's recommendation for all counts against you?"

"Yes, Your Honor!" Pastor N. O. Goode says meekly as his lead attorney puts his right hand on Pastor Goode's left shoulder to steady him.

"Has anyone coerced you or offered you anything in exchange for your guilty plea?" Judge Justus asks sternly.

"No Your Honor!" he responds trembling.

"Then it is the judgment of this court that you be sentenced to twenty-five years to life for second degree murder, assault with intent to murder, and being a felon in possession of an unregistered firearm. In addition, you are hereby sentenced to twenty-five years to life for misappropriation of funds, wire fraud and embezzlement, with all sentences to run concurrently." Judge Justus does not try to conceal her disgust and irritation with Pastor Goode.

"Whoa," all the people in the courtroom shriek as Pastor N. O. Goode, after hearing the sentence, trembles nervously then falls forward clutching his chest.

"Oh no!" shouts a smaller group of people sitting in the courtroom. Pastor Goode's wife, Marie Antoinette, who is sitting directly behind the defense table, starts to weep uncontrollably, then faints into the arms of her son, Jabez, and daughters, Delilah and Salome.

"Somebody call a paramedic," Judge Justus shouts!

The bailiff rushes over to the defense table and looks confused as to whom he should try to assist first, Pastor Goode or his wife.

The morbid curiosity of the crowd causes everyone to press forward to see what is happening with the Goodes. Pastor Goode appears to be having a heart attack, and his wife is just out cold! *"Please stand back, please stand back,"* the paramedics shout as they push their way through the throng of people in what seemed to be a monumental task just to get near the Goodes.

"Step back! Step back, please!" the burly Latino paramedic says,

dropping to his knees opening his medical bag and grabbing the stethoscope from around his neck to attend to Pastor Goode.

"Yes, get back and let the paramedics do their job," the bailiff shouts rudely, pushing people back, not caring about their age or gender.

"Hey, don't push my grandmother like that," the young lady says as the bailiff pushes her grandmother and makes her wig sit even more crooked atop her head."

The paramedics call for an additional team. The first EMT to arrive places Pastor Goode in their ambulance and rushes him to University Hospital while the second team attends to Reverend Marie Antoinette Goode, Pastor N. O. Goode's wife.

2:24PM Two Days Later. The Living Room of Ms. Loulabelle Jenkins, Long Time Member of the 9th Street New Harvest Missionary Baptist Church

All the local and major news outlets have converged on the home of Ms. Loulabelle Jenkins, the 82 year old matriarch and sole surviving female founder of the 9th Street New Harvest Missionary Baptist Church. Ms. Jenkins sits on an old but well maintained sofa in her small but comfortable living room. She is attended by her twenty-one year old great granddaughter, Chastity. Chastity adjusts her grandmother's arm in a sling as Ms. Jenkins had been shot in the arm. There is a large framed painting of Jesus on the cross over her fireplace. It is obvious that Ms. Jenkins loves photographs of family and paintings of prominent African Americans as she has a picture of Dr. Martin Luther King, with John and Bobby Kennedy alongside a framed photograph of Malcolm X on one wall. The rest of the available wall space is well organized with family photographs that tell a decade by decade history of her family. The news crews are eagerly jockeying for space with their shoulder mounted cameras and microphones.

"Ladies and gentlemen, please be careful. I am willing to answer all your questions, but some of you are getting a little too close for my comfort," Ms. Jenkins says in a mild manner and very calm voice.

"Ms. Jenkins, Ms Jenkins," the news reporters all shout as they struggle one with the other to place their respective TV stations microphone directly in

Ms. Jenkins's face.

"One at a time," Chastity shouts, slightly irritated with the fact her and her grandmother's space is being invaded.

"You, the cute reporter from Channel 8, I'll take your question first," Ms. Jenkins says in a flirtatious tone, flashing her pearly white false teeth.

"Thanks, the tall pecan colored well dressed reporters says," slightly embarrassed by the compliment.

"Ms. Jenkins, I am Reggie Stoddard from Channel 8 News. Could you tell us the circumstances that led to Pastor N. O. Goode being sentenced to a lengthy prison term for a number of criminal offenses, **Deacons Fellowes and Haran being murdered** at the behest of Pastor N. O. Goode, and your being wounded in the right arm? What happened that led to the downfall of one of this city's most prominent and influential pastors?"

"Well Baby, it all started fifteen years ago when we were just a small storefront church and our previous pastor, Pastor Frank Jemison, got in trouble for getting three teenage girls in our congregation pregnant. You know there is an old saying that the worse thing that could happen to a politician or a preacher is to be caught in bed with a dead woman who is not his wife or caught in bed with a live boy! Well, Pastor Jemison beat that old saying through his un-Christian actions. Imagine a forty-five year old man enticing and sleeping with three babies!"

"Ms. Jenkins, I do not mean to rush you, but we have a news deadline to meet so could you get back to what brought on the ruin of Pastor Goode?" Denise Levine from Channel 5 asks looking at her watch.

"Hmmp!" Ms. Jenkins sighs because of her perception of the reporter's rude intrusion. "Well, after Pastor Jemison was discovered to be the baby's daddy for three teenage girls, we had a church meeting and Pastor Jemison was forced to resign. Then we had a search committee but could not find a suitable replacement locally. Then lo and behold one Sunday while one of the **Deacons** was about to deliver the morning message, Pastor Goode and his family comes in and Pastor Goode tells the congregation that the Lord sent him to us to be our pastor.

He said, and I remember this as if it was yesterday, that if we allowed him to preach that Sunday and did not feel he was the man for the job, he would leave and never come back again. Well he preached one hell of a sermon."

"Big Momma!" Chastity exclaims in disbelief.

"This is gonna be on television!"

"What Baby? "Hell" ain't no bad word! It's in the Bible! Now where was I? Oh yes, Pastor Goode came in and preached this sermon that had most of the people shouting and running up and down the aisles. He sure could preach back then. Yes Lawd! He sure could preach back then! But they been saying lately he gets his sermons right off the Internet, and that's just plain lazy! Well, we had our search committee interview Pastor Goode and had him give us his references and application and such."

"That was a joke, Big Momma. He made all that stuff up and tricked y'all. That's what he did!" Chastity says sarcastically.

"He has never told the truth about anything from day one! He is a world class liar. He and his stuck up prissy wife!" Chastity continues.

"He lied about his education! He lied about his and his wife's qualifications! He lied about his wife having all them college degrees when she had a degree in Physical Education and a certificate in Religious Education. He made us believe she had a PhD in Religion. The Bible says that what is done in the dark will eventually come into the light! He just lied, lied, lied. The only thing he did not lie about was the fact that he had a job as a manager with the federal government! Other than that, he tricked y'all," Chastity says visibly irritated, squirming on the plastic covered sofa next to her great grandmother.

"Yeah Baby, he lied. He fooled us, but he was a good preacher when we was in the storefront church. You can't deny that. He was a good preacher," Ms. Jenkins says stoically.

Ms. Jenkins continues to tell her story how she was one of twenty-one original members that started the 9TH Street New Harvest Missionary Baptist church in the basement of one of the original deacon's home who was a reformed big time hustler. The TV crews slowly withdraw from Ms. Jenkins's living room as the cell phones of the reporters go off with messages of other breaking news events that their stations want them to cover. The only reporter to remain after about an hour and a half is Reggie Stoddard, who approaches Ms. Jenkins and says,

"Ms. Jenkins, I think you have a great human interest story that a lot of people would be interested in reading, so I would like to come back over the next few weeks to get all the history and facts about what happened at your church. With your permission, I would like to write about you, the church, and the story of Pastor Goode. Of course I would share any profits from the book with you. Do we have a deal?"

"You mean you would write a book about what happened at New Harvest and try to sell it and then give me some money just for telling the story?" Ms. Jenkins asks in disbelief.

"Yes ma'am! That is exactly what I mean. The story of Pastor Goode's crimes and fall from grace was one of the most widely covered news stories this year. I can not guarantee you the book will sell, but I think it has great potential to be a best seller!"

"Young man, I have always trusted you because you come across so well on TV and now in person as an honest person. Yes, we have a deal!" Ms. Jenkins says joyfully extending her right hand to shake his hand.

"All right then. How soon would you like to get started?" Reggie asks.

"Baby, we can start tomorrow! You know that Pastor Goode and I was very close and he used to call me his confidence," Ms. Jenkins says, trying to hide her attraction to this much younger man.

"You mean confidante, don't you Ms. Jenkins," Reggie says politely.

"Yeah, confidante. That man told me his whole life story like he was confessing to a priest in that booth. I knows all there is to know about that man. I can tell you some stories,..."

"Okay ma'am, that's very good. You can tell me all you know about Pastor Goode when we meet." Reggie closes his notebook and starts to rise from his seat.

"Stop calling me ma'am! My name is Loulabelle. Please call me Loulabelle," Ms. Jenkins says coyly.

"Okay ma'am, I mean Loulabelle. How does 5pm sound?" Reggie says trying to ease his hand out of Ms. Jenkins's hand.

"Five is good. I'm not going anywhere. So I'll see you at 5pm tomorrow," Ms. Jenkins says flirtatiously, smiling from ear to ear.

4:45PM The Next Day

True to his word, Reggie has arrived for his first interview with Ms. Jenkins. Chastity opens the door and escorts him into the kitchen where Ms. Jenkins is preparing what most people would consider a Sunday meal. She has prepared fried catfish, fried chicken, green beans, mashed potatoes and gravy, candied yams, cornbread and home-made dinner rolls, and for dessert, sweet potato pie. She did all this even though one of her arms is in a sling.

"Umm! Does it smell good in here!" Reggie says as he sits in a chair in the dining room that Chastity, who is blushing, points to.

"Ms. Jenkins, did you do all of this cooking just because I was coming over?"

"Sho did Baby. It's been a long time since I had a good looking man in my house," Ms. Jenkins responds laughing deliriously.

Chastity and Reggie join in the laughter. They eat, then Reggie pulls out a digital recorder, turns it on and just listens as Ms. Jenkins relates the rise and fall of Pastor N. O. Goode.

11:52am Sunday, May 8th Fifteen Years Ago. Pastor Goode Preaches His Trial Sermon

The storefront which is the home of the 9th Street New Harvest Missionary Baptist church sits on the corner of 9th and Cyprus Streets. It is a shotgun room with windows only on the Cyprus street side. The church building is narrow, very narrow, only about thirty-five feet wide but is very long. It used to house a prominent African American book store. The three windows of the church are covered with multicolored plastic which creates the illusion of stained glass. The choir stand and pulpit are on a crudely constructed removable stage floor that is only a foot from the ground and is made from one inch thick 4x8 eight feet pieces of plywood. Each 4x8 foot section is built on a frame that is similar to the structure of a backyard deck and braced by 6x6 inch posts. The plywood is covered with worn blue carpet purchased from a Boat Show at the city's Convention Center a few years ago for a very discounted price.

It is early May, and it is unusually hot for this time of year. So hot that the fake stained glass windows are opened as far as they can be and the back door that used to lead into the stock room is also opened halfway, but there is a heavy chain lock on this door to prevent any intruders with ill intent. There are three ceiling fans that are only circulating hot air and uniformly make an annoying whining and ticking sound. Each of these fans appears not to be fastened properly to the ceiling and could fall down at any moment.

"Whew, it is sho nuff hot in here!" Sister Betty Ward, an elderly woman about eighty, says to her sister, Beatrice.

"Girl, you know you ain't said nuthin but a word! It is hotter in here than it was in our old church down in Springville, Mississippi!" Beatrice says, vigorously working her funeral fan like so many other members of the congregation.

While the congregation of New Harvest Missionary Baptist Church resides in a storefront, its congregation is fiercely religious and has many dedicated workers in God's vineyard. It has a choir that can hold its own with some of the major church choirs in the community. The lead female vocalist is Sister Shirley Garrison. Even when she is wearing her choir robe, one could easily see that she is a beautiful and shapely dark skinned sista whose voice is indescribably rich in its tone. Every time she sings, the spirit just takes over, and on this day Reverend N. O. Goode had to wait several minutes for the congregation to calm down to a point where he could commence his sermon. It was obvious to a few people who are watching Reverend Goode intently that he was totally taken aback by this sista's presence, her voice and her beautiful smooth and flawless skin. He was also a little intimidated by the way she held the congregation in sway for such periods of time by simply singing a stirring gospel song. He waits patiently until the church, which is still feeling the spirit, has slowly calmed down.

"Amen, Amen, Amen," Deacon Ronnie Culbertson says, wiping his forehead feverously to remove the profuse sweat.

"Thank you Jesus! Thank you Jesus," Sister Netty Reynolds, a pleasingly plump sista of about forty shouts repeatedly, fanning herself as she slowly sits down in the folding chair.

There is a constant chorus of "Amen," and "Thank You Jesus" that is accompanied by a great deal of invigorated shouting as people who had been on their feet for the full extent of the song sung by sister Garrison finally and slowly start to take their seats.

Reverend Goode slowly rises from the huge Pastor's imitation leather wing back chair. His strides to the pulpit that is in desperate need of varnishing are slow and deliberate. He looks to his left, then to his right, and nods his head in a way that suggests he is totally impressed with the choir, especially Sister Garrison. His nods also suggest he approves of and is very pleased with their singing. Sister Garrison is feverously fanning herself and loosens the top two buttons of her choir robe exposing the profuse beads of sweat cascading down her neck.

In what seemed like an hour, Reverend N. O. Goode shouts nervously, "New Harvest, let's give our choir another hand. Didn't they give the Lord tremendous praise through that beautiful song?"

The congregation erupts into more shouting and clapping of their hands. The organist hurriedly slides back onto his stool and is rocking from side to side, his head bobbing from left to right. If you could not hear the music being played, you would think he was performing at an R&B concert. The choir director takes this as a signal, jumps to her feet, and dramatically leads the choir into another stanza of the song they thought they had finished. Her direction only serves to push the choir to sing more and more enthusiastically. Reverend Goode takes a step back, bows his head, and is appreciative of the fact that he has a few more minutes to calm himself before he delivers his sermon. He remembers his promise that if the congregation did not like his preaching on this his trial sermon, he would leave and never return. He realizes what is at stake and wants this job, BAD! "Thank you Jesus," he says under his breath.

He looks out into the congregation of about 70 people and winks at his wife. Then he notices one of the four ushers, Sister Niecy Goodbody, lean over at the end of one of the aisles of folding chairs to pass a fan from the Nevitts, Rogers & Wilson Funeral home to a woman of about forty who is sweating profusely.

God sure knew what he was doing when he gave that sister that body, Reverend Goode thinks to himself trying to keep a straight face.

"Thank you Jesus," an elderly man of about eighty shouts as he slowly rises from his seat, bracing his stance with his cane. "Thank you Jesus for all you've done for me," he shouts even louder.

"Praise God," Sister Loulabelle Jenkins shouts, tears welling up in her eyes.

The praising of God was infectious and overwhelming, and it seemed that it would never stop. So many members were caught up in the spirit that Reverend Goode had to extend his arms and politely give the signal for everyone to be seated. This, however, does not immediately stop the boisterous praise which was coming from every corner of the congregation. Most of the members of the choir were going off! The musicians were going off! The deacons were all on their feet giving praises to God like they were in attendance at a sporting event. Even some of the children were caught up in praising God and were jumping up and down in a trance-like state as a result of the choir's powerful delivery of the song. Finally, the shouting and praising dissipates to a point of almost whimpering and heavy breathing where Reverend N. O. Goode can break in and say, "Whew! Praise God! Praise God! That was a beautiful rendition of a wonderful gospel song. I hate to interrupt or interfere with the Holy Spirit, but we must follow the admonition found in I Corinthians, Chapter 14 verse 40, which instructs each of us to do things decent and in order!

Let me say again how blessed and thankful I am to deliver my trial sermon on this glorious day. I know it is a little warm, and I promise not to keep you long, but I want to talk about building this church into the great church the Lord planned it to be. Certainly this is a great church! You can feel the love and sincerity once you enter this sanctuary. But this church, the 9th Street New Harvest Missionary Baptist Church is slated by God's divine intervention to be one of the most prominent churches in this great city of ours. If we only follow the word of God, we will in a few years see such phenomenal growth that we will bear witness to the awesome plan of God for this church. So let us stand as the word of God is read."

The entire congregation rises to their feet, except twin girls who appear to be about six years old. They have fallen fast asleep on the back row of folding chairs, one leaning on the shoulder of the other whose face is pressed against the wall. They both are sweating from the intense heat in the sanctuary.

Reverend N. O. Goode surveys the room to insure that everyone has a Bible in hand, then says, "The scripture for my sermon comes from I Corinthians; Chapter 3, the seventh through the fifteenth verse. The topic of my sermon is: Building a Greater Sanctuary, based on the foundation laid by The Expert Builder, Jesus Christ! Please locate this scripture in whatever translation of God you may have and read silently along with me as I read from the New International Version of God's Holy word."

Reverend N. O. Goode reads,
"So neither he who plants nor he who waters is anything, but only God, who makes

things grow. The man who plants and the man who waters have one purpose, and each will be rewarded according to his own labor. For we are God's fellow workers; you are God's field, God's building. By the grace God has given me, I laid a foundation as an expert builder, and someone else is building on it. But each one should be careful how he builds. For no one can lay any foundation other than the one already laid, which is Jesus Christ. If any man builds on this foundation using gold, silver, costly stones, wood, hay or straw, his work will be shown for what it is, because the Day will bring it to light. It will be revealed with fire, and the fire will test the quality of each man's work. If what he has built survives, he will receive his reward. If it is burned up, he will suffer loss; he himself will be saved, but only as one escaping through the flames."

"You may be seated," Reverend N. O. Goode says self-assuredly, his confidence rising and his nervousness subsiding. His posture indicates he is feeling so confident he knows he is going to do well, very well. He looks left then right, then reverses that process as he scans the audience looking directly at each person sitting in the sanctuary. His purposeful intent is to make direct eye contact with each congregant. This is a technique he learned in his Toastmasters club.

He looks lovingly and longingly at his wife, then tries to sneak a look at Sister Goodbody, whose well proportioned body fits snuggly and curvaceously in her usher's uniform. She is standing like a sentry at the entrance to the sanctuary's double doors. She is dressed in a very tight, light blue usher's uniform whose hem is about four inches above her knees showing her well-proportioned and shapely caramel legs. She is wearing white gloves.

"Oh MY God, it is too hot in here," sister Goodbody says as she fans herself vigorously with a group of church bulletins in her left hand while she clutches a handful of contribution envelopes in her right hand that rests on the top of her perfectly round butt. She catches Reverend Goode's glance and thinks to herself shaking her head in disgust,

Hmm, is he trying to make eye contact with me? He's a married man! I hope I won't have to put him in his place in front of the whole church and his wife! I get so tired of all these married men trying to hit on me!

Reverend Goode casts another glance in Sister Goodbody's direction and thinks to himself, Damn, she is bad! Lord please help me stay focused on your Word this morning.

The entire congregation awaits Reverend Goode's sermon with great expectations. The consensus was he got off to a good start with his scripture based sermon's topic. It was a topic that resonates with all the adult members because they have been waiting desperately for a shepherd who will take them out of this old storefront church in a decaying inner city neighborhood. After all, he said that if he did not sway them with his trial sermon, he would never bother them again. That remark led to the people thinking he was either very good or very arrogant. In about forty-five minutes they would surely find out.

Reverend N. O. Goode composes himself, then starts preaching his sermon. Within the first five minutes, he has the bulk of the congregation clapping and shouting and saying amen in a thunderous chorus. The atmosphere in the hot storefront church is most electric. Most of the seven deacons are on their feet clapping with their arms outstretched over their heads. All the deacons, with the exception of Deacon Harvey Jacobs, have loosened their ties, rolled up their long sleeves, and removed their suit jackets. The few people in the neighborhood who pass by are amazed by the reaction to this man who showed up from nowhere and has the church demonstrating their acceptance of his sermon through their consistent and increasingly loud shouting and praising of God.

Same Day. Forty-Five Minutes Later

Reverend Goode has preached a very uplifting sermon. The atmosphere in the sanctuary is as electric as it was earlier after Sister Garrison's solo. Sweating profusely, Reverend Goode steps back up to the pulpit, then with the swagger of a country preacher, emphatically says, "If there is anyone in this House of God who is looking for a church home, then you can not find a better church home than this. I can tell by the spirit in this room that this congregation is dedicated to the Lord and one day, one day soon The 9th Street New Harvest Missionary Baptist Church will be in a huge sanctuary where we will have a day care center, assistance for the homeless, a credit union, an elder care center, and a community center to keep our young people off these mean streets in an environment where they will learn to grow to be responsible, God fearing adults!

This may sound like a far fetched dream, but if we just work together in the spirit of the Lord, anything is possible! If you feel like you are missing something in your life, now is the time to come and be a part of the body of Christ, a member of this wonderful church. Will you come? Will you come?"

Stepping back just one step, Reverend Goode sees that more than a few people are caught up in the Holy Spirit.

"Come my sister and my brother," he says, as he points to a young couple who look like they are unsure as to whether or not they should join the church. The couple slowly rises from their seats in amazement, thinking that Reverend Goode has read their minds. He had not read their minds, just their body language which they had no idea was speaking volumes about their indecision.

"Come, my sister and my brother," Reverend Goode exhorts, motioning with his hands for them to make that long walk down the aisle to the pulpit.

Caught up in the moment, and thinking that God is talking to them through Reverend Goode, the couple walks unsteadily and nervously, arm in arm down the long aisle to the front of the church. The congregation, as if from a cue, erupts into deafening applause and incoherent shouting as the couple is joined by six other people, each walking single file down the aisle. One of them is a young lady about Twelve years old whose mother stands with tears of joy streaming down her face as she repeats in a somewhat frantic refrain,

"Thank you Jesus! Thank you Jesus for letting my Baby see she needs you!" The young lady's mother shouts as she raises her hands over her head, looks toward the heavens, and starts running in place.

Another of the six people is a young man of about Twenty-four who is dressed in Hip Hop gear, the drooping baggy jeans, expensive sneakers, a throwback Baltimore Bullets jersey with a red, white and blue Baltimore Bullets throwback baseball style cap. He is also wearing three gold chains. He does not appear to have any family with him, but the congregation is electrified to see someone from the neighborhood join their church.

"Glory be to God," shouts an elderly, petite woman whose extreme age has taken its toll on her body. She sits leaning forward almost slumped over in a wheelchair.

"Will one of the deaconesses please come forward to take the names of these future members of New Harvest?" Reverend Goode asks, his heart pounding as he looks to the first row on his left where all the deacons' wives sit.

Deaconess Ethel Monger, wife of Deacon H.O. Monger, quickly rises to her feet while grabbing a legal pad positioned at the end of the row of chairs for such purposes. She takes the names of all eight people.

"Reverend," Deaconess Monger says gleefully. She is unable to conceal her happiness with the fact that the church has increased its membership by eight people and Reverend Goode has yet to be installed as New Harvest's permanent pastor.

"Reverend Goode, we having coming to us with Christian experience, Mr. and Mrs. Theo Lane," Deaconess Monger says, almost forgetting how to conduct this portion of the service.

"Welcome Sister and Brother Lane. Do you have a comment?" Reverend Goode says enthusiastically.

"Yes Reverend," Theo Lane says, his wife Gladys crying tears of joy. "We've been looking for a new church home and decided to try a smaller church since we've been members of a mega church for years. We felt lost in the crowd in our old church, so here we are! Your message was so inspiring that we both just looked at each other and said this is it. This is our new church home and new church family. We want to be led by a sincere Reverend that is a true servant of God, not a Reverend who only wants to get rich pimping God's word. So Reverend, we are ready to join your congregation and start working in a ministry."

"Glory be to God," Reverend Goode says exuberantly. "My brother, I agree you have come to the right church. I know that God sent both you and my family here, but I must confess that I am not the permanent Reverend here. Actually, the sermon I preached was my trial sermon!"

"What?" Brother and Sister Lane say seemingly amazed that Reverend Goode is not the main man! "Are you serious?" Theo Lane asks still looking like he is in disbelief.

"That's right my brother! I am not the permanent pastor yet, but pray that I am selected as the shepherd of this wonderful congregation."

"Well, in that case we will not join today but will continue to come to this church, and if you get selected, we will join, otherwise we will continue our search for a new church home," Theo Lane says as he gently grabs his wife's hand and motions to her to retake their seats.

"But my brother, you should still join this church even if I never become the pastor! This is a wonderful and awesome church, so please come back and become a member. I am sure that whatever ministry you and your wife join, you will be an asset to the Lord and His work here!"

The congregation of New Harvest listens intently to the dialogue and is overwhelmed with Reverend Goode's stance that this young couple should join the church even though he might not become the pastor. The deacons all look at one another and nod their heads in approval, all but one.

Deacon Gabriel Fellowes just stares at Reverend Goode with no discernible expression on his face.

As the Lanes finally reach their seats, the entire church is still stunned by their actions. Deaconess Monger regains her composure and introduces the young man in the Hip Hop gear.

"Reverend Goode, we have coming to us for baptism, brother Jabin Haran."

"Brother Haran, both Jabin and Haran are Biblical names aren't they?" Reverend N. O. Goode asks quizzically.

"Yes sir. Jabin means "intelligent" and Haran means "enlightened!"

"Well Brother Haran, do you have a comment for us?" Reverend Goode asks vigorously shaking the young man's hand.

"Yes I do, sir! I promised my grandmother I would do two things. One, get my GED then go to college, and two, join a church where the word of God was being taught. I know I'm young, but my grandmother passed away last week and we buried her on Saturday. I will get my GED in a couple of weeks, so I thought I'd come in here and check out this church since its in my hood, I mean neighborhood. I only went to church as a child and was dragged into the church house by my grandmother cause my mother died when I was nine. In these days I only go to church if it's a funeral or a wedding, and I don't feel comfortable on either occasion. But, I promised Big Momma, so here I am, standing in front of all these people and keeping my promise," the young man says, tears welling up in his eyes as he looks upward as if his grandmother is an angel flying overhead.

Wiping the tears from his eyes with the sleeves of his pristine white tee shirt, he continues by tearfully saying, "Big Momma, you meant the world to me, and I know that the only way I'll get to see you again is to join a church, so I'm gonna give this church a try. Save a place for me in heaven, but until I get there, I'm keeping my promises!"

The entire congregation is on their feet, crying tears of joy, and Reverend Goode is no exception. He has pulled his handkerchief from his shirt pocket and is wiping both the beads of sweat and tears that are simultaneously cascading down his face.

"And a little child shall lead them," Reverend Goode shouts into the microphone.

"Whew, laud!" Reverend Goode says, placing his right hand on the left shoulder of the young man. "Do you accept Jesus Christ as your Lord and Savior?" Reverend Goode asks emphatically.

"Yes I do," the young man says, still wiping the tears from his eyes, his head bent back, elbows bent, and his hands lifted upward.

"Then we will accept you as a member of New Harvest Missionary Baptist Church's family, pending your baptism."

The young man returns to his seat on the front row reserved for those joining the church or in need of prayer. Sister Goodbody has maneuvered her way down to the front row of folding chairs with a box of tissues and sits next to the young man offering some tissue. Her usher's uniform is so tight, one could swear that she was snuggling up to this young man. Deaconess Monger continues to introduce the rest of the candidates for membership.

Church service ends with a rousing benediction by Reverend Goode. He hurriedly makes his way to the front doors of the church where he is greeted warmly by the congregation. He gets compliment after compliment on how well he preached and ran the service. He reaches out to shake the hands of all the congregants which creates a virtual roadblock at the doors. His wife and children are still near the pulpit casting a loving glance at him for a job well done.

Sister Garrison, who sang the song that tore the church up, makes her way through the long line. She has taken off her choir robe and shows a beautiful burgundy dress that fits her curvaceous body just right! Reverend Goode looks at her trying to hide his lust and thinks to himself, *My God! Lord, please remove any lustful thoughts from my heart and mind.*

"My sister, you have an outstanding voice. If I become Pastor, I might need some voice lessons from you. Do you teach vocal classes?" Reverend Goode says eagerly, holding her hand and caressing it gently.

"No, not really," she responds.

"Well you might want to consider teaching voice. You have such a gift, such range, and of course I would pay you."

"Well sir, I must decline your offer because I do not have the time to teach voice. I have a career that keeps me very busy," Sister Garrison responds, trying to pull her hand out of Reverend Goode's hands. He is clutching her hand and looking her right in the eyes.

"Well daughter, think about it," Reverend Goode says noticing that many people are looking at him and seem to be wondering why he is talking to her so long when there is a long line and it is HOT in here!

Reverend Goode lets Sister Garrison go, a little perturbed that he can not look at her lustfully without making it obvious to the others waiting to shake his hand.

Damn she's fine, he thinks to himself, as a short stocky woman with bulging green eyes and no neck approaches him for a handshake and to make a comment.

Approaching her car and using her automatic door opener, Sister Garrison says to herself, 'There is something about that man that makes me suspicious. He's married and he held my hand like a playa trying to impress me with how soft his hands are. And what is this junk about me giving him voice lessons, she says, swinging her legs into her car. She starts the engine and drives off a little perplexed.

"Reverend Goode, that was certainly one of the best sermons we have heard in this church in a long time. We need more sermons like that, and when it comes up for a vote, I promise you have my vote to become our next pastor," a short pencil-thin sista says, batting her eyes and holding Reverend Goode's hand as if she were a massage therapist.

In comparison, she is so short she has to crane her neck to look Reverend Goode in the eyes. He finds himself in the same position he had placed Sister Garrison. He wants this woman to let his hand go, but she continues to hold his hand tight as if they were Crazy Glued together.

"Well thank you so much. I truly appreciate your comments and hope to be your pastor one day. Oh, please excuse me because there are so many people in line waiting to talk to me. Have a nice day."

This sister ,realizing he has brushed her off, rolls her eyes as she looks behind her at the line of people, most of whom are women. Rudely brushing by some other congregants standing by and blocking the door, she thinks to herself, I didn't want to talk to your tired butt anyway. You don't know what you are missing because we could have had a good thing going like I had with Deacon Monger. He just messed it up for us by marrying that skinny witch who never lets him out of her sight!

Another sister, who appears to be in her sixties and has a face like an unattractive man in drag, pushes her way to the front of the reception line.

"Reverend, I just wanted to tell you how much I enjoyed your sermon," Sister Ernestine Faye, a short, plump, high yellow sister with freckles and extra nappy red hair that is faded and balding due to excessive hair treatments over the years, says.

"Yes Reverend Goode, I just loved your message, and it was right on time for this here church," she says, her false teeth making a clicking noise as she grabs her chin trying to adjust her dentures without taking them out of her mouth.

"Where are you from, my sister," Reverend Goode asks warmly noticing a strong southern accent.

"I'm from Ratcheer, Mississippi," she responds smiling.

"Ratcheer, Mississippi!" Reverend Goode says enthusiastically.

"I am from Wiesport," shaking Sister Faye's hand.

Sister Faye closes the short distance between them by rushing up to Reverend Goode and hugging him like he was her long lost son.

Startled by Sister Faye's reaction to him, Reverend Goode tries to catch his breath as this sister's grasp around his waist is a little too tight, a little uncomfortable. Matter of fact, it is very uncomfortable, given her height which places her chin in his chest and her bulging stomach pressing his groin area.

"Well Reverend, I bet we knows a lot of the same peoples, so I want you and your family to come over to my house for dinner one Sunday. And don't worry, I'se can cook. Just ask anyone in this church. They's gonna tell you Sister Faye can really cook!"

"But my sister, I may not become the pastor of this church. Are you sure you want my family and me to have dinner at your house?"

"Excuse me," Sister Faye says, cutting off Reverend Goode. "I have a sixth sense bout things like that. You let me worry if you gets to preach at New Harvest," Sister Faye says boastfully after releasing Reverend Goode from the crushing bear hug. She simultaneously looks to see if the sweat coming from both of them has wrinkled her bright pink dress. Her taste in clothes leaves a lot to be desired. This dress looks homemade and styled from the forties. Sister Faye is in her mid-sixties, and she is not a Lena Horne look-a-like.

"C'mon Junior, Tina, and Alberta," she says to her three children who range in ages from 19 to 26. "Momma doesn't feel like cooking today cause it is so hot. We're gonna eat dinner at Juanita Mae's Cafe. Okay?"

Reverend Goode is still shaking the hands of some congregants, many of whom are enduring the oppressive heat so they can tell him how much they loved his sermon. The funeral fans are being feverishly worked by men, women and children, creating an artificial tropical breeze. As the people leave, they hand their fans to the two ushers, Sister Goodbody and Brother Casanova Riley. Brother Riley's wife patiently sits at the rear of the church monitoring her husband's lustful stares over the top of his rose tinted designer eye glasses that are perched on the bridge of his nose.

I do not know why I stay with this man. The children are all grown and out of the house. I make good money, so I do not need him financially, but as unfaithful as he is, he is a good father and grandfather, and he still knows how to make me feel so special, Sister Riley thinks to herself.

Being a true player, Brother Riley looks at his wife and puckers his lips as if to give her a kiss. She smiles in return but notices that the gesture was merely a distraction as her husband slyly leans back to take a long look at Sister Goodbody's behind.

Damn! he thinks to himself, checking the crowd so he will not get caught looking at Sister Goodbody's butt. There are some beautiful women in this church and I'm going to get that. Yes sir, Brother Riley thinks to himself as he collects yet another funeral fan. He then smiles at Sister Goodbody who is unaware of his lustful leering.

The deacons, seven in number, are all huddled near the pulpit, watching how Reverend Goode is working the crowd.

"They like him! They like him a lot!" Deacon H. O. Monger says, shaking his head up and down as an affirmation of his observation. Given how the people reacted to Reverend Goode, we might want to have a joint meeting so we can make him an offer to become the Pastor. I don't know about you, but I was impressed, very impressed how he ran the service today," Deacon Monger says directing his comments to Deacon Isa Crooke, Chairman of the Deacon Board.

"He did preach one hell of a sermon, and he had the people on their feet several times," Deacon Ronald Bennett, an elderly, tall and well built man in his late seventies says while both of his hands are perched on his cane.

"We think we could work with him because we are the real power," Deacon Isa Crooke says trying to whisper. "So if you guys like him we can have him come to our monthly combined Deacons and Trustees meeting. We can interview him informally and if he checks out, we can make him an offer. It's been almost a year since we had a fulltime pastor, and this church won't grow until we get situated with a permanent pastor. He's hungry, that's obvious to me, so he'd be unlikely to not go along with how we do things here," Deacon Crooke says, making authoritative eye contact with the other deacons. After all, it's his money that keeps the church afloat. He then gets confirmation of his plan as they all shake their heads in agreement.

"All right then, I'll tell him we want him to submit an application for the job of "Pastor" with a resume and three references. Agreed?"

"Sure,"

"That's fine,"

"I'm good with that," the other deacons respond in unison.

"Okay H.O., go tell him that we want to talk to him in the Deacons Office before he gets out of here. He'll probably come talk to us anyway when he's done meeting and greeting the people. He wants this job bad, so go tell him to come back to the office before he and his family leave."

"Okay, I'm on it," Deacon H. O. Monger says as he slowly moves to the front of the reception line, moving past families with children, young couples and some elderly folks who took some time to stand on their feet before they got in line.

Reaching the front of the diminished line of people, Deacon Monger steps next to Reverend Goode and says, "Reverend Goode, we'd like to see you in the Deacon's office when you are done here. I promise it will only take a few minutes."

"Okay, that's fine," Reverend Goode says, smiling, thinking to himself that they must have been impressed. "I should be there shortly," he tells Deacon Monger, wishing these people would hurry up and not take all day complimenting him.

You would think the heat in this place would get them out of here, but I must have done a great job with my sermon. Why else would the people stay in this long **_LINE_** to thank and compliment me, and the Deacon's want to see me, too! Thank you Jesus, N. O. Goode says to himself, looking at his wife who is fanning their children who are all asleep and full of beads of sweat covering their faces.

Deacon Monger enters the small and cramped Deacons' Office and informs the other deacons that Reverend Goode will join them shortly. The Deacons' Office is about eight feet wide and twenty feet long. New Harvest has a ceiling about fifteen feet high. The beige, glossy paint on the walls is cracking in spots and screams for a new paint job. There is an old roll-top desk at the back of the office that is covered with old church bulletins, used Sunday School books and other debris that should be thrown away. There are several folding chairs, the kind one would see at a funeral parlor that are stacked against the wall. The rest are being used by the seven deacons, except for Deacon Isa Crooke, Chairman of the Deacon Board.

Deacon Isa Crooke sits in an old, faded, burgundy leather wing chair looking like the king of some small, impoverished country. He sits very erect, looking very dignified and has his hands clasped over the top of a fine mahogany cane with a gold handle. He is a tall slender man, about six two with silver permed hair. He is wearing a shiny, grey suit with a tie and shoes to match. He also has a huge ring on each finger that would serve him well if he were to get into a fight as this collection of rings, encrusted with various gemstones, looks like a set of brass knuckles. Rumor has it he was a big numbers man, and a rival tried to have him killed. Deacon Crooke was shot four times and survived but was left with a permanent and very noticeable limp, which explains his use of the elaborate gold handled mahogany cane. He has a "special" chair on the front row of the sanctuary as he is not only a founder of New Harvest but its chief financier. He owns the storefront where New Harvest holds its services. Deacon Isa Crooke impatiently looks at his Rolex watch just as Reverend Goode enters the Deacons' office.

"My apologies gentlemen, but your congregation kept me in the receiving line for such a long time thanking me and complimenting me about the sermon I delivered. By the way, how do you feel I did?"

Leaning forward with his glasses sliding down to the bridge of his nose, Deacon Isa Crooke sternly asks, "Nah Brother Minister, you tell us how you think you did?"

Stunned by the question to his question, Reverend Goode replies after pausing for about four seconds, "We'll have to give all glory, praise and credit to the Lord."

"But that's not what I asked you, Reverend. So again, HOW DO YOU THINK YOU DID?" Deacon Crooke asks in an impatient and bullying tone.

Surveying the small, cramped, and certainly overheated Deacon's Office, Reverend Goode, using a panoramic view, searched the facial expressions of the other deacons for support before he responds to Deacon Isa Crooke's terse questioning.

"Well Deacon, I believe that through God I did a great job of reaching

New Harvest's congregation by both teaching and preaching God's word. I made my examples so basic, even the children understood my message. But again, I have to give all praises to the Holy Spirit for being with me when I was preaching," Reverend Goode says, wiping his sweat generated from the heat and Deacon Crooke's grilling interrogation.

"That's what we wanted to hear, Reverend. We wanted to hear you give credit to the Lord but at the same time take credit for what you did. After all, we're all human, right?" Deacon Isa Crooke says emphatically.

"Right," Reverend Goode says, finally relaxing and sitting back comfortably after taking a seat in one of the folding chairs.

"Well Reverend, we are prepared to place your name in consideration for the Pastor-ship of the church before the congregation. If I push it, you will be selected without a problem. But our offer, of course, is dependent on whether or not you are willing to be the Pastor of this poor-in-money but rich-in-spirit and praising-God church," Deacon Crooke says as he lets his cane rest between his thighs and extends his right hand to Reverend Goode as an indication that he is consummating a deal.

"Am I willing?" Reverend Goode says, trying to contain his excitement.

"Yes, Yes!" I accept your offer to be New Harvest's Pastor, Reverend Goode says enthusiastically.

"But aren't there two considerations on your part, Reverend?" Deacon Isa Crooke asks, as if it were a trick question.

"Two considerations?" Reverend N. O. Goode asks, trying not to fall into a trap set by the cagey Deacon Crooke.

"Yes, two considerations," Deacon Crooke says, still leaning forward and sternly looking into Reverend Goode's eyes.

"You never asked us about salary, and you did not ask us if it was okay for you to talk to your wife," Deacon Crooke says, smiling sheepishly.

Still trying to conceal his beaming smile, Reverend Goode says, "Well gentlemen, I guess I am so overwhelmed with the offer to be the shepherd of this fine congregation that I really did not think about the salary. I have a good full-time job with good benefits working as a mid-level manager for the Highway Commission," N. O. says with so much excitement in his voice. "And as for my wife's position, she will support me no matter what! She knows how bad I want to be Pastor so that I might answer my calling to preach and teach the word of God. I know she will be happy that you offered me the job!"

Smiling like he just bought a sixty-thousand dollar car for two grand, Deacon Crooke says, "Well Reverend, we wanted to be fair with you, so how does $400 a week sound?"

Without any hesitation, Reverend Goode responds, "Fine! Just fine!"

Deacon Crooke extends his right hand to Reverend Goode, and Reverend Goode ecstatically stands to shake Deacon Crooke's hand as if Deacon Crooke was the Pope.

Regaining his composure, Reverend Goode says, "Thank you gentlemen. I promise to not let you down. I will work with you to make this the best church in this metropolitan area."

All the deacons with the exception of Deacon Crooke and Deacon Fellowes stand to shake Reverend Goode's hand. Reverend Goode notices that Deacon Fellowes is slowly rising from his seat, never taking his eyes off of him, and seems to be checking him out with great suspicion.

Finally, Deacon Fellowes approaches Reverend Goode and says, "Well, my brother, I pray that you will help us increase the flock of this church. I also pray that we will always work in concert as it is written in I Corinthians 14:40, to always do things decent and in order."

"Oh we will, my brother, we will!!" Reverend N. O. Goode says, still mentally floating on a cloud.

"Well gentlemen, is there anything I need to know? Anything I need to be prepared for before I share this most wonderful news with my family?" Reverend N. O. Goode asks.

Slowly rising from his throne-like seat, Deacon Isa Crooke says, "Yeah Pastor, there are two things you need to know. One, we have a standing Deacon's meeting every Thursday evening from 6pm to 8pm. We want you to be part of that meeting until we feel you have learned how we do things here at New Harvest. And two, we expect to announce you as the new Pastor at the next Church Quarterly Business meeting with us this Saturday. The meeting will be done with the Deacon Board, you and the Trustees chairing the meeting before the church. You'd better be prepared to share your vision for this church with the congregation, and you'd better be good in what you say," Deacon Isa Crooke says, generating laughter from all the other Deacons except Deacon Fellowes, who now has made Reverend Goode uncomfortable because he seems to refuse to smile and acts like he knows something bad about him.

What is with this brother? Reverend Goode thinks to himself with a nervous grin on his face. Why is he gritting on me?

Returning his focus to Deacon Crooke, Reverend Goode, now potential Pastor Goode, thinks to himself, this guy, Crooke, must be running things here, but it does not hurt to gather a few troops to ensure that I'm selected as Pastor. If I am to have a problem with any of these guys, it will be this brother Deacon Fellowes. I just do not get his drift. He can't know anything about me, so what's his problem?

"Well gentlemen, it is getting late, and I promised my wife I'd take her out for dinner after church," Deacon Crooke says, slowly rising from his chair, breathing heavily, which is typical of a man of his poor health. Surviving being shot four times has taken its toll on him physically.

All the deacons except Deacon Fellowes rise as if they were in court, and the judge rises to leave the courtroom.

"Yeah, we better get out of here," Deacon Monger says, quickly moving over to Deacon Crooke's side to help him get to his feet. "Yeah, we'd better get out of here while we still have wives cause y'all know these women can not take the heat in all that makeup and fine clothes," Deacon Monger continues, trying unsuccessfully to be humorous.

Reverend Goode stands by the door and shakes the hand of each deacon as they exit the Deacon's Office. Deacon Fellowes is the last one to exit and just stares at Reverend Goode as he leaves the company of the other deacons. He shakes the Reverend's hand with a very firm grip, looks Reverend Goode in the eye, and says, "You don't remember me, do you?"

"No, I don't," Reverend Goode responds.

"Well, just give it some time, and it will come to you," Deacon Fellowes says abruptly, releasing his grip and hastily walking past Reverend Goode.

Damn! What the HELL is that brother's deal? Pastor Goode says, a little agitated by what he feels is Deacon Fellowes's rude treatment.

The Goodes have a late model Chrysler mini-van parked about a block and a half away from the church. Sister Goode leads their three sleepy children down the street single file. Upon reaching the mini van, Sister Goode uses her automatic door opener to open the sliding side door and watches as each child gets into the mini van. Jabez, the youngest, is nine, and he scrambles to the back seat so he might stretch out as if he were in bed. Salome, the oldest at fourteen, lets her twelve year old sister, Delilah, get in first in the middle seat, then enters the van, pulls the sliding side door with both hands, and ensures that her brother and sister have their seat belts on. She sighs deeply and wipes the sweat from the brow of her Baby brother, then her sister, then looks into her little purse and pulls out a mirror to check her hair, which is limp from the intense heat.

"Mommy, when are we going to the hairdresser?" she asks in an irritated tone.

"Soon, Baby soon," her mother replies, taking a very deep breath, then sighing in disgust as she stands outside the mini van waiting on her husband in the blistering heat! She waits patiently as her husband hastily saunters down the street toward their automobile.

Approaching the minivan, he pauses and stares at his wife, looking like he is about to explode with excitement.

Pastor Goode is so excited by the offer to become New Harvest's next Pastor, he forgets his manners and leaves his wife standing on the curb waiting for him to open her door, help her into the van, and close the door behind her.

"Nathan, Nathan, are you forgetting something and someone?" Sister Marie Antoinette Goode says, not trying to hide her sarcasm.

"Ah Baby, you know my mind is doing summersaults. How could I ever forget you?" He rushes around to her side of the car and with the skill of a doorman at an expensive hotel, opens her door, watches as she gracefully seats herself, then closes her door behind her. He then runs around to the driver's side of the mini van and hastily sits down, almost out of breath. "Whew!" he exclaims, as he just sits in his seat looking toward his wife.

The Goode's children are all fast asleep as Reverend Goode starts the mini van and turns the air conditioner on full blast, but the cooling agent must be low because all that is blowing on his family is slightly cool, not cold air. He shuts off the air, looks over at his wife again with a huge grin, says nothing for what seemed to be an eternity, then says, "Baby, they offered me the job as Pastor!"

Sister Goode looks at her husband in disbelief and says, "What?"

"Baby, I said they offered me the job as Pastor, and they're going to pay me $400 a week," Reverend Goode says leaning across his seat to kiss his wife but is restrained by his seat belt.

"$400 a week! Well we can certainly use the money! she says with a tense smile on her face.

"Baby, we are on our way. $400 a week today, but in a few years to come, I promise you we will have an expensive home in the best neighborhood, drive the most expensive cars, send our children to the best private schools, vacation in Europe and even dine with dignitaries like the President of the US of A!" N.O. Goode says, his voice rising, trying to be humorous but making a promise he truly plans to keep.

"Baby, in a few short years your family will see that you did the right thing by marrying me and that you did marry up as opposed to marry down."

"But Baby, my family loves you so why…"

"They did not love me for you at first," N. O. Goode says, interrupting his wife mid-sentence.

"They were not in favor of your marrying what they thought was some barefoot, overall-wearing, corn-bread-eating, fried chicken and watermelon-loving, itinerate, and illiterate, **coin-tree** boy from Mississippi!" Reverend Goode says, in an exasperated tone.

"Baby, I'm not saying nothing bad about your folks, but you come from money! A family that owned the largest janitorial service in this city." Your grandfather, Daddy Wainwright, even ran with some of this city's most powerful Blacks, preachers and politicians alike. Then here I come, virtually penniless and homeless, from a small town in Mississippi where my father worked as a driver and mortician's assistant in the town's only black owned funeral home. So I know your folks were not in favor of you marrying me when you had all those eligible, socially prominent brothers from all the rich Black families here."

"But Baby, I was not interested in them! I saw something very special in you," Sister Goode says, her chest heaving due to her deep feelings for her husband.

"I know Baby, I know," he responds with a touch of pride and conquest in his tone. "Baby, do you member how we met and where?" he asks, smiling.

Putting the minivan in drive but not focusing on the traffic, Reverend Goode slowly pulls out into traffic and is almost side-swiped by a 1989 silver Mustang that seemed to come out of nowhere. The Mustang's driver ignores two facts: 1) that he was doing fifty-five in a twenty-five and 2) it's Sunday and he is in close proximity to a church. Neither fact must have registered on him as he sped down the street. He gave Reverend Goode the finger and continued to spew out his litany of obscenities.

"N. O., are you okay?" Sister Goode asks out of breath, her hands crossed and clutching her chest.

"I'm fine! I'm fine! I guess I was not concentrating, and he just came out of nowhere!"

Checking his side and rear view mirror and looking over his left shoulder, Reverend Goode eases out into traffic and asks his wife again, "Baby, do you remember how and where we met?"

Turning in his direction, she says, "Yes Baby, I do!"

Reverend Goode takes a very deep breath and begins to reminisce about how and where he met his wife, Marie Antoinette Wainwright.

September 15, Twenty Years Ago in the Downtown State Office Building

"Hey N. O., did you dump the trash from the 6th floor break room?" Willie, the janitorial crew chief shouts in the direction of N. O., who has his back to Willie.

N. O. Goode does not hear him because he is listening to Frankie Beverly and Maze on his Walkman. N. O. is playing his music so loud that Willie can hear every lyric even though N. O. is wearing headphones.

"N. O, N. O., did you hear what I just asked you?" Willie yells down the long hallway as N. O. continues to push his trash bin, his body gyrating to the music. He is completely unaware of the fact that his supervisor is trying to get his attention.

"Damn it, that boy better get rid of that Walkman so he can hear me," Willie says, as he takes a roll of toilet tissue off one of the cleaning supply carts and hurls it at N. O., barely missing his head.

N. O. is startled by the roll of toilet tissue that bounces on the floor about six inches in front of him. Turning abruptly in Willie's direction, N. O. is fuming and rushes toward Willie. Just then, the elevator bell rings, the door opens, and Grandpa Wainwright, his son Eldridge and Eldridge's daughter, Marie Antoinette step out.

"Cool It!" Willie signals N.O with his facial expression. Willie knows that the Wainwrights are serious task masters, and any sense that their employees might be horseplaying on the job could lead to their immediate firing.

"Is everything all right?" Grandpa Wainwright, a tall slender and very dark, distinguished looking man asks in a very proper English accent.

"Oh yes sir," Willie is quick to respond.

"Yes sir! Everything is all right," Willie reiterates as he looks over at N. O.

with an, If you want to keep your job, you'd better play along, look.

"Well gentlemen, you know how I like to perform surprise checks on my crews to ensure that the quality of service my family prides itself in is taking place at the businesses we clean. So here I am, and it looks like you men are keeping this place very clean," Eldridge Wainwright says, imitating his father's distinguished and proper dialect.

"Have you gotten any complaints?" N. O. sarcastically blurts out to the sheer embarrassment of Willie.

"Ahhh, what N. O. means, Mr. Wainwright, is we do such a good job that no one here would have a reason to complain about our services. Right N. O.?" Willie says, as he begins to perspire more from being nervous than from the heat. After all, this is a climate controlled building and the temperature is about seventy two degrees.

"No Willie, what I mean is, have the Wainwright's gotten a complaint about what we do, especially what I do or what some folks think I should be doing. If I'm not doing my job to the satisfaction of our customers, then I want to know so I can do better. I'm here for one reason and one reason only, to make money!" N. O. says in a slightly defiant tone. He is still upset with Willie's use of the roll of toilet tissue as a projectile to get his attention.

"Well said," Grandpa Wainwright says." Well said."

"What is your name, young man," Grandpa Wainwright asks.

"His name is N. O. Goode," Willie blurts out.

"Willie, he has clearly demonstrated his capacity to speak, so please let him answer me," Grandpa Wainwright says in a scolding tone.

"Yes sir, Yes sir," Willie says nervously, his voice barely audible, his eyes exploring the floor.

"My name is Nathan Obadiah Goode," N. O. responds, looking at Willie, expecting another interruption.

"N. O. Goode? NO Goode!" Grandpa Wainwright says with a chuckle.

"Well N. O. I am Cleotis Wainwright, founder and owner of this company, and I like a man to speak his mind. I also like a man who is not afraid to get his hands dirty to make an honest dollar doing honest work. How long have you been working for us?"

"About seven months sir," N. O. responds, his anger subsiding since Willie threw the roll of toilet paper at him.

"Well Willie, you better keep your *eye* on this young fellow.

He may be your boss one day," Grandpa Wainwright says, smiling.

Willie begins to frown and does not speak out of turn, knowing that Grandpa Wainwright is not one to make jokes.

Finally he says, "Yes sir. Yes sir, Mr. Wainwright!"

"Willie, I know you know my son and granddaughter, but N. O., I do not think you have had the pleasure. N. O., I would like you to meet my son, Eldridge heir to the Wainwright Empire, and his daughter (my granddaughter), Marie Antoinette Wainwright."

N. O. hastily removes his rubber gloves and thrusts his right hand rather crudely at the almond colored and statuesque Marie Antoinette Wainwright.

Surprised by his crude manner but impressed by his physical appearance even though he is wearing coveralls, Marie Antoinette says, "It is a pleasure to meet you, Mr. Goode."

N. O. is equally impressed with Marie Antoinette and says, trying to be charming," It is a very nice pleasure to meet, I mean, make your acquaintance, Ms. Wainwright."

Both Grandpa and Eldridge notice the attraction emerging between the two, but Eldridge is not appreciative of this janitor holding his daughter's hand beyond the necessary time to properly greet someone.

"Marie, it is time for us to go!" Eldridge says rather sternly as he nods his head to Willie and N. O in a gesture suggesting he is dismissing them.

Back to the Current Day

Reverend Goode pulls up to a modest three bedroom bungalow in a working class neighborhood. It is obvious that most of the families in this neighborhood take great pride in their homes and neighborhood as all but two of the lawns out of thirty homes have manicured lawns. There is an annual neighborhood block party where prizes are awarded to the three homes with the best kept lawns and landscaping. Reverend Goode has never won any awards for his property as he is content just to keep the grass mowed and edged, and the shrubbery trimmed. When it comes to focusing on his yard compared to the lot of his neighbors, working outdoors just is not his thing.

After parking in front of their home, Reverend Goode comes around to the passenger side of their van and helps his wife out. All of the children get out of the van stretching and yawning, their clothes sticking to them from their sweat. The air conditioner in the van does not work well, so Reverend Goode has the front windows rolled down and the side window vents open. Sister Goode guides their three children into the house, then to their bedrooms.

"All right, take your church clothes off and put some play clothes on," she instructs them as she kicks off her heels and plops down on the sofa, caressing her feet one at a time. I can't wait until I break these shoes in. My feet are killing me, she says to herself as she sits in an unladylike position unbuttoning the top two buttons of her blouse. "Whew! It is hot in here," she says. "Oh Lord, give me strength! My feet hurt so bad!"

After what only took seconds but felt like hours of torture, she finally reaches the wall separating the small living room from the dining room. This is where the thermostat is mounted.

"Eighty degrees! Honey," she shouts to her husband as he struggles to bring his briefcase and the bags of carryout chicken dinners into the house. She is stepping in place as she now needs to go to the bathroom.

"Yes Baby, what do you need?" N. O. asks.

"Can you do something to lower the temperature in this house?" she shouts, not realizing N. O. is standing right behind her.

"Sure Baby," he says, pulling her to him and wrapping his huge hands around her waist, pushing her breasts upward.

"Now N. O., you know that the children are awake and it is much too hot for us to do what is on your mind," she says, moving away from him slowly and smiling teasingly.

"Well, I was thinking that since we got such good news today, we might celebrate," he says, smiling and licking his lips.

"Celebrate!" she says, pretending to blush.

"Look, you get this house cooled down and maybe, just maybe we can open up a bottle of that good wine we have been saving and celebrate when the children have gone to sleep!" she says, fanning herself.

"Your wish is my command," he says, throwing his suit jacket over the back of one of the dining room chairs.

N. O. turns the thermostat to 58 degrees, then bounds down the basement stairs to get a couple of oscillating fans to start the cooling process. Just as he plugs in the second of three fans the telephone rings. Marie Antoinette Goode answers.

"Hello. Yes, he is here. Please hold on," she says with a puzzled expression on her face as she hands N. O. the telephone.

"Hello, this is Reverend N. O. Goode. How may I help you?"

"You can give me the $200 you promised me for a job well done, Cuz!" the person on the line says, laughing.

"Theo, Theo, is this you?" N. O. asks, happily surprised.

"You bet it is, Cousin! How did you like our performance as two dedicated church going people looking for a new church home? Call them people in LA and tell them to polish a couple of them Oscars cause me and Brittany deserve 'em for the way we came across as a sincere Christian family looking for a new church home," said Theo Lane, the husband who made the impassioned speech about joining New Harvest when the doors of the church were opened. "That led the congregation to believe we were joining New Harvest because we thought N. O. Goode was the permanent Pastor!"

"Theo, that was an amazing performance," N. O. says jubilantly while his wife looks on, puzzled.

"N. O.," N. O.'s wife tries to interrupt but stands mute after N. O. puts his index finger over his lips in the vertical position to signal, "quiet please!"

N.O. then covers the mouthpiece of the telephone and says to his wife, "Baby, why don't you go and make sure the children are ready to eat dinner. I promise to not be on the telephone much longer."

Sister Goode nods her head in agreement and leaves the room, her feet still aching and swelling from her too tight shoes.

"Yeah Cousin, that was an Academy Award winning performance, and I thought it was a real nice extra touch to get the young brother who talked about keeping a promise to his grandmother to join in your performance," N. O. says excitedly.

"Well N. O., I can't take credit for young blood. I thought you hired him as backup to us, so if you didn't hire him, then he must've really liked your sermon!"

"You mean you did not pull that guy into the mix?" N. O. asks startled.

"Nope! Never saw the brother before. It looks like you got the gift of gab, and it worked on at least one person in that church," Theo says somewhat amused.

"Well, praise be to God! Praise be to God! I was so nervous, and I knew that your being there would help me pass this first test at New Harvest. And by the way Theo, I got the job," N. O. says proudly.

"Oh yeah?" Theo asks.

"Yeah, they gave me the job pending the approval of the congregation and their paying me $400 a week!"

"$400 a week. Then we needs to renegotiate our original deal.

The $200 fee is now $300," Theo says, trying not to laugh.

Both N. O. and Theo laugh for about thirty seconds when Theo says, "Look Cuz, you just made it over the first hurdle, so now we have to get you in permanently. Let me think on it for a few days, and I will come up with a scheme to get you in there permanently, but remember, Cuz, if you become Pastor because of my help, you'll owe me," Theo says, turning his tone from friendly to strictly business.

"Now why did you even go there, Theo?" N. O. asks disappointedly.

"Hey Cuz, I ain't trying to be cold blooded, especially to family, but if you recall, you're the one who got me involved in the hustling game. You're the one who taught me to look out for number one, then everybody else in the family, **AFTER I GET Mine.**" Theo says with increasing seriousness. "CUZ, it's like what Wesley Snipes told Allen Payne in that scene in New Jack City. "Friends is friends and business is business' This is business! You got your game, the preaching game, and I got my hustles, the hustles you taught me. If anyone knew the game of conning people and running the women, it was you, Cuz. It was you!" Theo says sarcastically.

"Look Theo, I know you find this hard to believe, but this is no hustle for me. I really want to preach. I remember as a small child when your momma, my momma, and Big Momma, used to take us to church, and I saw how those well dressed preachers with their shiny new cars would have the church house rocking with their big words and fancy style of talking. I said to myself right then that I want to do that when I grow up. Forget about being a doctor or a lawyer or a policeman. I wanted to be a well dressed, smooth talking preacher. So that is why I went to the Baptist Seminary to learn the word."

"The word? What word?" Theo asks, extremely puzzled.

"Cousin, the word just means the words in the Bible. I learned how to preach God's word! I was called to preach and teach God's word, so just be patient and continue to help me. I have a dream, a vision that one day I will be one of the best known pastors in this country, and when I do, I promise there will be something in it for you," N. O. says in the manner of a politician.

"We're talking money, Cuz, right?" Theo asks in a very serious tone.

"Yes, of course," N. O. responds.

"All right then cause you know I ain't into no church. I want what I'm gonna get now, not in some heaven," Theo says sarcastically.

"Okay, Theo!" N. O. says exasperated.

"Look Theo, let me talk to you later. Me and the wife have to feed the children and put them to bed, so I will talk to you soon."

"Okay Cuz. I will come up with something to get you into that church cause I heard that even though the church is small, they got a few members with some serious cheese. I even heard that one of the deacons hit the Big Lotto a few years ago. Okay Cuz, like I said, we'll be talking soon. Later, N. O."

"Later, Theo."

"Lord help me stay focused on what lies ahead for me. I want you to bless me and my family so I will dedicate myself to teaching your word to your people."

"N.O. Oh, excuse me, honey, I did not notice you were praying," Marie Antoinette Goode says, as she abruptly enters the dining room.

"That's okay, Baby," N. O. says, still reflecting on his conversation with Theo.

"By the way, N. O., who was that on the telephone? The voice sounded so familiar."

"Oh that was my cousin, Theo, who I grew up with like a brother. He was calling to congratulate me on getting the job at New Harvest."

"But Honey, we just arrived home and have not talked to anyone. How did he know you had the job?"

"That was him and his wife who joined New Harvest, when I opened the doors of the church!"

"But N. O., if he is your cousin, why did he not say that..."

"Baby, I am exhausted. Can we eat, then talk about this later!"

N. O. says, his head down and his energy level diminished by the call.

"Fine!" she responds sharply.

There will be no celebrating tonight, she thinks to herself.

"Daddy, do we have to go back to that old, hot, stinky church?" Salome, the Goode's oldest child asks staring at her father intensely as she sticks her fork into her mashed potatoes as if she is not hungry.

"Well Baby girl, they have offered me the job of Pastor at that church," N. O. says, searching for the real question behind the question posed by his daughter.

"Well Daddy, I think you can find a much better church to preach for, and with air-conditioning and real pews. That church was just too old, too small, and too dirty for us," Salome responds, lowering her eyes, staring at her fast food chicken dinner on a styrofoam plate.

"Salome, I am just starting out as a preacher, so I have to start small, then work to build that church to a big church."

"But Daddy, why do we have to start small? Why can't we start with a bigger church, a real church, not some old store turned into a church. There has to be some real church somewhere in this city that you could preach at. Great Grandpa Wainwright is always telling me we deserve the very best, and that church is not the very best!"

Taking a deep breath to control his frustration with Salome's comments, N. O. responds, "Baby girl, even Great Grandpa Wainwright started with a small business that he grew over several years. I want to do what he did. Start small and end up big. Please be patient with your father. I have big plans, and one day you will be happy with what we will have as a family. Right Baby," N. O. says looking over at Marie Antoinette.

"Ahhh, yes, that is correct N. O," Marie Antoinette responds both sarcastically and reluctantly.

"Yes baby, listen to your father. He has **BIG PLANS** for this family."

"Daddy, Delilah," the second oldest Goode child quips.

"Yes, Sweetie!"

"Daddy, how long will it take for you to get a bigger church? Will I be able to have my own room?" Delilah asks with a degree of enthusiasm.

"Sweetie, one day not only will you have your own room, when you are old enough, you will have your own car and the best clothes, fine jewelry,"

"N. O!" Marie Antoinette yells.

"Stop filling that child's head with a lot of nonsense. A lot of dreams."

Chuckling and leaning back in his chair in the dining room, N. O. snaps back, "Baby, if we don't have dreams for our future and share those dreams with our children, what is the purpose of living. It is our dreams that give us the motivation to try and do better for ourselves. Look at me. I started as a simple worker in a meat packing factory and part-time janitor working for your granddad, and look at me now. I went from working on the line to being the Budget Director at the very factory where I was making about $13.00 an hour. And now, I have a good government job. I have a BA degree in Finance, and a Certificate of Completion from the Cloverdale Bible Community College. WHY! Because I had a dream that one day I would be like all those well dressed, nice-car-driving, big-house-living preachers I used to see and admire in my old neighborhood."

As N. O. looks across the table, he sees that his stern speech is upsetting his wife and children. Each of their children is frozen in motion with either a fork or a piece of chicken in their hands.

N. O. continues, "Look Baby, I don't mean to seem like I am upset, but we should never squash the dreams of our children. What would it hurt to let them have dreams, big dreams?"

Abruptly rising from her seat and throwing her paper napkin onto the table, Marie Antoinette Goode makes a dash to their bedroom, holding her left hand over her mouth as if she were about to throw up.

"What did you do to Momma?" Jabez asks his Dad with a hateful look on his face.

"Yeah, Daddy, why did you have to talk to Momma like that," Delilah asks as she gets up abruptly and heads along with her brother to their parents' bedroom."

Knocking on the bedroom door, Jabez says, "Momma are you all right? Momma, is everything okay?"

"Momma, are you okay?" Delilah asks in a concerned tone.

N.O. and Salome still sit at the table. N. O. is baffled by what has just happened and asks Salome, "Don't you want to go and check on your mother, too?"

"No, Daddy, I'm okay sitting here with you. Momma will be okay after she stops crying."

"Crying?" N.O asks, surprised by his daughter's comment.

"Yeah, Momma cries a lot when you are not here, especially when she talks to Granddaddy and Grandmother on the telephone."

"Do you know what they talk about?" N. O. asks, his elbows on the table and his face buried in his hands with an expression indicating his puzzlement.

"They talk about how Momma should be living in a bigger house, have better clothes, that kind of stuff."

"Salome, Salome," Delilah yells at her older sister.

"Come here right now!"

"Okay," Salome says timidly as she slips out of her seat at the table and makes her way toward her parents' bedroom.

"Salome, what have I told you about telling our secrets to Daddy? What have Mommy and I told you about girl's talk? Delilah says indignantly.

"I'm sorry, I'm sorry, Delilah," Salome says in a tense and subservient tone, slightly above a whisper.

"All right Salome, but do not let me have to talk to you again about this. There are some things us girls need to keep from Jabez and Daddy! Do you understand?" Delilah says, still scolding her big sister with her speech and eyes.

"What are you two talking about?" Jabez asks after going to the bathroom to get a box of tissues and rejoining his sisters.

"Nothing much," Delilah and Salome respond in unison.

"Nothing at all," Delilah reiterates.

Knocking on their parents' bedroom door, Jabez, Delilah and Salome are finally told they can enter by their mother, who is sitting at the foot of the bed, still in tears. They close the door behind them. Jabez hands his mother the box of tissues while Salome and Delilah both sit on opposites sides of her and throw their arms around her.

Meanwhile, while sitting at the dining room table, N. O. thinks to himself, "so the high and mighty Wainwrights are still filling my baby's head with a lot of nonsense about how I'm not a good provider and how she could have had the pick of the litter in this city's eligible **RICH** bachelors? Hmm!

This is the story of my life, I have always had to prove myself to everybody, and now I have to prove myself to my own wife. But that is okay. I will show those damn Wainwrights they have a diamond in the rough that will evolve into the Hope Diamond! He rises to go to his bedroom and sees his daughters comforting his wife and his only son with his arms folded across his chest standing guard inside his bedroom near the door. When he attempts to enter, Jabez blocks his admission and says sternly, "Now is not a good time for you to come in, Daddy. Momma is upset with you."

N. O. stares at his son as if he was a traitor and stomps back down the hallway to the dining room and tries to finish his dinner. Damn those Wainwrights! They are getting my own flesh and blood to gang up on me, N.O. mutters to himself. I hate them! I hate them with a deep purple passion, he mutters to himself, ensuring that he is not overheard by his children.

"Momma, what's wrong?" Delilah asks," trying to comfort her mother.

"I am okay, children. Mommy needs some time alone. Please go and finish your dinners. I'll be out in a few minutes."

"Okay," the children all say in unison as they slowly walk out of their parents' bedroom single file looking back at their mother.

"Please close the door behind you."

"Yes, Mommy," Delilah says, pulling the bedroom door tight, shaking her head in disbelief.

Marie Antoinette pulls the comforter and sheets back, then puts her right-hand between the mattress and the box springs and pulls out a nine by twelve inch manila mailing envelope and slowly pulls on the adhesive tab that has signs of having being opened before.

She then pulls out a stack of ten or more recent photographs of a red bone woman in the company of two teenage boys. One could see from the photographs that at one time in her life the woman had a nice body but has put on a few pounds in all the wrong places. The boys are obviously her sons because there is a very strong resemblance to the woman, but there is something familiar, very familiar about the boys that disturb, Marie Antoinette. She unfolds a letter that she has obviously read before and reads,

"Mr. Eldridge Wainwright,

 Enclosed, please find the photographs my operative in Mississippi has taken that offers conclusive proof that your son in-law, N. O. Goode, is the father of two illegitimate and dependent children, (sons) born to a Ms. Sylvia Weekes. Ms. Weekes gets public assistance for their sons with the benefits for the oldest son, Nathaniel, about to be exhausted because he is approaching eighteen years of age. Public records suggest that Mr. Goode has not paid any child support to either child and has denied paternity of said children.

 It is also worthy to note that Mr. Goode has a criminal record for criminal offenses such as petty larceny, carrying a concealed weapon, pandering for prostitution, possession of a controlled substance, and distribution of marijuana. All of these records were expunged four years after his cases were adjudicated per a plea bargain years ago, but my operative is well connected and was able to get a friend in the county courthouse to provide us with this information with the understanding that we could never use this information as it would jeopardize my operative's source's job. Local records indicate that since Mr. Goode has been a resident of this state, he has avoided arrest; however, my operatives here have discovered that when he first arrived in this community he was involved in distributing small amounts of marijuana and cocaine. He was never arrested but was known to have some criminal associations, some of whom are incarcerated at this writing. He also discreetly associates with a cousin who is a known felon.

This information was acquired via a wiretap of his current residence.

My assessment is that your concerns about Mr. Goode's character and integrity are well founded. As it is said in the streets, "He bears watching." In all fairness, it is possible that he has turned his life around after his past encounters with the legal system.

I hope that you have found our investigative work to be more than satisfactory and hope that you will use our services in the future. If you would like to extend our surveillance of Mr. Goode, we would welcome the opportunity and offer you a modest discount on our fees for our services.

Sincerely,
John Templeton
J. A. Templeton & Sons, Private Investigations"

Damn you, N. O! How are you going to provide for our three children when you have two sons you have never told me about in Mississippi? Those boys have your build, eyes and head! Are there any more children by different women lurking in the woodwork? What if this woman finds out where you are and seeks back child support? Oh N. O., what have you done? What have you done to our family? Marie Antoinette says to herself as she places the photographs back into the envelope, reseals it, then secures it under the mattress as far as her arm would reach. She then remakes the bed as if nothing has happened.

"Lord, give me the patience and strength to deal with what will obviously happen in the future. You know how much I love this man, and he has never shown me any disrespect or any to our children, but one day I will have to address this issue with him, one day soon," Marie Antoinette says aloud knowing she is alone in the bedroom. She quickly walks over to the mirrored closet doors, straightens her dress, wipes the tears from her eyes, and prepares to go back to the dinner table. She opens the bedroom door and walks to the dinner table as if she were a runway model exuding a great degree of poise and grace.

"Baby are you okay," N. O. asks cautiously, sensing something is wrong.

"I am okay! Now everyone finish their food so we can have dessert," she says in response.

"Dessert?" the children yell in a chorus.

"Yes, dessert. We have ice cream and cake, but you must eat all your food," Marie Antoinette says, avoiding eye contact with N. O.

"Baby, are you sure you are okay," N. O. asks nervously.

"Yes, I am okay, but we need to talk, N. O. We really need to have a long talk," she blurts out, not trying to hide her disgust.

"Okay Baby, we'll talk," N. O. says, sensing that he is in serious trouble.

Did she catch me checking out that fine usher, Sister Goodbody, N. O. quizzes himself. He is completely off-track, completely oblivious to the seriousness and severity of what is plaguing Marie Antoinette.

After everyone finishes their meals, Marie Antoinette directs the children to get ready for bed, and they all joyfully comply. It has been a very long day for them and they are ready to go to bed without any whining.

After she makes sure the children are all in bed and asleep, she goes back into her and N. O.'s bedroom and retrieves the envelope from under the mattress. Holding it as if she is not sure whether or not this is the right time to confront her husband, she steps back toward the bed and is about to hide the envelope when she notices N. O. standing in the doorway.

"Baby, what is wrong?" N. O. asks nervously, still puzzled as to what the problem is.

Marie Antoinette begins to weep softly and flings the envelope at N. O., hitting him in his chest.

"This is what is wrong," she says, as she plops onto the bed covering her face with both hands."

"N. O., how could you deceive me like this? What am I supposed to say to my family who was not in favor of my marrying you in the first place! What are we going to do, N. O? And more importantly, what are you going to do about your other family? I know my dad will want me to get a divorce! What are you going to do N. O? What are you going to do?" Marie Antoinette asks, her face still buried in her hands and her sobbing becoming louder and louder!

Sighing deeply, N. O. says, "Baby, I am sorry, but my boys' mother did not want me to have anything to do with my sons because I no longer loved her. So, to punish me, she kept me from my sons, and when I tried to make contact with them, she hid them from me. Baby, I promise you I tried to take care of my boys, but their evil and vindictive mother prevented me from being in their lives. She even turned her whole family against me. They would take my boys and hide them every single time I tried to make contact. Baby, I tried. Honestly I tried!" N. O. says, slowly sitting on the bed caressing Marie Antoinette tenderly, kissing her on the nape of her neck, then rotating her body in his direction so he can kiss her on the lips.

"Oh N. O., are you telling me the truth?" she asks, her anger subsiding and her naiveté oozing from her words.

"Yes Baby, I am telling you the truth! I have never lied to you, and I do not plan to start now. Now that your dad has helped me locate my sons, I will do what I have wanted to do for a long time and support them!," N. O. says as he rolls Marie Antoinette on her back and starts to simultaneously kiss her tenderly as he starts to unbutton her blouse.

"Oh N. O," she says as she slips her hand to the night stand and turns off the lights with a remote control.

Back at Ms. Jenkins's House

Noticing that Ms. Jenkins is beginning to nod off, Reggie abruptly says, "Well Ms. Jenkins, I really enjoyed the meal, and I certainly enjoyed your insights into Pastor Goode's past. What an incredible memory you have. And you say he confided all of what you told me to you? Why do you think he trusted you so much?"

"Well Reggie, I knows that I am not a busybody in the neighborhood or my church, so he trusted me for that reason. Also, due to the fact that I was the top mother of the church, I have influence with the deacons, trustees and the rest of the church members. But I also kinda think he saw me as a mother figure since he lost his mother many years ago when he was a very young man."

"Okay. I see," Reggie says standing and stretching because it has been a long session with Ms. Jenkins.

He stretches again then says, "Please excuse me. When can we meet again to work on the book?"

"Tomorrow, Baby. Tomorrow. And I will make you another big dinner," Ms. Jenkins says before Reggie interrupts her and says, "Ms. Jenkins, if I eat like this every time I come over here, I will gain too much weight. How about if I stop at Giuseppe's Pizza and bring a couple of their Italian salads? Is that okay with you, too, Chastity?"

Her eyes bulging with glee and anticipation from the thought of having a celebrity in her house Chastity says, "Certainly, or I can make us a big salad. What kind of dressing do you like?"

"Chastity," Ms. Jenkins interrupts. "Stop being so forward. If I didn't know any better I would think you kinda like Reggie."

Reggie just smiles and Chastity thinks to herself, "If you only knew how much I like this man. He is so **FINE!** And he's intelligent with a good job, too!"

The Next Evening Back At Ms. Jenkins's House

Like a child waiting on Santa Claus, Chastity peers through the curtains at her grandmother's house, waiting eagerly for Reggie to get out of his car and ascend the steps to the porch. Once Reggie has made it to the porch, Chastity abruptly yanks the door open and says, "Hi Reggie! May I help you with those bags?"

"Sure," Reggie says, noticing that Chastity is wearing an extremely tight pair of jeans and an equally tight top that clearly shows off her well sculpted and well proportioned physique. Damn! This girl could give Beyoncé a run for her money when it comes to having a tight body, Reggie says to himself, trying to disguise the fact that he is very impressed with Chastity's build.

"What is that I smell," Reggie asks as he hands Chastity a couple of the bags from the Italian Pizzeria and takes his oversized backpack off his shoulder and places it on the floor.

"Oh, its one of those fragrances that I bought from one of the Muslim vendors at the Flea market," she responds coyly.

"Oh, I meant, is that sweet potato pie I smell coming from the kitchen? I told your grandmother she didn't have to cook anything, but I love her sweet potato pie," Reggie responds, completely oblivious of Chastity's constant stares.

"Oh, I'm sorry. Your fragrance is nice, very nice, but that sweet potato pie aroma has really got my attention," Reggie says apologetically, sensing he has hurt Chastity's feelings.

"Reggie's here," Chastity yells in the direction of the kitchen with a tinge of disappointment in her voice.

"Well, bring him back here chile. Where's your manners?" Ms. Jenkins yells back in a slightly happy and simultaneously irritated tone.

"These young folk of today have no manners. I told that girl a thousand times, manners will carry you farther in life than money, but she just doesn't get it."

Reggie and Chastity walk side by side and enter the kitchen as Reggie looks intently at all the family pictures on the living room and hallway walls.

"Well Baby, I mean Reggie, are you ready to get started with the interview?" Ms. Jenkins asks as she leans forward and gives Reggie a kiss on his cheek. She is trying not to get any flour from her apron on his sports jacket.

"Well, wouldn't you two like to eat first," he responds, taking the same seat at the kitchen table he occupied on his first visits.

"Well, you and Chastity can eat because I had a snack when I was fixing the pies. I made one for you to take with you, but you've gotta promise me one thing, ya hear?" Ms. Jenkins says looking very serious.

"What is that Loulabelle," Reggie says, remembering she does not like to be called ma'am.

"You can't give not one slice; not one crumb of this pie to any of your girlfriends," she says, trying not to laugh.

"Not a problem. I don't have a girlfriend, let alone girlfriends," Reggie says smiling.

"What's the matter? You do like women, don't you?" Ms. Jenkins asks seriously.

"Grandma," Chastity interrupts, slightly surprised and embarrassed by her question.

"No, Ms. Jenkins, I love women, especially African American women, but my hectic work schedule does not allow me much time to socialize, and since I am a Christian, I don't do the bar scene," Reggie responds, seemingly not surprised or insulted by Ms. Jenkins's question.

Ms. Jenkins and Chastity make eye contact acknowledging the fact that Reggie is single, a Christian, and more importantly, **_AVAILABLE!_**

"So no girlfriends, huh," Ms. Jenkins asks like she is a prosecutor and Reggie is a defendant on trial for his life!

"Yes ma'am, Yes Loulabelle. No girlfriends," Reggie quickly responds, smiling.

"Okay then, that's settled. Let's get back to the Pastor Goode story," Ms. Jenkins says, washing her hands in the kitchen sink then grabbing some large bowls from her cabinets for the salad Reggie has brought.

"Okay, where was I? Oh yeah, I was talking about how that rascal came to be Pastor of New Harvest. Well, the next thing that happened was," she continues with her story. She seems to be in a trance-like state as Reggie listens intently.

Chastity sits as close as possible to Reggie during Ms. Jenkins's discourse to the point of making it uncomfortable for him to move like we all do when we sit in the same spot for hours.

"Okay, the next important thing that happened was that Pastor Goode had to get voted in by the congregation at the next quarterly Church Business meeting. Was he smooth or what? He was so impressive, and he even got me to fall for his tricks and smooth talk.

"Oh he's a crook all right," Chastity quips. "He's a real con man," she continues.

"Anyway Reggie," Ms. Jenkins continues, "This is what happened."

Saturday, 6:00p.m. Fifteen Years Ago at the 9th Street New Harvest Missionary Baptist Church Quarterly Business Meeting

Reverend Goode has been asked to address the small but growing membership of the storefront church and to provide the congregation with his vision for the Church.

Reverend Goode, who is wearing a size too small sports jacket and a golf shirt, struggles with the buttons on his sports jacket. He soon realizes the futility of trying to button his sports jacket and simply gives up.

His nervousness very apparent just by his fidgeting stance, he waits to be introduced by Deacon Isa Crooke, chairman of the New harvest Deacon Board.

"Good evening New Harvest. I see some new faces and assume you are interested in joining our church or have recently come up to join New Harvest when the doors of the church were open. Here at New Harvest we try to follow the scriptures about our church meetings, and that scripture is found in 'I Corinthians 14:40,' where it reads, *DO THINGS DECENT AND IN ORDER!* So, I am asking that we be aware of the fact that time is precious, and we need to get here on time so we can get out on time. Our meetings are supposed to start at 6pm, and end at 8pm, but when people come in twenty, or thirty minutes late, that slows down the process because we have to go **BACK** over some of the agenda items to bring everyone up to speed."

Deacon Fellowes thinks to himself, we need to start on time and end on time as long as we have a quorum and not worry about the latecomers keeping up. It is on them to stay caught up by being on time!

"First on our agenda," Deacon Crooke continues, "is the introduction of Reverend Nathan Obadiah Goode, whom the Deacon Board has made a tentative offer to become the next Pastor of New Harvest."

Deacon Crooke is interrupted briefly by boisterous applause from the small group of New Harvest members who regularly attend the Business Meeting on time.

"Hallelujah," shouts an attractive woman of about seventy whose beautiful silver hair is matched by her elegant silver and very stylish jogging suit. One can tell from her appearance she is a woman of exceptional means because her wrists are adorned with a series of diamond studded bracelets. Her earrings are also studded with at least 2.5 carat diamonds.

"Praise God! Praise God," shouts Ms. Loulabelle Jenkins, the Main mother of the church, her gray hair exposed at her temples under her not so expensive wig.

"That's what I'm talking about," shouts Deacon H. O. Monger as he stands like a proud parent applauding as if one of his children was taking a bow after performing in an elementary school play.

Stretching his arms to signal he wants the shouting and cheering to stop, Deacon Isa Crooke, "Okay! Okay! As I was about to say, we will hear from Reverend Goode in terms of his vision for this church, and we will vote whether or not we should make him our permanent Pastor," he says in his usual pompous, intimidating and arrogant tone.

His tone borders on a threat as the people instantly become quiet and return to some semblance of order and decorum.

Quickly rising from his seat on the front row of the church, N. O. Goode virtually leaps to the pulpit and positions himself directly behind the podium. He then scans the sanctuary from left to right, then right to left as if he is looking for a specific person.

Leaning into the microphone and clearing his throat N.O. says, "I want to thank the Deacon Board and the congregation of New Harvest for giving me this opportunity to speak to you and share with you my three point vision for the growth of this church. But before I do that, I want to introduce my lovely wife, Marie Antoinette, and our wonderful children, Delilah, Salome and Jabez."

Reverend Goode's wife and daughters stand and are acknowledged by the sixty plus people attending the meeting. The children are all sleepy and are sitting uncomfortably on the old worn out chairs placed close enough to resemble pews. Jabez, the youngest son, has stretched out in a fetal position and has fallen asleep. Delilah, having made eye contact with her mother, nudges Jabez, who slowly stands, rubbing his eyes vigorously in an attempt to awaken himself.

"Thank you all for the warm reception of my family. I also want each of you to know that we will not allow ourselves to get the big head, thinking that we need to be placed on a pedestal in this church. We will work as hard as any other family in New Harvest to ensure that this church becomes the best and largest House of God in this community, if not the nation! If the floors need to be mopped, we will mop the floors! If the sanctuary needs to be painted, we will buy our own brushes and help paint the sanctuary! If we are fellowshipping with another church with a meal, we will help prepare and serve that meal! We are here to work in the service of the Lord and will do whatever it takes to build this church to glorify our Lord and Savior, Jesus Christ!"

"You tell them Rev," a man on the second row behind N. O.'s family shouts while he stands and applauds enthusiastically.

"Yes Lord, this is the kind of man we need at New Harvest," the lady in the silver jogging suit shouts with twice as much vigor as the man who preceded her.

Reverend Goode's fervent delivery of his theme of being a true servant is warmly received by all the members of the congregation as the rest of the people assembled at the church meeting join in the loud and very vocal approval of N. O.'s comments. By this time the number of participants in the church business meeting has grown from about sixty to seventy-five folks.

Some people were born to go to work and come to church late, Reverend Goode thinks to himself, upset that people keep straggling into the room fifteen to twenty minutes late. He looks and sees who he has been waiting on to make an appearance, his cousin, Theo Lane, and his wife. Theo has an additional five or six couples with him as they all struggle to find seats in different areas of the small storefront church.

Marie Antoinette notices their arrival and wonders why they do not sit together as opposed to purposefully dispersing themselves among the congregation.

What is this all about? she ponders, looking over her shoulder at Theo and his wife.

N. O. Goode and Theo make eye contact, and Reverend Goode looks approvingly at Theo as if to give him a thumbs-up. Theo's arrival makes N.O feel reassured that he will be successful achieving his agenda tonight.

N. O. clears his throat again and says, "Before I share my three point vision of the direction I might assist New Harvest, please allow me to tell you a little about myself." I am one of five children, born and raised by devout Southern Baptist parents in rural Mississippi. My dad was a deacon who worked in the towns only black-owned funeral home, and my mother was a domestic. They taught me many Christian values such as honesty, decency, and devotion to God, family, and country, in that order. I was educated in my hometown's public school system. I have traveled across this country and have worked various jobs such as construction, on the line in factories, and even as a janitor. By the way, God blessed me to meet my lovely wife one night while I was working my second job as a janitor for her grandfather and father's, Wainwright's Janitorial Service. I said all that to say that I am not afraid of hard work. I promise that, in addition to my efforts, should you choose me as your Pastor, my wife and family will also work hard in this vineyard, called New Harvest."

N. O. is again interrupted by applause. When the applause subsides, N. O. continues, "In terms of my qualifications, I am a member of New Zechariah Full Gospel Baptist Church, where I accepted my calling to the ministry under Pastor Renaldo Barrington III. Pastor Barrington is my mentor, and he tutored me as I studied under him to one day be prepared to have my own church. I am also a graduate of the Wycliffe-Cloverdale Bible College in Paducah, Kentucky. I have a Bachelors degree from that institution in Theology and am currently taking courses online to fulfill the requirements for a PhD in Divinity from the John The Baptist University of Theology."

Deacon Isa Crooke sits in his throne-like chair with his hands perched atop his gem studded cane and shakes his head in a manner that suggests he is happy to hear they are getting such a qualified shepherd of New Harvest's flock.

Stepping back a few inches from the podium and vigorously wiping his brow, N. O. continues, "I am not the only member of my family who is well educated and brings a lot to the table because my lovely wife, Marie Antoinette, is a graduate of Guyton Business College where she holds a degree in Regional and Urban Planning. She is employed in this field by the state government, where she is a Senior Urban Planner.

"So, I say all this not to boast but to let you know that should you vote me in as your next Pastor, you will have someone who brings a lot of knowledge, skills and abilities to serve you as the Pastor of this wonderful congregation."

Deacon Isa Crooke stands and leads those in attendance in a rousing and thunderous applause of approval. Taking a silk handkerchief from his left pants pocket, Deacon Isa Crooke says, "Well, Reverend, tell us what you would do to build the membership of this church if we were to make you Pastor."

Showing a slight degree of nervousness, looking at Deacon Isa Crooke, then the congregation, Reverend N. O. Goode says, "I thank God for this opportunity to share my vision with all of you. I know that God sent me to New Harvest to assist you in the fulfillment of His mission that is recorded in the Book of Life in Heaven. So what follows is not necessarily my vision. Rather, it is the vision ordained for all of us here at New Harvest.!"

Pausing just long enough to take a very deep breath, N. O. reaches to the shelf under the podium, lifts a huge tumbler perched on the podium's shelf and takes a sip of ice water. He then continues, "God's vision for New Harvest comes in three logically connected phases. First, we will increase the membership of New Harvest within the next seven years by going out into the community, going door to door, street corner to street corner until we will require a much larger sanctuary. After all, we are a Missionary Baptist church, so we will become Missionaries in this community. Yes, if we implement God's plan, we will need a sanctuary that will have classrooms for Christian education and other Christ-based activities for our congregation, such as the Boys and Girl Scouts, Day Care, and a Credit Union to assist those in our community who can not get a loan from the large lending institutions because their income is below the poverty line. So how will we accomplish this you might ask? Well, that takes us to the next phase in God's vision for New Harvest. We have the structure that God wants us to have by the proper teaching of tithing in this church!"

N. O. is temporarily interrupted by the thunderous applause of the participants in the business meeting, most notably, Theo Lane and his crew who are all on their feet applauding vigorously.

Continuing, N.O. says, "Third, we will have the best Youth department of any church in this city because we want to build a larger church and ensure it continues to exist long after we are all gone on to glory. How do we do that? We teach our children to love the Lord, and logically, when they become of age, they will move New Harvest to an even higher level as one of the premier churches not only in this city but in this country."

"Preach," Deacon Monger's wife yells.

"Halleluiah," several people shout excitedly, showing their approval of N. O. Goode's three point vision for New Harvest.

N. O. backs away from the microphone waiting for the amens and increasing loud applause to subside. He scans the audience trying to do a quick head count of those who are showing their approval of his vision. His eyes become fixated when he notices Sister Goodbody who is sitting in the front row. She is wearing a very tight top and some even tighter short jeans.

Damn, that girl has a body on her: he almost blurts out as he surveys the contour of her body; her ample breasts, her tiny waist, wide hips and her enormous thighs.

Lord give me strength, he says to himself, still fixated over Sister Goodbody who notices his stares and is enjoying the attention. He finally snaps out of his trance-like state when Deacon Isa Crooke says, "New Harvest family, we are ready to vote on whether what we just heard from Reverend Goode is sufficient grounds to appoint him our next Pastor. All those in favor will show their support of Reverend Goode," Deacon Isa Crooke says before being interrupted by Deacon Fellowes.

"Excuse me Deac, but before we vote, don't we want to ensure that only New Harvest members vote on this very important issue, the future shepherd of this flock? The Word says that we must do everything decent and in order. I see several unfamiliar faces in the church this evening, and we don't want the vote to be swayed either way, for or against Reverend Goode by nonmembers," Deacon Fellowes says calmly while staring relentlessly and impolitely at Reverend Goode without a smile.

"Well, I see your point my brother, but many of the peoples here have been in our services before. But okay, let's do this! Will all the members of New Harvest please stand so we can do a head count?" Deacon Crooke says, a little irritated by Deacon Fellowes comments, which he knows are right.

Rising from his seat, Theo Lane, Reverend Goode's cousin, says, "May I ask a question?"

"Sure," Deacon Isa Crooke responds.

"Well, me and my wife came up to join the church, but we have not been extended the Right Hand of Fellowship. So, are we able to vote, because technically, anyone who wants to join, even if they were to join tonight, should be allowed to vote on the new Pastor. Otherwise, we could have stayed at home."

"He's got a point," one of the men that came in with Theo says loudly.

"Yeah, I agree with that brother because I want to join this church because I heard what a good preacher Reverend Goode is from a friend in this church. I'd join tonight if y'all would open the doors to the church!" says another member of Theo's group sitting across the sanctuary from Theo and his wife.

Theo and his plants have started a commotion in the church meeting, and many people are agreeing with them. Anyone who wants to join on the spot should be able to vote.

Rising from his seat near the middle of the church, brother Jabin Haran raises his hand to ask a question like he is in high school. Deacon Fellowes recognizes his attempt to be recognized and shouts over the boisterous conversations surrounding the voting question.

"We can all sing together, but we can't all talk together. Let us do things decent and in order. Please allow the young brother an opportunity to speak," Deacon Fellowes retorts, his tone twinged with irritation.

"Good evening, y'all. My name is Jabin Haran, and my grandmother used to be a member here. Some of you might remember that I joined this church because I made a promise to my granny. Okay," he says, taking a deep breath.

"Since we have an issue of who is a member and should have the right to vote, why don't we wait to the last Sunday of the month, which is only two weeks away, and anybody who has joined by then can vote. That way we would be sure that we do things like my brother said, in order and decent."

"Decent and in order" a chorus of members say, correcting him.

"Yeah, that's what I was trying to say. Personally, I like Reverend Goode and feel he is a good man, but I understand what the Deacon, what's your name brother?" he says, looking at Deacon Fellowes.

"Fellowes. Deacon Fellowes."

"Right! Like Deacon Fellowes said," Brother Haran says.

"Why should we have to wait two weeks when we plan on joining the church right now?" one of Theo Lane's crew asks, seemingly upset with brother Haran's idea of a delay.

"Yeah, I'd like to get this vote over tonight," Gladys Lane, Theo's wife says, with a smug expression on her face.

N. O. Goode looks at the deacons, then his wife and family, then the overall congregation. Whew! This might be a close call, but I have to give Theo credit for bringing in some folks to sway the vote in my favor if the vote goes down tonight. And if I get in, I'll owe him big time! N. O. says to himself, taking another look at Sister Goodbody, then looking over at his wife, Marie Antoinette.

That sister makes me want to go back to my playing days, but I must be cool until I get in the job as Pastor. Then I'll have to play this situation by ear. I can't get hooked up with this sister, no matter how bad she is, until I know if she'll be discreet, N. O. thinks to himself as he continues to absorb all the commotion created in the church about who is eligible to vote tonight.

"Deacon, Deacon Crooke, may I propose a possible solution to our dilemma?" N. O. asks, leaning directly into the microphone and talking as loud as he can to get everyone's attention.

"Certainly, Reverend," Deacon Isa Crooke responds, happy there is a break in the confusion brewing in the church.

"Well Deacon, I suggest that you and the seven members of the Deacon Board vote whether or not there is a vote tonight or if the vote is delayed, as my young brother suggested. Since there are seven of you, there can not be a tie, and I assume those assembled here tonight will abide by your decision." N. O. says, trying to hide his sinister smile and intent.

"That's a very good idea," Deacon Isa Crooke says, lifting his arms to the congregation in a manner that suggests he wanted their approval.

"All those in favor of the Deacon board deciding this voting issue, please raise your hands."

All but twelve of the people in the church raise her hands. Most notably, Deacon Fellowes does not raise his hand. Rather, he stands in a defiant pose with his arms wrapped across his chest. When Deacon Fellowes sees the majority vote for N. O's option, he just stands mute looking over at Brother Jabin Haran who also did not raise his hand in support of the Deacons making the decision on a vote that night.

"Okay, it's settled then. We will cast our votes tonight. All in favor of installing Reverend N. O. Goode as the next Pastor, the next shepherd of New Harvest Missionary Baptist Church, please say, aye!" The ayes were so boisterous that there was no need to ask for those who were not in favor, but Deacon Isa Crooke then asks, "All opposed?"

Only the same twelve people opposed, realizing they were defeated.

"Okay then, the deacons will retire back into the Deacon's Office where we will discuss and vote on whether or not we have another vote tonight to install Reverend Goode as our next Pastor," Deacon Crooke says loudly into the microphone as he points to the deacons letting them know to go into the Deacon's Office.

This is not right, Deacon Fellowes thinks to himself.

"I've got this! I've got this," N. O. says to himself trying to suppress his glee.

Back in the Deacons' Office

"Let's get this over with," Deacon Crooke says abruptly and impolitely to the other deacons.

"Deac, it seems you have already made up your mind, and there is no need for discussion," Deacon Fellowes says, in an exasperated tone.

"Well, I want this man as the Pastor because I believe I can work with him,…"

"You mean "control" him," Deacon Fellowes says interrupting Deacon Crooke.

"Be that as it may. I feel he's the best deal we can get right now. We can mold him to be the Pastor we want him to be because he wants this job badly," "But,…"

"No buts, Deacon Fellowes. We need to vote, get out of here, and get back with the people," Deacon Crooke says in a mean spirited tone, interrupting Deacon Fellowes who just shrugs his shoulders in disgust.

"Okay deacons. All in favor of having the installation vote tonight, say aye."

"Aye," all the deacons with the exception of Deacon Fellowes say, their heads bowed in a very subservient manner.

"Okay, that is it. Let's go back into the sanctuary and see what the people say," Deacon Crooke says in a triumphant tone.

The deacons reenter the sanctuary and call for the vote, and N. O. Goode is installed as the second Pastor of New Harvest Missionary Baptist Church.

N. O. vigorously shakes hands and hugs each deacon, showing his gratitude but he is rebuffed by Deacon Fellowes.

What is with this brother? N. O. asks himself, realizing that he is not one of Deacon Fellowes fav five.

N. O. is still ecstatic and wants to run over to Theo to give him a manly hug, but he does not want to make it apparent that they know each other. They make eye contact, and that eye contact says, "We did it!"

The business meeting begins to slowly wind down with most of the people going over to N. O. and expressing their congratulations as they exit the church. Some of the women are a little too brash, too bold in the manner they either hug or hold N. O.'s hand, so Marie Antoinette decides to move closer to where her husband is standing so she can hear what these women are saying as they congratulate her husband. She pays extra attention when she sees Sister Goodbody easing her way through the line of well-wishers and jockeying for position to be fourth in line to congratulate the newly installed Pastor N. O. Goode.

I hope I don't have to set that sister straight about her inappropriate behavior towards my husband! She looks like she is undressing him with her eyes. If she thinks I am meek, then she has another thing coming! I have enough problems with his little secret, Marie Antoinette thinks to herself, rolling her eyes and making every effort to ensure Sister Goodbody knows she is the object of her negative attention.

"You better watch how you approach my man," Marie Antoinette murmurs as she rouses her sleepy children, never taking her eyes off Sister Goodbody. She slowly positions herself within striking distance of her husband and the line of well-wishers like a lioness in tall grass about to pounce on her unsuspecting prey.

"Well, congratulations," Sister Goodbody says coyly as she stands in a sexy pose, flaunting her more than ample hips while softly placing her right hand in N. O.'s hand. She is wearing some very tight jeans and a tube top that shows her extraordinary figure.

Damn she's fine! N.O thinks, almost blurting out his inappropriate and lustful thoughts.

N.O. clasps his hands over hers, making a sandwich of her hand and his. He notices she is a little nervous because her breasts are heaving and her palms are very moist. He softly strokes her hand between his to the total irritation of Marie Antoinette who has intensified her concentration on this situation.

"N. O! N.O!" Marie Antoinette yells, trying to maintain her sense of decorum.

"Dear, would you mind giving me a hand with the children?" she says, staring Sister Goodbody down. She has a look that leaves no room or need for interpretation. Get away from MY MAN! she screams internally.

Noticing Sister Goode's irritation, Sister Goodbody slowly pulls her hand from between N. O.'s.

Clearing her throat, Sister Goodbody surveys the room before she addresses N. O.

"Well, again, I want to say congratulations. And I hope you will enjoy being the Pastor of this small but growing congregation. See ya Sunday," she says, waving at N. O. over her shoulder, swaying her shapely hips and butt in such a way that most of the men and women in the sanctuary are in complete awe.

Damn, all the men seem to be saying silently as they watch this marvel of God's creation.

Slut" all the women seem to be saying silently as they enviously watch her exit the building.

"Reverend, Reverend," Deacon H. O. Monger says, adjusting the volume of his voice upward, realizing that his new Pastor is more than slightly distracted.

"Yes, Deacon. What is it?" he responds.
"We need to get these folks out of here because it's getting late and we have to prepare for communion in the morning."

"Okay, fine," N. O says, moving toward his wife and children.

"Honey," he says to Marie Antoinette, who does not open her mouth but gives him a "Do not Honey me look."

It is going to be a long ride home, N. O. thinks to himself. A very long ride home.

"Well ladies and gentlemen, it is time for us to vacate the premises because our wonderful Deacon Board must return back here early to prepare for the Lord's Supper. I, I mean my family and I will see you all in the morning," N. O. says as he looks over to his wife to gauge just how angry she is. As the people walk by single file, he shakes their hand and pats them on the back, smiling like he had just won the largest lottery jackpot ever. His eyes dart down the single file line when he sees Sister Tricia Hamilton, New Harvest's most gifted vocalist just a few feet away.

Man, does this congregation have some fine women, N. O. thinks as Sister Hamilton gets closer and closer. N. O. looks at her intently. She has a body that rivals Sister Goodbody's, but she is more modest in her attire. N. O., however, notices her fine brown frame and greets her, staring at her breasts.

"What's your name, my Sister? I remember that song you led the Sunday I preached my trial sermon. Wow! You were beyond gifted," N. O. says shaking her hand and gently rubbing her back as if to get her aroused.

Sister Hamilton abruptly pulls away with an expression on her face that she is silently saying, Wait a minute! You do not know me like that, and besides, you are married.

This activity is being keenly observed by Marie Antoinette, who is struggling to keep her composure. She is fuming.

Sister Hamilton tries to fake a smile as she attempts to get as far away from N. O. as possible. "Have a good evening," she says, trying to be polite.

"May I have my hand back?" she says with a slight degree of frustration and irritation in her tone.

"Oh sure, my Sister. I meant no harm. I am just trying to get to know all the people in the congregation, especially those who have such a wonderful God given gift like you."

"Thanks, and have a good evening," she says, quickening her pace as she exits the building.

What an idiot! What a letch! she thinks as she opens her car door with her remote.

Finally, all the folks have left the building. N. O. turns in the direction of his family, focusing on Marie Antoinette. She is still suppressing her anger. They exit the sanctuary walking down the street with their children in tow. Finally they reach their van, and the sleepy children's bodies wave from right to left, then left to right as they struggle to stand straight. When all of the children are loaded in the van, they drive home, a trip that only took about twenty minutes but for N. O. seemed like an eternity. He finally pulls into their driveway and Marie Antoinette wakes the children and tenderly gives each one a kiss on the forehead as they disembark from the van.

N. O. opens the front door of their house and holds it while each of his children files past him. Marie Antoinette slowly steps past N. O., walking sideways. Her stare clearly sent the message to N. O., "You have really hurt me by disrespecting me with your actions tonight."

N. O. was correct; it was a very long ride home. Marie Antoinette just stared blankly out the windshield never saying a word.

N.O. goes into the living room, turns on the television, kicks his shoes off, and flops on the sofa. Ten minutes later, Marie Antoinette appears behind the sofa clutching a pillow, a blanket, and some sheets.

"Baby, what's up?" N. O. exclaims nervously.

"We'll talk in the morning," she responds exasperated.

"N. O., I am hurt! Very hurt by your lack of respect tonight. I saw how you were looking at those women, especially the one with the tube top and tight jeans. When you add your sons down south to how you are disrespecting me in public, you show me you have the ultimate contempt for me and our marriage. And you claim to be a man of God,..."

"Wait a minute, Baby; I am a man of God."

"Huh, some man of God! My father was right about you! You are nothing but an opportunist. You are only with me because I am a stepping stone to where you feel you will be in the future. You are a user! And I promise you, you will not use me to get into the right social circles, and you are certainly not going to play me for a fool right in my face. N. O. I want a divorce!"

"A *divorce,*" N. O. shouts, jumping up from the sofa and running back to where Marie Antoinette was standing with the linen and pillows still in her hands. N. O. attempts to hug her, but the linen separates them. With tears streaming down his face, N. O. says, "Baby, I am sorry. I was just trying to be friendly with all the New Harvest members, so when you thought I was paying too much attention to those other women,..."

"Stop N. O., stop," Marie Antoinette says bitterly, mindful of the fact that the children might hear them.

"You did not caress the fat and ugly duckling women the way you did some of the others, especially the two shapely girls, one with all her stuff hanging out. You caressed both of them in a very inappropriate manner. I saw you! I saw what you did! So do not make me think you think that I am *stupid!*"

"But Baby, a **DIVORCE!** N. O. shouts.

"Keep your voice down. I do not want you to wake the children up! Look, we will talk in the morning, but we are through. This marriage is over!" Marie Antoinette says fiercely and adamantly, rolling her eyes.

Ring! Ring! Ring! The ringing of the telephone immediately interrupts the argument between N. O. and Marie Antoinette. They both reach for the telephone, but N. O. retrieves it first. Marie Antoinette watches N. O.'s facial expression change and she can hear the muffled voice on the other end of the telephone. With a dazed look, N. O. slowly hands the telephone over to Marie Antoinette as if he was passing her a glass filled with nitroglycerin. Looking at N.O and realizing something must be wrong, she places the telephone against her right ear and says, "Hello, this is Marie Antoinette."

"Mrs. Goode, this is Captain Baxter Phelps, Chaplain of the U. S. Coastguard. Are you home alone, or is someone with you?"

"Who are you and why is it your business if I am home alone?" Marie Antoinette asks tersely.

"Well ma'am, it is my sad and unfortunate duty to inform you that your parents and grandparents were lost at sea," Captain Phelps responds, trying to maintain his composure.

"What?" Marie Antoinette screams in disbelief, tears streaming profusely down her cheeks.

She starts to waver like a willow in a windstorm, and N.O rushes to her side and props her up. She continues to scream in agony. She screams so loud that all three of their children are awakened and rush to the living room.

"Mommy, what is wrong?" they all shout.

"Mrs. Goode, Mrs. Goode," Captain Phelps says patiently with a great deal of compassion in his voice.

"Yes, yes, "Marie Antoinette says softly with her husband and children encircling her and holding her up. If they were not there, she would probably have fainted.

"Mrs. Goode, if I may continue. Your family members were cruising in the Caribbean on their sailboat. All the sailboat operators were notified by the Coast Guard of the potential dangers of the storm. They were advised to make it back to the nearest port. It appears that your family ignored the warning, possibly thinking they could make it to their destination, the island of Anguilla. The storm obviously took them by surprise in terms of its intensity. It appears that your family tried to make it back to their port of origin but got caught up in the midst of the storm. They subsequently sent out a distress signal, an SOS about four nautical miles southwest of Anguilla. We dispatched a cruiser, but when it arrived we discovered their sailboat had been capsized by the storm. Their sailboat was floating upside down. Apparently, they had all gone below deck to ride out the storm, but the sailboat took on too much water and eventually submerged, trapping them all inside. The storm was so fierce that their boat was swept toward a small remote island where it crashed on the reef. We have retrieved their bodies and will let you know when they can be viewed for positive identification. I am so terribly sorry and will stop by to see you tomorrow morning."

Crying hysterically, Marie Antoinette says in a barely audible voice, "Thank you." She places the telephone back in its cradle crookedly, and N. O. straightens it so they might receive other calls.

"Mommy, what is wrong?" Delilah asks in total amazement.

"Granddaddy and Granny Wainwright, Great Grand Daddy Wainwright, and his new wife, Hilda are gone," Marie Antoinette says as N. O. helps her sit on the sofa.

"Gone? Gone where?" Jabez asks.

"To heaven, son. They have all gone to heaven," N. O. responds, sensing Marie Antoinette's immeasurable grief.

"Oh my God! Oh no!" Salome exclaims wailing.

Delilah does not say a word and weeps uncontrollably as she sits next to her mother wrapping her arms around her mother's waist, shaking her head wildly.

"No Mommy, no. They can't **ALL** be dead!"

Jabez just stands mute like a guard at Buckingham Palace, trying not to show any emotion but he breaks and starts to cry uncontrollably.

N. O., sensing the opportunity to manipulate this tragic event to his advantage, sits on the sofa next to Marie Antoinette and strokes her hair. He reaches for a box of tissue on an end table and gently places the box in front of Marie Antoinette.

"Here you go Baby," he says, tenderly taking deep breaths while holding the box of tissue. He patiently holds the box of tissue in such a way as to not interrupt the comfort that Delilah is extending to her mother. Marie Antoinette pulls three tissues in rapid succession from the box, hands one to Delilah, and uses the other two in a futile attempt to stem the Niagara Falls-like tide of tears streaming down her cheeks.

N. O. slides closer to her and says, "Baby, leave everything to me. I'll talk to The Coast Guard and make the necessary arrangements to have your folks brought back here for a proper burial. Just trust me, Baby. Just give me this chance to prove how much I love you," he says, kissing her gently on the forehead.

Marie Antoinette is so devastated by the news of her family members, she almost forgets that moments earlier she was proposing divorce to N. O.

"That's wonderful of you since we both know how some of my family feels, I mean felt about you. I am not up to dealing with the funeral arrangements or anything like that," she says before being interrupted by N. O.

"Baby, I have your back and always will have your back. Just trust me. I will take care of everything," he says, wondering if she has forgotten about her threat to leave and divorce him.

"Thanks, Baby," she says as the telephone begins to ring. Many people call during the remainder of the night because the Wainwrights are one of the city's most respected and prominent families. When the local Television channels report the tragic news, many folks call the Goodes to express their condolences. People call and call all night long.

Back at Ms. Jenkins's House where Reggie is getting tired but is intrigued by Ms. Jenkins's incredible gift as a "Story Teller"

"Well Ms. Jenkins, I think we have covered a lot of material for the book. I must admit to being very impressed with your ability to recollect all these facts. Tell me before I come back on tomorrow what did happen that kept Pastor Goode and his wife together after the deaths of her family members? Why didn't she divorce him?" Reggie asks arching his back and stretching his arms into what looks like a human "Y."

"Well, Baby, this here story gets deep, real deep," but Pastor Goode was so gracious and loving to his wife during the time of her grief that she toned down her anger for months," Ms. Jenkins responds.

"Yeah, and he was smart enough not to even look at, let alone talk to any of the pretty women in the church. That calmed his wife down big time!" Chastity blurts out. Her grandmother looks at her with a silent and scolding look.

"Who's telling this story?" she remarks with a stern look at Chastity.

"That's all it took?" Reggie asks.

"Well, there was the fact that old man Wainwright," Ms. Jenkins says before being interrupted by Reggie.

"You mean Mrs. Goode's Grandfather, right?" Reggie asks.

"Yes, the older Mr. Wainwright," she responds.

"You see, Sister Goode was kinda locked into a situation where she more or less had to stay with Pastor Goode," Ms. Jenkins says, slowly rising from her chair, clutching her cane.

"Old man Wainwright married this real young, pretty thing younger than his very own granddaughter. She got him to change his will, and he did. He was a horny old bastard!"

"Grandma," Chastity shouts, wincing.

"I'm sorry, Baby! Anyway, the changes in the will made her executor and gave her the bulk of the old man Wainwright's estate. Eldridge and his heirs were only assigned ten percent of the total estate. I'm telling ya, the girl was smart! Real smart!"

"But I am a little confused about something," Reggie states.

"What's that?" Ms. Jenkins asks.

"Well, it seems to me that Eldridge would have contested the will revisions at its initial filing, suggesting that his father was not of sound mind and incapable of making the right decisions about how his estate was to be handled. After all, it was Eldridge who really built the business into where it is today, right?" Reggie asks, still puzzled and bewildered.

"Well Baby, Eldridge was fighting the changes in the will. To be honest, I don't understand why he and his wife were on the boat with his step mom unless he was planning to push her overboard.

He hated that girl because she was conniving and treacherous," Ms. Jenkins says after taking a sip of coffee.

"I tell ya, she was smart, real smart and turnt around and convinced old man Wainwright that Eldridge was plotting against him, and the will was revised again making her the sole beneficiary of the Wainwright Empire. Eldridge was furious, but again, he couldn't have been too furious because he went on the trip to the islands with them."

"Do you think Eldridge planned to use the trip to convince his father that his new young wife was a schemer? Do you think he felt that he could show his father that after all he had done over the years he had shown his loyalty and deserved to be treated better in the will?"

"Anything is possible, Reggie. Anything is possible. But I guess we'll never know now, huh?" Ms. Jenkins says as she begins to nod off a bit.

"After she convinced the old man to change his will a second time, the pretty young thing had a will of her own drawn up making her twenty-one-year-old son from a previous relationship the sole beneficiary of the old man's estate in case sumpthin happened to her. She had the bulk of the old man's money placed in a Trust Fund, and when the elder Wainwrights were killed in that storm, the youngster got all the money."

"But didn't Pastor Goode and his wife try to get a portion of the estate by going to court?" Reggie asks in disbelief.

"Oh yeah, they tried, but Pastor Goode picked some sto' front lawyer friend of his who did not have the best of reputations."

"What kind of lawyer did you say, sto' front?" Reggie asks, puzzled.

"She meant storefront, Reggie. He was a **sto' front** lawyer," Chastity says, slightly turning her head to the right so as to not laugh at her grandmother's country dialect.

"Oh, okay," Reggie says, biting his bottom lip so he, too, would not burst into delirious laughter at Ms. Jenkins's butchering of the English language.

"Anyway, Reggie, Pastor Goode's lawyer was sleazy and dishonest, but he and Pastor were tight. They knew each other way back when, and Pastor probably owed him a favor. Damn, I know more about the law than that fool did!" Ms. Jenkins replies, twisting her neck trying to get some relief from a crook in her neck.

"Anyway, the judge ruled against Pastor and Sister Goode. And Sister Goode was so upset with Pastor because his choice of a lawyer left her almost completely out of the will. She found out her cheap ass daddy did not leave her much in his will, and she got zero from her granddaddy's will. This was the beginning of Sisters Goode's desire to get even with Pastor Goode, and did she ever. First, he has the two sons he never told her about, and then he hires a buddy that causes her to lose her inheritance," Ms. Jenkins says, still fidgeting with her neck.

"What do you mean, Ms. Jenkins?" Reggie asks.

Before answering, Ms. Jenkins looks at the clock on her dining room wall, and realizing another thirty minutes have passed, sighs and says, "Well Reggie, that's another story for another day! Ms. Jenkins must put these tired old bones to bed. So we can continue on tomorrow."

"Okay, Ms. Jenkins, I'll see you and Chastity tomorrow at around the same time if that is okay," Reggie says, putting his micro recorder and note pad into his book bag.

"Okay, Baby," Ms. Jenkins says, smiling as she watches Chastity rise and walk Reggie to the front door.

"Goodnight Ms. Jenkins," Reggie says, noticing the lustful look in Chastity's eyes.

"Good night, Reggie," Ms. Jenkins responds.

Chastity walks down the long hallway from the kitchen to the living room. Her gait is almost like a school girl skipping next to the little boy she is infatuated with. Reggie is a little nervous because he senses that there will be a conversation when she lets him out the door that will make him very uncomfortable.

"All right Reg, calm down. It might not be as bad as you think it is. You don't want to blow this. You have a book deal hanging in the balance. She's a bad girl and all that, but her speech, age and maturity leave a lot to be desired. If you've got to let her down, let her down easy!" Reggie says to himself, slowly taking deep breaths.

"Reggie, I know I'm a few years younger than you. I don't have your type of money or education, but do you think it is possible that we could hang out sometime?" Chastity asks, standing all up in Reggie's space.

"Chastity, I told y'all I don't have or want a girlfriend right now. I want to get my career as a credible journalist started, so I do not think it advisable that we start seeing each other now."

Now, Chastity thinks aloud. So he's saying that I do have a chance but not right NOW, Chastity thinks with a huge smile.

"Okay Reggie, I will wait until you are ready, but I had to tell you that you are a fine and very well dressed man that I could easily fall in love with, so I'll be cool for now," Chastity says hugging Reggie, burying her head in his chest, rocking from side to side.

Becoming aroused, he very abruptly says, "Hey look, I have a deadline for a story I must submit for tomorrow's newscast, so I have to run. See you tomorrow, okay?" he says, dashing out the door like a fireman leaving the fire station on a fire call.

Standing in the doorway watching Reggie get into his car and drive off, Chastity slowly closes the door and thinks to herself, I know he likes me, I just gotta work on him. That brother is so fine!

2:35pm the Next Day in Reggie's cubicle

Reggie feverishly types his notes from his sessions with Ms. Jenkins into his laptop.

"This sad but true story has the makings of a Pulitzer," Reggie says to himself with an ink pen clutched in his teeth.

Ring, Ring, Ring!!!

"Hello. News room. This is Reggie. How may I help you?" Reggie says, recognizing the number displayed on his caller-id.

"Reggie, this is Chastity and,..."

"What's up Chastity? You sound excited," Reggie says, a little annoyed Chastity has called him at his office.

"It's my grandmother. She's sick, real sick," Chastity says excitedly.

"What!" Reggie exclaims.

"Yes Reggie, she's very sick and wants to see you before it's too late."

"Too late? What do you mean too late" Reggie asks, annoyed, suspicious and concerned.

"Look, Reggie, I've gotta go see about my grandmother cause it seems like you aren't concerned about her. I'll be here for another twenty minutes or so and then, never mind, forget it. You got other more important stuff to do," Chastity says as she slams the old wall mounted telephone in the kitchen into its cradle.

"Chastity! Chastity," Reggie shouts, then notices he has attracted the attention of all his colleagues on the newsroom floor, all of whom are standing and looking over the tops of their cubicles like a bunch of nosy neighbors.

Damn, I hope this girl isn't playing me, Reggie says to himself as he hastily grabs his cell phone, notebook and book bag and heads out the newsroom. Reggie rushes to the elevators and frantically pushes the down button repeatedly and impatiently.

"Finally," he says, when one of the three elevator doors opens. He rudely pushes his way past Kendrick, the copy boy that has a cart filled with video tapes and printouts to be viewed by the various film editors on the news room floor before the 5pm newscast.

"Where ya going Reg?" Kendrick, asks, wondering why Reggie is in such a big hurry.

The door to the elevator closes before Reggie has time to respond.

On the way to Ms. Jenkins's house, thoughts of Ms. Jenkins possibly being on her deathbed race through Reggie's mind. After all, he has become very fond of her while working on the book. Yet, he is suspicious of Chastity's intent. Is her grandmother really sick? If she is so sick, she needs to be rushed to a hospital. If he is expected to rush over to Ms. Jenkins's house, why hasn't Chastity called for an ambulance and asked Reggie to meet them at a local hospital? Is this just a ploy to get Reggie over to Ms. Jenkins's house so Chastity can spend some extra time with him?

That girl better not be playing me, Reggie mumbles to himself over and over again until he arrives in front of Ms. Jenkins's house. Everything appears okay, normal. There is no ambulance in front of Ms. Jenkins's house. No crowd of neighbors whose morbid curiosity induces them to stand in the intense heat to see what is going on. Nothing! Nothing seems out of the ordinary. He parks his car and rushes to the front door and knocks on the door as hard as he can. He finally hears Chastity say, "Who is it?"

"It's me, Reggie."

"Oh, thank God," Chastity says as she goes through the process of unlocking the two dead bolt locks and slides the chain lock off the door. After all, this is not one of your better neighborhoods in the city. Even though Ms. Jenkins is well known by all her neighbors, it is still dangerous because the youth of today in her neighborhood do not have the same values as their parents.

"Oh Reggie, I knew you would come over," she says coyly, exuding all the sexuality she could muster.

"Chastity, what's up? Where is your grandmother, and why are you dressed in a bathrobe if your grandmother is sick, or how did you say it, real sick?" Reggie asks his voice climbing and anger rising.

"Oh, I said that just to get you over here, Reggie. I wanted to show you how much I care about you, and I plan to show you just how much I love you," Chastity says, untying the belt to her terrycloth bathrobe and dropping it from her smooth and symmetrical shoulders to the floor, exposing the rest of her very nude and extremely curvaceous body.

Reggie winces, his obvious discomfort and stress clearly showing on his face. He tries to suppress his anger over being duped but mentally, and more importantly, physically he likes what he sees. He really likes what he sees!

"Whew!" he sighs deeply, trying to hide his erection which Chastity instantly notices and is overjoyed by her obvious effect on Reggie.

"Girl, put that robe back on. Nothing can and is going to happen between me and you. I told you I am not looking for any relationship right now. I am trying to get my career on track," Reggie says as Chastity approaches him, hugs him in a tender caress and gets on her tip toes to gently nibble on his left ear lobe.

"Stop that!" Reggie says as he *ssslllooowwwyyy* pushes Chastity away from him.

"Girl, what are you trying to do, get me fired and lose the book deal with your grandmother? Where is she anyway?" Reggie says as he has both hands on Chastity's shoulders keeping her at bay.

"Oh, today is her day to feed the homeless at the Malcolm X Center. She'll be gone for a couple more hours, so stop playing. You know you want this!" Chastity responds stepping back, showing the exquisite contour of her body. She then slowly turns around as if she were on a rotisserie. She makes sure that Reggie gets more than an eyeful of her tempting and flawless body.

"Jesus, this girl is something else," Reggie says as he steps backward, placing his hand on the door knob.

"Look Chastity, I have got to get back to the newsroom, so please, please do not do this again. I am not ready for a relationship."

"You mean you are not ready for a relationship with somebody like me, don't you," Chastity blurts out before Reggie could finish.

"No, that is not it, what I'm trying to say is that ..."

"Oh, I know what you are trying to say, that a girl like me from the hood is not good enough for some big time TV reporter because you have better options."

"Could you shut up for one minute, Chastity?" Reggie yells, not concerned if anyone outside might hear him.

"Look, you are a nice, beautiful girl, and the fact that you are from the hood has no bearing on why I do not want to get involved with you."

"That's a lie! You know you think I am not on your level," Chastity blurts out again, interrupting Reggie.

"Chastity," Reggie yells, That's not it, damnit! I am in love with someone else, but she's involved in a relationship with another man."

"So what's the problem, Reggie? She don't love you, so why can't we?"

"Chastity, I am a very focused man. I love this woman, and I know she loves me, but we had our problems in the past and those problems drove her into this other man's arms. I can not love you or anyone else for that matter until I know where her heart really lies. Listen to me," Reggie says loudly, sensing Chastity is about to interrupt him.

"Listen, do you want to be in a relationship with a man who loves another woman? Are you willing to be the other woman and never the main woman? No, I do not think so," Reggie says sternly as Chastity begins to weep softly and begins to pull the bathrobe back over her body.

Reggie reaches over to Chastity and hugs her. He then rocks her in his arms and says, "Look, you are a very attractive young woman, and you have one of the best bodies I have ever seen, but you are too young for me for one thing, and I am not, never have been, and never will be a player! I don't like being hurt, so I will not hurt you by using you for sex because that is all a relationship between us could ever be," Reggie says, still hugging Chastity and kissing her lightly on her forehead.

"But Reggie,.."

"What Chastity?"

"Whatcha gonna do if your girl marries the other man? What you going to do then?" Chastity asks tears still streaming down her cheeks.

"Honestly, I don't know. I don't know what I will do if that were to occur. I do know how I will feel though."

"How Reggie, how would you feel?" Chastity asks, tearfully looking up at Reggie while standing flat on her feet, her heaving breasts pressed firmly against his sternum.

"Like dying. I would feel like dying if she were to marry him. I have a difficult time as it is just knowing that she is in his arms, and forget about the thought of her sleeping with him. It just tears me apart inside," Reggie says, releasing Chastity and shaking his head in disgust as he takes a step backward.

"Look, if it is going to make you feel uncomfortable, then maybe I need to stay away for a few days. I can make an excuse so your grandmother will not get suspicious about my not coming over here every day," Reggie says, opening the two dead bolt locks but leaving the chain lock engaged.

Sighing deeply and repeatedly, Chastity finally says after a momentary pause, "Reggie, I love you and I'm gonna wait and see what happens with this woman you are all caught up with, and I promise to be cool, so please don't stop coming by," Chastity says, her words interrupted by her sniffles.

"Are you sure my coming by won't be a problem?" Reggie asks, waiting for what he hopes will be a sincere confirmation from Chastity.

"Yes Reggie I promise. I won't act a fool around you and my grandmother. I promise!"

"Okay then, I will see you later this evening," Reggie says as he opens the front door and hugs her, then hastily moves to his car. Chastity stands mute by the open door, her robe open at the bottom and her right leg and thigh prominent as Reggie takes one last lustful look at her.

Whew! She is a bad girl but ... Reggie thinks to himself as he starts his car and drives off.

Chastity stands in the doorway and watches Reggie drive away. She locks the door like she were locking the doors of a jewelry store at closing time, then slowly walks down the narrow hallway to her bedroom. Once there, she plops onto her bed and opens a scrapbook. The scrapbook is full of news articles about Reggie. She opens the scrapbook as far as it will expand and holds it across her chest, crying.

"Oh Reggie, we belong together," she says mournfully as she rocks sideways until she finally falls asleep. Hours pass and she is awakened by the sound of her grandmother turning her keys in the dead bolt locks.

"Chastity, Chastity!" Ms. Jenkins shouts through the narrow gap caused by the sliding chain lock on the door.

"Yes, Momma Loulabelle," Chastity says as she struggles to get into a pair of tight jeans and throws on an extra large T-shirt.

"I'm coming."

"Chile, what have you been doing? And look at this house. Girl, you knows that Reggie will be here in a few hours, and I do _**not**_ want him to see this house messed up. Have you started to cook?" Ms. Jenkins asks Chastity in a stern tone.

"Well, I had started getting everything ready," Chastity says, her head down as if she were embarrassed.

"Well girl, you'd better get to work! That handsome young man will be here shortly, so we've got a lot a work to do."

"Yes, Momma Loulabelle," Chastity responds sheepishly, rushing into the kitchen ahead of her grandmother to assist in preparing tonight's dinner for her beloved Reggie.

The same day, same time, Pastor N. O. Goode's room in the Intensive Care Unit of Mercy Hospital.

The Goode family surrounds N. O. Goode's bed in the ICU. He is in an oxygen tent, and Reverend Marie Antoinette Goode is in a prayerful pose as she and her children await the doctor's prognosis.

"Mrs. Goode," the doctor says, entering the room looking like he has not slept in a month, hair disheveled, and in desperate need of a haircut and shave.

Extending his right hand, he then says, "I am Doctor Clark Hudson."

Marie Antoinette shakes his hand with a definite lack of enthusiasm.

"Doctor," she barely utters.

"Mrs. Goode, I have to be honest with you. Your husband has suffered a massive stroke, and it is my fear that if he recovers, he will be in a vegetative state for the rest of his life. I noticed that he signed to be on the organ donors list. Is that correct?"

"What are you talking about?" Jabez asks hurriedly.

"Certainly you are not talking about taking my dad off life support so you can give his organs to other people, are you," Jabez continues, his anger obvious, his nostrils flaring.

"That's right," Salome interjects.

"You are not going to let my daddy die!" We want him to stay on life support until he recovers."

"But Miss, that is very unlikely. You may consult with another physician, but the prognosis is going to be the same."

Delilah simply stands mute. She begins to pace back and forth along the left side of her father's bedside with the beeping sounds of all the life monitors about to drive her crazy. She is completely oblivious to all the peripheral conversations.

Doctor Hudson scratches his right temple, sighs deeply, then says, "It's your call, but if he were my loved one, I would not want to see him like this for another year or two! He will only waste away right in front of your eyes. But again, it's your call!"

"But he's not your family, so we will make the decision," Delilah says, finally speaking up and hugging her mother.

"Okay, okay," Dr. Hudson says, shrugging his shoulders and sighing as he exits N. O.'s room. He looks over his shoulder to see who is watching him, then pulls his Black Berry off his belt and enters a linen closet where he redials the last number called.

"Hello, Dave. Look, we might have to wait for another candidate because I could not convince this family to pull the plug on the guy who was a big time crooked preacher here in the city. Naw, naw, his heart is perfectly fine. He had a massive stroke, so in essence he is brain dead. I gave the family my spiel about not wanting to see him on life support for a long time, but they wouldn't bite, so we'll have to either come up with another plan for this guy's family to change their minds or find another candidate. But this guy is a very good candidate for your brother's heart transplant surgery. Now remember, when I pull this off and get your brother a heart, you will owe me $50k, right? Okay, good. Look, I have to go," Dr Hudson says as he is interrupted by a housekeeper coming to get some clean sheets and pillow cases.

"Oh excuse me Doctor," the housekeeper says backing the huge laundry cart on wheels into the linen closet. She never lifts her head up while she navigates her way around the now silent Dr. Hudson.

6:30PM Ms. Jenkins's House

I sure hope this girl doesn't act out on me this evening, Reggie thinks to himself while turning off the ignition to his car. He sits in the car a few minutes, mentally preparing himself for some type of confrontation.

"Well I guess the longer I sit here, the longer it will take for me to find out what Chastity is thinking and what she may have told her grandmother. I hope that she is cool like she said she'd be so I can get the information for my book done as soon as possible."

Reggie slowly walks up the path to Ms. Jenkins house and knocks on the door.

"Is that you, Reggie?" Ms. Jenkins asks from a distance

"Yes ma'am, it's me," Reggie responds, wondering why Chastity is not answering the door.

"Hey Ms. Jenkins, it's good to see you, as always," Reggie says, struggling to keep his backpack on his shoulder as he stoops to hug her.

"Where's Chastity?" he asks.

"Oh, I don't know what is wrong with that girl. She said she wasn't feeling good, so she's in her room taking a nap."

Hmm! Taking a nap. That's good, very good, Reggie says to himself as he follows Ms. Jenkins through the house.

"That's her room right here if you want to knock and see if she wants to see you," Ms Jenkins says teasingly.

"Ah, no ma'am. That's okay. If she is taking a nap, I don't want to disturb her," Reggie says, almost tip-toeing his way past Chastity's bedroom door.

Inside her room Chastity hears the dialogue between her grandmother and Reggie. She desperately wants to burst out of the door and hug Reggie. However, rejection is not new to Chastity, and even though Reggie is fearful of an unwarranted outburst, she has reconciled herself to the fact that she must play it cool, very cool if she has a glimmer of a chance to be his woman.

"Lord, you know I don't ask you for much, but please let this man see some qualities in me that will make him want me for more than just my body. It's hard out here, Lord, for a good woman to find a good man, and you done dumped a good man in my lap. I take that as a sign that you want us together, so please show me a way to get with this man!" Chastity prays. She turns back over and lays in a fetal position. She clutches a community magazine which has a full page picture of Reggie on its cover and an associated article talking about his award winning news stories. She is so hyped up she tries to sleep but can not because she feels tightness in her chest, the tightness that we have all experienced when we have loved someone who did not love us in return.

"C'mon Baby and have a seat," Ms. Jenkins says as she heads to her stove to retrieve one of the four pots to prepare Reggie a plate.

Feeling rather awkward and extremely pensive, Reggie looks down the hallway expecting Chastity to exit her room with a weapon of some sort, maybe a butcher knife like the shower scene in the movie, *Psycho*. But still no Chastity. After Ms. Jenkins puts sumptuous portions of food on his plate, Reggie finally relaxes and is jolted back into reality when Ms. Jenkins asks,

"Baby, are you all right?"

"Oh sure, Ms. Jenkins. I'm good!"

"So where was I, Reggie?" Ms. Jenkins asks, in a slightly sexy tone as she tries desperately to slide into her chair at the table. After all, he is a very handsome man and she wants to give him the impression that she is a classy woman, a classy old woman.

"Well you were telling me about how Pastor Goode got his start at New Harvest and his plan to build the church into a mega church," Reggie says as he makes the necessary adjustments on his micro-recorder to record this session.

"Ms. Jenkins, what I really would like to focus on this evening is how Pastor Goode was able to grow New Harvest to the point it is today. What specifically did he do to take New Harvest from a small storefront church to the mega church it is today? Just how did he do that?" Reggie asks, trying to be polite but also trying to rush Ms. Jenkins along. He senses she enjoys his company and takes her time relating her story because the longer it takes to tell the story, the longer Reggie will grace her with his company.

"Well Baby, he's a very good preacher, but he ain't that good of a teacher. That's why he and Brother Haran were always at each other."

"You mean Jabin Haran, the Sunday School teacher turned deacon?" Reggie asks, as he slides his micro recorder closer to Ms. Jenkins's plate that is covered with sweet potatoes, roast beef and gravy, mashed potatoes and collard greens.

"Yeah him! If anyone should've been the Pastor of New Harvest, it should've been Brother, I mean Deacon Haran. That boy must've grew in the spirit cause when he first joined, he wasn't nothing but a thug. Be he turned his life over to the Lord and studied like nobody's business. And after a while that boy sho could teach. You see it was the people who started out helping Pastor Goode that eventually saw through him and brought him down," Ms. Jenkins says, stretching and twisting in her dinette chair.

"Okay, we can get to that later," Reggie says, slightly exasperated.

"What I'm trying to get a handle on is how did a man like N. O. Goode, a truly gifted and mesmerizing speaker, a man who was nobody's dummy, how did this man achieve such heights in the ministry, then have a dramatic fall from grace? Even you've said he was a real bright guy. So how did he get caught up in a situation that led to his being charged with massive embezzlement of funds and complicity in murder? "Reggie says, trying to be polite and show the proper respect to his elder. After all, it was Ms. Jenkins who Pastor Goode had confided all the sordid details of his nefarious schemes.

"Well, we needs to go back to when Pastor Goode first came to New

Harvest, he identified who was who and what was what.

"I'm not following you, Ms. Jenkins? Who was who and what was what?" Reggie asks perplexed.

"That's just an old country term meaning he cozied up to the deacons and trustees who he thought had the power and pacified those who didn't. He appeared to be everybody's friend, but all he wanted was to gain power by getting close to the people with the power. He was a smart politician cause he'd also flatter people like me who had lots of respect at New Harvest," Ms. Jenkins says, as if she made some very profound and philosophical statement.

"Huh," Reggie says.

"Okay, I have it! Who was who and what was what!" Reggie says with an obvious degree of clarity emerging from his tone.

"Look, Pastor Goode was a smart politician first," Ms. Jenkins says.

"He figured out from Jump Street who had the power, who had the money, who had the influence, and who didn't have any of that at New Harvest," Ms. Jenkins says, smiling.

"You see, he courted Deacon Isa Crooke because he knew Deacon Crooke was a former hustler, a very good hustler. So he went to him first and played him like an old fiddle. He was always telling Deacon Crooke how much he needed his guidance and even went so far as to plan his sermons based upon what topics Deacon Crooke wanted to hear. And there was a time when Pastor Goode was a whooper."

"A whooper?" Reggie asks.

"Reggie, you mean to tell me you don't know what a whooper is? she says surprised.

"No ma'am! Please enlighten me," Reggie immediately responds.

"Okay, Reggie. A whooper is a preacher who has a method of starting his sermon out real slow and then he uses his voice like a musical instrument. He moans and groans and raises his pace of speech faster and faster during his sermon. His voice might start at the baritone range, then rise to a falsetto while he'd be grabbing the microphone and letting loud this gravelly sound from deep down his throat. If you've ever listened to James Brown and think about how he'd say stuff like, 'and da' "ah ha,' 'huh, huh,' that's what a whooper does. Just think about a preacher preaching like he was singing a James Brown song. That's whooping!"

"Wow!, I got what you are saying now, but I have heard N. O. Goode speak, and he was typically a very emotional preacher, but he was also a very articulate preacher," Reggie says, as if Ms. Jenkins had just explained the complexities of aerodynamics and he understood every complex detail of her dissertation.

"Yeah, he was articulate when you heard him in the latter years, but at first he was a serious whooper, one of the best in the city if not the country. But when he started pulling in the educated peoples, he stopped whooping and started preaching like he was the damn King of England. He was too proper for some of the older members. Some left. Some complained silently. The rest just died off. "

"Okay, so tell me more about his manipulation of the people like Deacon Crooke," Reggie says, eager to follow in this vein of the story."

"Well, what Pastor Goode did was to, what's that big word that means you kiss somebody's behind to get what you want from them?" Ms. Jenkins asks, rubbing her chin with her left hand, looking up as if the word she was looking for is written on the kitchen ceiling.

"Do you mean ingratiate?" Reggie quickly responds.

"Yes, what Pastor Goode did was ingratiate himself to Deacon Isa Crooke so Deacon would not only put pressure on the churches founding members, but he also called in a lot of favors in the community. There were a lot of people that owed Deacon Crooke favors, some big favors!"

"Like what?" Reggie asked.

"Well, Deacon knew men who were in the building trades, so he had them come and spruce up the sto front, and then Pastor Goode had these big press conferences every three month, giving Deacon Crooke all the credit. But the real purpose of the press conferences was to get the TV and papers to focus on Pastor Goode's plan to build the church. He was like a Marcus Garvey, a Black Messiah who was using the TV and newspaper to tell people they needed to hurry up and get in on a good thing on the bottom floor. Pastor was pushing Deacon Crooke in front of the cameras, then he would step in and put the finishing touches on his spiel. It worked like a charm because within the first year of these press conferences New Harvest's membership grew three times as big as it was before Pastor Goode became our Pastor."

"So what types of things was Pastor Goode doing?" Reggie asked.

"Well, he copied some of the Black Panther's programs from the sixties. He had a program that took food to the elderly sick and shut-ins. He had us able bodied senior citizen women provide before and after school child care with a hot breakfast in the morning and a light snack in the afternoon for the poor children in the neighborhood. He got Black and White college kids to come in and tutor the middle and high school kids in the evening during the school week. And my favorite program was how he arranged to take the senior citizens to the grocery sto, the malls, and even to the movies on every Saturday morning, rain or shine, so we could get out the house and have a good time together."

"Wow!" Reggie exclaimed. So Ms. Jenkins, how did he manipulate the other leaders in the church?"

"Well, he played up to all the mothers of the church and the pretty young women and created a ministry called the Pastor's Advocates. What we would do was to sell fried fish and chicken dinners, and every two weeks we'd sell breakfast for three dollars, and the profits would go straight to the pastor in a plain brown paper bag. I always thought that was a little crooked, but who am I? Of course he asked me to be the Leader of this ministry cause I was known to be the best cook at New Harvest. I never touched the money though! No sir! We had a treasurer who handled that. I think she gave pastor some cause she was always pushing her fat self to the front of the line every time we had a dinner at the church."

"Gave the Pastor some what, Ms. Jenkins?" Reggie asks playfully, knowing what she was talking about.

"Boy, you know what I'm talking about!" Ms. Jenkins says as she lightly hits Reggie on his left arm, laughing.

"She'd always be batting her long fake eye lashes at Pastor, and I even saw her put a fifty dollar bill of her own money into one of the brown paper bags before she gave it to Pastor after we had sold a bunch of fried fish and chicken dinners," Ms. Jenkins says, scratching her head through her wig with a pencil she was using to write down the numbers she planned to play the next day.

"So how did he grow the church so fast? Ms. Jenkins," Reggie asks again politely, yet impatiently.

"Look Reggie, I knows you wants to get your Oscar for writing this story, but you need to let this old lady tell her story the only way she knows how, from beginning to end. I can't keep up with you if you expect me to jump all over the place because I'se got to tell you how it was told to me by Pastor Goode. And he told me like I was a priest and he was making a confession."

Reggie sits back in his chair slightly disgusted but realizes Ms. Jenkins is right. She must tell the story the way she knows how, no matter how long it takes.

Ms. Jenkins senses Reggie's impatient, then says, "You young people are so much in a hurry all the time. Where you have to go so fast and what are you going to do that is so important when you get there? Let me tell you how Pastor came to confide in me. You see, when he first started preaching, I fell after tripping on a torn piece of the carpet in the church. That was when we was still in the sto front. I didn't know it, but I had fractured my ankle. Pastor insisted that I go to the hospital and get an x-ray. I didn't think that I needed to go, but he insisted, so there I went off to the hospital in the church van. Pastor followed us in his family van and stayed at the hospital with me until I was released. He told the people at the hospital the church would cover my expenses, and he stayed with me until I was released. So we became good friends from that day on until he got into trouble with the law."

"So you are telling me just because he was so attentive to you, you began to trust him and he began to trust you?" Reggie asks leaning forward with an intense look on his face.

"That's right," Ms. Jenkins responds immediately. "I had his back, and when people would say things about him like he was inexperienced, I would come to his defense, especially against some of them deacons."

"What are some of the things some of the deacons said about Pastor Goode?" Reggie asks, ready to hear some juicy gossip.

"Well, Deacon Fellowes used to always say, HE BEARS WATCHING! And when Brother Jabin Haran got on the Board, he used to say Pastor needed to study more and that Pastor's sermons were real weak and that he got most of them off the computer, that he copied other preachers sermons and preached them like he wrote them himself.

"Weak," Reggie says, startled.

"Oh yes, they got into a serious war at some of the Bible Studies because Brother Haran knew that word better than Pastor, and at first, people thought he was just trying to show off, show everyone what he knew. But as time went by, we got to see that what Pastor was teaching us was not always biblical, especially what Pastor said about giving and working in God's vineyard."

"Hmm," Reggie sighs in disbelief.

"Yeah, I'm gonna miss brother Haran. He knew his stuff! You could tell he was a man who loved the Lord and studied as much as he could. He was one hellava Sunday School teacher," Ms. Jenkins says, as if she was reminiscing about the good old days.

"Grandma," Chastity says as she appears in the doorway clutching her half-length bathrobe tightly at the area under her breast and just above her waist. She is clutching the bathrobe so tight on purpose to show off her shapely hips and her bulging thighs, and her legs are not bad either.

Wow! That girl could be a Jet Beauty of the Week, Reggie thinks, trying not to let Ms. Jenkins notice how he is looking at Chastity.

Girl, now you know I've taught you better than that. Why are you in here with that short robe on when we got male company in the house? What you trying to do, give Reggie an eye full?" Ms. Jenkins asks.

"Why you in here anyway? I thought you weren't feeling good," Ms. Jenkins continues.

"I just came to get some cold water and some yogurt," Chastity says, brushing past Reggie as she heads to the refrigerator. Her right thigh touches his left leg.

"Oh, excuse me Reggie," Chastity says coyly.

"Well hurry up and get out of here so Reggie and I can continue talking. I don't want you in here enticing this man," Ms. Jenkins says as she stands up and stretches.

"Yes ma'am," Chastity says in a very sexy voice looking at Reggie. She grabs a bottle of water and a cup of yogurt from the refrigerator. She opens both but never gets a spoon for the yogurt, dipping her forefinger into the cup, then provocatively licking her finger in front of Reggie. When she sees that her grandmother is distracted, Chastity opens her robe like a flasher in New York's Central Park exposing her nude body. She winks at Reggie and silently mouths, "You know you want some of this!" as she thrusts her hips forward.

Reggie looks at her smooth taut skin which is obviously well oiled and glistens like fine satin.

Reggie looks at Ms. Jenkins who is still distracted and sighs deeply.

Yes, I want some of that, but what is it going to cost me, he thinks to himself. This girl is crazy, but she is so fine and has such an exquisite body, Reggie continues to think to himself.

"Good night, Grandma. Good night, Reggie," Chastity says as she looks directly into his eyes first then at his groin to see if she got him aroused.

"Hmm," she says softly as she notices that she has made an impression on Reggie. A really big impression on Reggie.

Standing at the edge of the kitchen and the hallway, Chastity mouths to

Reggie, "This can be yours! All you have to do is ask."

She walks slowly with an enticing gait down the narrow hallway looking over her shoulder to see if she has captured Reggie's attention.

She has! Most definitely!

WHEW! Reggie thinks to himself.

Come on Reggie, let's get focused. Let's get back on the J-O-B! he thinks to himself.

"Okay Ms. Jenkins. Can we talk about how the riff got started between Pastor Goode and Deacon Jabin Haran? And what caused the problems with Deacon Fellowes and Pastor Goode? How did Pastor Goode go from being the Pastor of a church that had a membership of seventy-five to eighty parishioners to being the Pastor of a mega church with well over fifteen-thousand members? These two deacons seemed be very honorable men!"

"Well, you see Deacon Haran joined the church when he was about twenty-three. He was raised by his grandmother because his momma was a stone cold junkie, all strung out on that stuff all the time. She was either not around or locked up. She eventually died from an overdose when Deacon Haran was just nine years old. That caused him to act out, but his grandmother got him back on track by the time he was in high school. Before she died, he had promised his grandmother that he would get into the church, and he truly kept his promise. That young man studied and studied, and it was easy for everybody to see how serious he was about the Word. He eventually became a Sunday School teacher, and if you're asking me, he was one of the best, if not the best, at New Harvest," Ms. Jenkins says stretching and looking at a very old antique looking wall clock over her refrigerator.

"Oow, look at the time, Reggie! We need to stop here and continue on another day," Ms. Jenkins says as she begins to yawn over and over again.

"Oh, forgive me Ms. Jenkins, but when I come over here and listen to you, I lose all track of time. May I ask you one more quick question before I leave, well, actually two questions?"

"Sure Baby. What cha wanna know?" Ms. Jenkins says, slowly rising from her seat at the dinette table.

"Well, I would like to know why Pastor Goode hated Deacon Haran and Deacon Fellowes so much?" Reggie asks, also rising as he packs his things into his book bag.

"Well, they were two different men, so he hated them for two different reasons. I'm getting tired, so I will just give you a preview about why he hated Deacon Haran so much. We can talk more Thursday evening because I'm going to my sister's church for Bible study tomorrow evening," Ms. Jenkins says, getting a little impatient with Reggie's persistence.

"You see, Pastor Goode hated Deacon Haran because Deacon Haran exposed Pastor for his lack of study, his laziness in his studies and for getting some of his sermons off the Internet!"

"Off the Internet," Reggie exclaims in a surprised tone.

"Yes, Deacon Haran, who knew the Word, said that Pastor copied some of his sermons from the Internet and proved it at several Bible Studies."

"Wow!" Reggie says a little louder than usual.

"You see, Deacon Haran was serious about his Bible studies. He went to Bible College back in the day even before he taught Sunday School or became a deacon. So I understand he went to Pastor Goode in private and told him he knew he was getting some of his sermons off the Internet, then telling everyone when he was preaching, 'God gave me this to tell y'all, so don't be mad at me'"

"Wow," Reggie exclaims.

"Was any of that true?" he continued.

"Yeah, unfortunately it took those of us who supported Pastor Goode to see that. Even though he was a good preacher and could whoop with the best of em, he was not a good teacher."

"He fooled a lot of us, and like Brother Haran used to say, he was feeding us boloney and making us think it was steak."

"What?" Reggie asks confused.

"Deacon Haran used to always tell us in his Sunday School class that if you'd never seen a steak, tasted a steak, or smelled a steak and some con man, some false preacher came along and fed you boloney and told you it was a steak, then you'd believe it was a steak. He used to say that we needed to study the Word for ourselves so we could not be easily fooled by some slick-talking, fine-dressing pimp of a preacher. And was he right about Pastor Goode! He was feeding us boloney in his sermons and during his Bible Studies and was telling us it was steak," Ms. Jenkins says as she motions to Reggie to head down the hallway.

"Okay, okay," Reggie says, eager to hear more.

"I can take a hint!" he says, laughing.

"Okay, Ms. Jenkins, I will see you Thursday. Thanks so much for being patient with me. I am sure this book will be well received when we get finished.

People like to read about the mess that goes on in the church!"

"Will we get rich?" Ms. Jenkins asks in a halfway serious, halfway playful tone.

"There is a good chance it might sell well, but time will tell," Reggie responds.

"Oh Reggie, you said you had two questions for me. What is your other question?"

"Ah, I forgot," Reggie responds, knowing he wanted to ask if Chastity would be at home on Thursday because they were right outside Chastity's bedroom door.

We made a lot of progress tonight without Chastity's interference, Reggie thinks to himself. She is too much of a distraction."

8:45pm- Same Day Back in N. O. Goode's Hospital Room.

"Good evening, visitors. It is now 8:45pm and visiting hours will be over at 9:00pm. Please conclude your visit as the doors to the ICU will be locked promptly at 9:00pm."

The automated announcement blares over the public address system as Marie Antoinette Goode sits slumped in the huge, well worn imitation leather, but extremely comfortable chair next to her husband's bed. She is slowly hypnotized by the sound of the life monitors attached to N. O. The announcement has awakened her from a very deep sleep. She slowly opens her eyes and begins to reflect on her life with N. O. The love and admiration he heaped upon her early in their relationship. How he stood by her when her family passed away, lost at sea. The deception of his true motives to become a mega church Pastor and more importantly the devastation she suffered finding out he had sons from a prior relationship that he hid from her. Then she also could not forget his numerous betrayals with some of the women at New Harvest. Aware that her husband's notoriety gives her a few more minutes to spend in the ICU, she is slow to get herself ready to leave. She slowly drifts off to sleep and begins to dream, to reminisce about days gone by. Some days she wishes she could go back to. Others were filled with heartache and pain.

Early One Saturday Morning Years ago

N. O., dressed in a bathrobe and house slippers, goes out to the mailbox. He is a successful mega church pastor and lives in a 24,000 square foot palatial home in the suburbs. His house has all the trappings of success, a three car garage, a swimming pool, and a combination tennis and basketball court in his backyard. He counts among his neighbors a state legislator, a retired NBA basketball player and several wealthy entrepreneurs. As he saunters to the mailbox with a cup of coffee in his right hand and the newspaper tucked under his right arm he notices a small plain brown package protruding from the back of his over-sized mailbox. The kind of mailbox one sees on a rural road. He picks it up slowly and curiously looks over the package. He notices that this package has absolutely no postage marks. On one side of the envelope someone has scrawled in block text. "For the Eyes of Pastor Goode ONLY - View In PRIVATE!!"

N. O. shakes the package, then says aloud as an afterthought, "Could this be a bomb?"

But the package is so light in weight that he assumes it is okay. He looks right, then left down his street to see if anyone who does not look like they belong in his neighbor is around. He discovers he is the only person out at this time of the morning. Since it is early in the morning, he enters the house and tip-toes down to the basement where he has a huge family room equipped with a pool table, a well stocked bar with a rack of wine glasses hanging overhead, and a movie-sized big screen TV with twelve beige leather theater style seats, The basement has plenty of room to host a big family meal or a party with plenty of space for a dance floor. The basement is also well lit with rope lights around the dark grey base boards with the walls being painted a silverish tint. The ceiling is high, so unusually high that even Shaq would not have to stoop to stand erect in this basement. The walls are adorned with paintings, many of them originals with religious themes. He goes behind the bar and retrieves a cork screw which he uses to cut through the packaging tape on the package.

When he opens the package he finds three DVD's simply marked "Salome at her Best." There is a note attached that reads,

"View the videos and then expect a call. We will be in touch very soon."

"What the hell!" he says to himself as he balls up the note and throws it into the trash can behind the bar.

Maybe I ought to get that note and tear it up so Marie won't see it, he thinks to himself.

He tears up the note and stuffs the torn pieces into the right pocket of his bathrobe.

He goes to the DVD player that also contains his stereo system and surround sound and inserts the first of three DVD's. Using the remote control, he starts the DVD. The first thing he notices is the poor quality of this cheaply and crudely made movie because the color and the credits are amateurish at best.

"What the hell!" he says to himself again.

Horrified, he sees the Title of the movie, "Jezebel Booby's Sexapades, Volume 3." He then notices a voluptuous, tall and slender young lady that looks just like his daughter, Salome.

"Oh my God, that is Salome! What is she doing in a porno movie when she is supposed to be in acting and modeling school?"

In the opening scenes she is naked with three men, and it is obvious that she is no novice in terms of being in a pornographic movie. N. O. grabs his lips with his left hand, pinching them in surprise, disgust and embarrassment. He tenses up so much that he shudders. A chill runs down his spine.

"God help me. My baby is a porno star," he says just above a whisper.

N. O. continues to watch the DVD, not believing his eyes. His heart is racing, and he is filled with incredible dread. Tears well up in his eyes as he sees his daughter perform sexual acts with the three men that are expressly prohibited in the Bible, acts that the Old Testament says were punishable by *DEATH!* The men switch sexual positions with Salome, and one could easily see from her facial expression that she was truly enjoying her work!

Cursing, N. O. abruptly turns the DVD off and paces around his basement.

"How could this be? Where did I go wrong as a father? We let our Baby girl go to LA against our best wishes to pursue a career in modeling and acting, and this is what happens! This is what we get as trusting parents!"

Startled and still in disbelief to the point of being dazed, he removes the first DVD and plays the first five or six minutes of the other two DVD's and becomes even more heartbroken, disgusted and sad. He feels like throwing up as he knows if he is watching these DVD's, there must be other copies.

Who sent these to me? Are they planning to blackmail me? How long has Salome been doing these movies? N. O. ponders, as he continues to pace trying to figure out what his next move ought to be.

"Whew," he exclaims over and over again trying to get his thoughts properly arranged.

"Lord, if this is a test or punishment for my past transgressions, I pray that you will forgive me and see me through this almost insurmountable obstacle to my ministry."

"Damn Lord, what did I do to deserve this?" he says softly, ever mindful that his wife, son and other daughter, Delilah, are upstairs asleep.

He falls to his knees and begins to pray,

"*Lord, please guide my steps as I try to bring my daughter home. Help me understand how I could have raised a child in a religious atmosphere and now see her engaged in perverted sex acts with men not her husband. Please Father, help me find a way to break this news to my wife because I know if she saw these videos, it would kill her. Lord, please forgive me for my past transgressions against you and my wife and children, all my children! Amen.*"

Rising from his knees, N. O. collects the DVD's.

While pacing he hears a familiar voice. It is his wife, Marie Antoinette.

"N.O., where are you, Baby? What do you want for breakfast?" she shouts as she enters the kitchen directly above the basement. N. O. can even hear her open and close the refrigerator door.

N. O. looks around quickly for a place to hide the DVD's. He stashes them in the laundry room on a shelf behind a stack of towels that are folded but have yet to be taken upstairs and placed in the linen closet.

"Hey Baby, I'm down in the basement reading the paper. I will be up in a minute," N. O. says as he glances back at the shelf where he placed the DVD's to ensure himself they are well hidden. He walks toward the stairs, then notices the newspaper still has a rubber band around it.

Thinking quickly, he removes the rubber band from around the newspaper and scatters the sections of the newspaper on the floor next to his favorite chair, just in case his wife were to join him in the basement.

That's it. If she comes down here and sees the paper still rolled up, that might lead to a lot of questions, and I'm not ready to talk to her about Salome just yet!

N. O. quickens his pace but stops dead in his tracks to look in the direction of the place he hid the DVD's and the newspaper he scattered on the floor. Satisfied that everything looks okay and that his lie is covered, he scampers up the stairs to the kitchen to have breakfast with his wife.

"Baby what do you want to eat?" Marie Antoinette asks N. O. again, wondering why he has not answered her.

"Huh!" he responds.

"N. O., are you okay? You are walking around here like a zombie. Is anything wrong?" Marie Antoinette asks, a little frustrated since she just woke up.

"No Baby, everything is okay,"

"Well, if everything is okay, then let me ask you again, what do you want for breakfast," Marie Antoinette says cutting N. O. off while he was trying to answer her.

"Ah, I'll just have another cup of coffee. I'm not very hungry," N. O. says looking off into the distance.

"N. O., what is wrong? We've been married too long for you to sit here and tell me that something is NOT bothering you! What is it? Did you have another affair? Are there more bastard children in your past? What is it?" Marie Antoinette shouts as she realizes she is getting loud and that Jabez and Delilah are upstairs asleep.

Shaking his head in disbelief, N. O. responds, "Why is it that every time I am in deep thought, you bring up my past? I've apologized for my past indiscretions. What do you want from me? But if you must know, I received a strange package today in our mailbox."

"A strange package? What kind of strange package?" Marie Antoinette asks.

Sighing deeply, N. O. says in a very disappointed and frustrated tone, "It's Salome. While we were sitting here bragging on her accomplishments in modeling and acting school, she's been up to something else!" N. O. says as he sits at the kitchen table with his head clasped between his hands.

"Please do not tell me she is using drugs," Marie Antoinette says as she sits across from N. O. and softly pulls his hands away from his face.

"No, it's not drugs, or at least I do not think she is using drugs," N.O. says with a tear appearing in the corner of his eye.

"Please Lord, tell me she's not pregnant," Marie Antoinette says probingly.

"No, even worse," N. O. responds, trying to wipe the tear from his cheek while still holding Marie Antoinette's hands.

"What N. O? What could be worse than her being pregnant?"

"She's in some of those movies."

"What kind of movie are you talking about N. O? After all, we let her go to California to take modeling and acting classes."

"She is in some pornographic movies where she is performing lewd sex acts with two or more men at the same time," N. O. says, not looking at Marie Antoinette.

"She's doing what?" Marie Antoinette asks. "No N. O. That can not be. Not my baby! She's just twenty years old!"

"It's true Baby, I got these DVD's in the mail, and there is no doubt that it is Salome." N. O. says as he begins to cry in earnest.

Marie Antoinette moves to the chair next to N. O. and throws her arms around the neck of her husband.

"No, N.O. it can not be true," she says as she begins to weep.

Choking up, N. O. says, "I'm sorry, Baby, but it is true. We have to figure what we are going to do. We also need to find out what the intent is of the person who left the DVD's in our mailbox."

"You mean someone left copies of pornographic movies of our daughter in our mailbox?" Marie Antoinette asks.

"Yes, and whoever is doing this obviously wants money, probably lots of money, to keep this out of the press. I have been trying to think through this. Since she was in California, it is possible there will never be a connection to us and my, I mean, our ministry. That's what I'm banking on. So we need to kill this situation real soon, or we could lose everything I've, I mean, we've worked for."

"Well, the first order of business is to bring Salome home and have her see a therapist."

"Yes, Baby, that will be our first order of business. We'll let it leak out in the church that Salome is real sick, that we are bringing her home to take care of her," N. O. says.

"But Marie, what if she doesn't want to come home?"

"Oh she's coming home all right. After I talk to her, she will not have a choice. She'll listen to me because we are very close. Even more closer than Delilah and I are, and you know how close Delilah is to her momma. Salome is coming home and will abide by the rules we set down. Trust me!" Marie Antoinette says with a self-assured tone.

"When the kids get up and get out of the house, we can go down stairs and see her DVD's. As a father I am so terribly disgusted by what she permitted to happen to her in these sordid movies," N. O. says.

1:03PM Later that afternoon at the Goode Residence

"Okay Baby, before we talk to Salome, I think it is important that you watch a portion of these horrible videos," N. O. says.

N. O. retrieves the three DVD's from his hiding place and inserts one into the DVD player and pushes the play button. Immediately, Marie Antoinette starts to cry, her chest heaving, her hand over her mouth as she sees her baby daughter in complete undress perform sex acts that she thinks are unspeakable.

Noticing his wife's obvious distress, N. O. stands next to her and hugs her hip to hip.

"Turn that disgusting video off," Marie Antoinette yells, breaking N. O's embrace and stomping across the basement where she stands and cries uncontrollably.

"Please N. O., please turn that trash off!" she says emphatically.

N. O. quickly adheres to her demand.

"We must find a place to hide these so Jabez and Delilah will not find them," he says as he closes the jewel case that contained the DVD.

"You can burn them or throw them in the trash as far as I'm concerned," Marie Antoinette says while she frantically paces back and forth across the basement floor.

Ring, ring, ring!

"Who can that be?" N. O. asks looking at his wife with a perplexed look on his face. He slowly walks to the gold plated antique wall mounted telephone, lifts the receiver and says,

"Hello, Goode residence."

"I assume you've watched the movies, huh?" the electrically altered muffled voice on the other end of the telephone asks sarcastically.

"Who is this and what do you want?" N. O. yells into the telephone as his wife gets closer to try and hear the conversation. They lean in together, shoulder to shoulder in a feeble attempt to both hear the person on the telephone.

"It's not about what I want. It's about what you want! Do you want to keep your position as Pastor of New Harvest? Do you want to maintain your status in the community, make the kind of money you make?" the person on the other end of the telephone says stepping up the aggressive tone.

"Okay, I knew this was about some way to extort me, what is it you want?" N.O. asks. .

"Look, we are not going to let you trace this or any future calls. Call the police, and copies of the videos will be sent to every major news outlet in the city and to select members of your church with a nice explanation of who Jezebel Booby really is. Ya feel me? We'll be in touch!"

Click!

"N. O., what do you think they want from us?"

"Money Baby, money!" N. O. responds as he simultaneously hangs up the telephone and throws his arms tenderly around his wife.

"Oh N. O., what are we going to do? Just how do you plan to handle this? Her head buried in N. O.'s chest."

"First things first, Baby. We need to get out to California and bring our baby girl back, then we will deal with these blackmailers. I need to make a call, so why don't you go upstairs and call Salome, but don't tell her we know anything about her videos. Baby, call her and try and remain calm and feel her out, and I'll make a few calls to see what we can do about these extortionists."

"Okay, N. O.," Marie Antoinette says as she tenderly kisses her husband, then runs upstairs to call Salome.

When N. O. is sure she is out of earshot, he dials his cousin, Theo Lane.

"Hello," Theo snaps, showing his exasperation and irritation with this intrusion.

"Theo, this is N. O."

"Yeah, I saw your name come up on my caller-id, what's up?"

"Look Theo, I have something I need to discuss with you and would prefer to do it in person," N. O. says just above a whisper.

"Well, I'm kinda busy right now. I'm visiting a sick friend who needs the laying on of hands, if you know what I mean," Theo says, chuckling, not appreciating the import of N. O.'s request.

"Theo, I know you are busy. You are always busy, but this is very serious and very important. I really need your help," N. O. says in a pleading tone.

"Okay Cuz, since you're family, I'll come over in about two hours, how's that?"

"Theo, I would prefer if we met somewhere where we may talk in private," N. O. responds.

"Damn, Cuz, this must be serious. Okay, how about meeting me at Crazy Louie's used car lot. That shouldn't draw any suspicion," Theo responds.

"That will work," N. O. responds.

"Let's meet there in two hours, okay?" N. O. asks, silently praying for a positive response.

"Okay Cuz, two hours and we meet in front of Crazy Louie's used cars," Theo says sighing deeply to let his cousin know he is interfering with his plans.

Given Theo's criminal past, he will know how to handle these blackmailers, N. O. thinks as he hangs up the telephone and heads upstairs to change clothes so he can meet Theo.

"Who was that?" Shandrica, one of Theo's girlfriends asks.

"Oh, just a buddy needing a favor."

"Are you sure it wasn't your wife or another one of your girlfriends?" she asks sternly as she applies make-up in the cheap motel bathroom.

"C'mon! You know after Gladys, there is no other woman in my life. Besides, the two of you are more than a notion, and oh, by the way, you're *married, too!*" Theo laughs as he stands behind Shandrica, wrapping his arms around her waist and gently kissing her on her neck.

"Ooooh, Theo! You'd better stop because we both need to get out of here," Shandrica moans, thrusting her head backward and enjoying the tingling sensation derived from Theo's light and tender kisses.

"Ooooh Theo," she moans again as he turns her around abruptly, kisses her passionately then picks her up and carries her into the bedroom and gently drops her on the bed.

Back at the Goodes about thirty minutes later

"Did you call Salome?" N. O. asks his wife who sits on the side of their bed looking despondent.

"Yes, but I did not get an answer. I tried to be cheerful and left a message asking her to call me. I just said we had not heard from her in a while and were just checking to see if she was okay."

"Well, we'll have to go out to LA and bring her home. I have a meeting to go to see what I need to do about this blackmail situation, but when I get back, let's start making arrangements to head out to LA to bring our baby girl home, N. O. says as he puts on an expensive hooded navy blue jogging suit.

"N. O. who are you meeting with?"

"Baby, some of the things I might have to do and the people I might have to deal with about the call we got should not concern you. Just trust me. Trust me Baby!" N. O., says as he nervously struggles to snap the band of his bejeweled Rolex watch.

"I will be back in a couple of hours, and we can talk then. Trust me, the less you know, the better off we will be," N. O. says as he tenderly plants a kiss on Marie Antoinette's lips.

She looks up at him, sighs, then simply says, "Okay N. O., I will put all my trust in you!"

One Hour later in front of Crazy Louie's Used Car Lot.

Crazy Louie's is the leading used car dealer in this metropolitan area. He has a two acre lot that seems to have an endless inventory of pre-owned vehicles. It has been said that the very best place to hide is in plain sight. Meeting in front of Crazy Louie's seems to be the ideal place for Theo to meet N. O. The level of activity on the lot plus the fact that N. O. is in street clothes offer little chance of them being recognized in the throng of people who are attracted to the Carnival-like atmosphere at the car lot.

Theo is sitting in his white-on-white late model Jaguar XJ6 when N. O. nervously approaches from the passenger curbside of Theo's car as if he were about to make a drug deal. Theo has parked a little too close to a fire hydrant, so N. O. has to tap on the window.

"Hey Cuz, why don't you get in?" Theo asks, throwing his hands out and hunching his shoulders as if to say

"What's your problem?"

"Theo, you are parked a little too close to the fire hydrant and I'm afraid that I will nick your door if I try to squeeze in. Could you pull up a few feet?" N. O. asks looking left then right to see if he is being observed by anyone on this busy street.

Theo responds, "Okay Cuz, okay!"

N. O. quickly slides into the front passenger seat, then takes a deep breath and sighs.

"Whew! Theo, I really need your help."

"Well, hope whatever the hell it is that it is important enough for you to make me miss out with my girl, Shandrica," Theo says interrupting N. O.

"It's beyond serious, Theo."

"Well Cuz, get to it! What's up?" Theo says, pulling his sun glasses down to the bridge of his nose as he leans in N. O.'s direction.

"It's Salome."

"Salome, she ain't hurt or nothing?" Theo asks in halted speech.

"Someone sent Antoinette and me some DVD's of Salome, and they were pretty disgusting."

"How do you mean they were disgusting?" Theo asks with a very puzzled expression.

Sighing deeply, N. O. says, "Well, she is in some nudey movies,..."

"Nudey movies? You mean pornos?" Theo exclaims, surprised.

"Yes, I guess the correct terminology is pornographic movies," N. O. says, trying to mask his deep embarrassment.

"Damn, Baby girl went to Cali and got into the porno biz! I'd never believe it in a million years," Theo says shaking his head vigorously in total disbelief.

"But that's not all of it, Theo. The person who sent us the movies of Salome is trying to blackmail me."

"How much they asking for?" Theo asks, engaged more than ever in the conversation.

"The caller has not asked for any money yet and said we better not go to the police or he will send copies of the movies to the press and certain members of the congregation. So I need your help, Theo. I mean, I have no idea what to do".

"Well Cuz, the first thing is that you need to listen to them and not get the police involved. You got a good thing going at the church, and we don't want to mess that up. How are you and Marie set money-wise, just in case they ask for big money?"

Well, I got a half a million in a safe in the house and another $1.5 million in an offshore account. Plus, I got about sixty thousand combined in my checking and savings account. That money plus my salary is all the IRS knows about." N.O. responds looking up at the ceiling of Theo's car as if the figures he spoke of were written there.

"Okay, okay," Theo says, "Who do you think is behind this? What do you think he has to gain? There is something seriously wrong with this picture cuz! And I ..."

"I have no idea Theo! N. O. says, interrupting Theo. We do not know that many people in LA and who would try to hurt me like this? All the people we know out there are pastors, and most of them have more money than me. So, why would they ..."

"Cuz, who says the person behind this is in LA?" Theo says, exasperated. "Think Cuz, think! Who do you know here who has connections in LA?

"Wait a minute," N. O. says, angrily. "A few months back there was a conference out in LA for deacons, and guess who represented New Harvest?"

"Who Cuz?"

"Deacon Haran and Deacon Fellowes!"

"I don't know Cuz. They don't like you, but they ain't that street smart in my opinion to come up with a plan to blackmail you. We are talking about a federal offense, and they ain't built for no federal prison time!"

"But Theo, who else could it be? Especially Deacon Fellowes. He obviously has something against me!"

"Cuz, we will have to give this situation some more serious thought. I am going to have some people I know check those brothers out. But again, I just don't see them being that hard or that crooked, especially, since they are always fighting my moves on the Trustee Board."

"I do not know Theo! I just do not know! This whole situation is suspicious."

"Yeah Cuz, but we gotta come up with a plan real quick so when they ask you to drop some big money on them we will be prepared. You need to determine how you are going to get the money they ask for without arousing any suspicion in the community or New Harvest. No matter what, Cuz, I got your back."

"Thanks Theo," N. O. says, leaning over and hugging Theo.

"Cuz, you've always been there for me, so I gotta do what I gotta do. Besides, we can't let somebody mess up our good thing at New Harvest," Theo says trying to inject some humor into a tense situation.

"Look Cuz, I'm gonna call in some outstanding notes I have on the streets and try and come up with about $100 grand in the next couple of days. Do you think that will help?"

"People owe you that kind of money Theo?" N. O. asks.

"Yeah, Cuz. Let's just say I'm a smart business man! Cuz, you need to be able to come up with some serious cash, too. I never heard of a blackmailer taking a check! Think about how much you and the Misses can come up with quickly just so I'll know if I have to go deeper into my stash. I'm gonna do all I can Cuz, even if I have to borrow some big money from a loan shark, cause I know you're good for it. And Cuz, if my people get wind of who is behind this, we won't have to pay out any blackmail money! Just money to dispose of our problem!"

"But Theo, I do not want anyone hurt behind this."

"Cuz, ain't they trying to hurt you? Besides, what happens to whoever it is ain't your worry. What you don't know you can't tell. I will handle this! Nobody gets over on me and my family!"

Pausing for about thirty seconds, and now looking down at his feet, N. O. finally says, "Well, I think I can come up with about $200,000 because I don't want to give them all my cash in the safe."

"Okay Cuz. But, we gotta be prepared that they, might ask for more. Here's what we need to do. I might have to spend a lot of time at your crib. So when they call, you can let me be on the phone with you and I'll negotiate with them about how much they want because it's obvious to me they want cash, some serious cash to stay quiet. The other consideration is that we got to get some type of guarantee that they will not come back later and ask for more money. They may accept a little money at first, then try to bleed you dry by asking for additional payments over time. We must be careful about that!"

"Thanks, Theo. I knew you would know what to do," N. O. says as he leans over and shakes Theo's hand vigorously.

"Not a problem, Cuz, because we're family and have to look out for one another. But you will owe me though," Theo says with a robust laugh.

"Heh, heh," N. O. laughs nervously, knowing full well that Theo will come back at some later date looking to be compensated for his assistance.

Back at the Goode's Residence

Ring, ring, ring!

Marie Antoinette is sitting at the kitchen table looking at a family photograph album and is reminiscing about how perfect her children seemed to be when they were young. She slowly gets up and walks like a zombie toward the wall mounted telephone.

"Hello, Goode residence."

"Momma, this is Salome. Did you call me?" Salome asks in a puzzled tone.

"Yes Baby, and it is so good to hear from you."

"Is everything okay? You sounded like something was wrong?" Salome continues, still puzzled why her mother's call seemed distressed.

"Whew!" Marie Antoinette sighs, choking up before she responds.

"Momma, what is wrong? I know you, and I can tell something is up. Did Daddy hit you again? He better not have hit you. If he did, you need to call the police like I did when he hit you before I moved out here to go to acting and modeling school," Salome says, her voice rising. because she is about to explode in anger.

"No Baby, Daddy did not hit me," Marie Antoinette responds as she starts to cry.

"Then what is wrong, Momma? What is wrong?"

"Salome, come home! Please come home."

"Why Momma? Why do you want me to come home?"

"Baby, Daddy went to the mailbox today and there was a package that did not come from the post office that was stuffed in our mailbox."

"So what was in the package?" Salome asks, still puzzled as she interrupts her mother.

"Baby, there were some dirty movies on DVD's that you were in and,…"

"What, someone sent you some DVD's with me in them?" Salome asks, startled to find out her parents have found out how she was making a living in LA.

"Momma, I'm sorry, but I met this man, and I thought I was in love with him. He made me believe that we would get married and that if I only did a few of these movies, he could get me into legitimate movies and nobody but his friends in the movie business would know. He also said that if I did a few movies, he would only sell them overseas. Nobody else would know about them. I only did a few."

"But Baby, whoever sent the movies is asking us for money, probably lots of money. Your daddy says that we are going to be blackmailed."

"What?" Salome asks angrily.

"Yes, they are threatening to send the movies to the TV stations and members of the church."

"Momma,..."

"Salome, please come home so we can get this situation straight," Marie Antoinette says, interrupting her daughter while trying to maintain her composure.

I knew something like this was going to happen. Salome has always been our wild child, a free spirit. But I can not show how upset I am or she will refuse to come home. She is our most stubborn child, Marie Antoinette thinks to herself.

"Momma, I can't come home right now, I am under contract."

"I hope you do not mean under contract to do more of those movies," she yells into the telephone before she catches herself and tries to calm down.

"Look Baby, I am sorry I yelled, but don't you see if you continue to do those types of movies, you will put your daddy and me in jeopardy?"

"Momma, I do not care about Daddy, but I do care about you. Daddy has always been more than a little shady, and how you can keep forgiving him for beating you and cheating on you is just mind-boggling to me," Salome sternly states to her mother.

"But Baby, your father has not hit me in a while, and..."

"Yeah Momma, he has not hit you in a while, but just you wait! He'll get upset with someone at the church and pretend he is turning the other cheek there, putting a show on for the congregation only to come home and start slapping your cheeks. He's dangerous, Momma. Why do you think I was so set on leaving home?"

"Baby girl, I know you love your father. He is a good man, and he does not mean to get so upset."

"What the hell are you talking about, Momma? He's the most self-centered, egomaniacal, manipulative, disloyal man I have ever met. If I had stayed home, I would probably have killed him!"

"Ooh Salome, you can not mean that!" Marie Antoinette says with tears cascading down her cheeks.

"Momma, leave him, and I'll come home and live with you, Delilah, and Jabez. Otherwise I'm staying here in LA."

"Salome, I can't leave your father. First of all, I do not have any money. You know he controls all the finances in this house."

"Oh great, you just gave me another descriptor for Daddy, he's a control freak. He has to have his way ALL THE TIME, or he makes everyone in the house miserable."

"But Salome,"

"Momma, again, if you want me to come home, I will only come home if you get your own place."

"But Salome, my leaving him would ruin your father's ministry which he has worked so hard to build. He's done so much to build New Harvest that if I left him now, people would question why and that would cause the church to split."

"Momma, you just don't get it, do you? Daddy didn't build that church because he is a righteous, God fearing man! He worked so hard as you said because he has a gift for public speaking, a gift for being the world's greatest phony, and most importantly, the world's greediest man. He only went into the ministry because he loves money and women, both of which, are readily available to him at New Harvest. Has he fathered any children yet?"

"You should not be so hard on your father. He has his faults, but I still say he is a good man. Look at the house we live in," Marie Antoinette says in her most persuasive tone.

"So what, Momma! We have a huge home that the people at the church bought and paid for, and he talks about the members like dogs. Even those members that kiss his ass on a regular basis like Trustee Bass, Deacon Monger and Deacon Crooke,..."

"Salome, let's make a deal. If you come home, get a **respectable job,** and after one year you don't see any improvement in your father, then you can go about your business as long as you promise not to go back to making those horrible movies. Baby, aren't you afraid of catching some disease like AIDS by being in those movies?"

"No Momma! All the actors have to get tested on a regular basis, and through the aid of trick photography we use protection that the viewer never sees. I have nothing to worry about!"

"But Baby, it is so unnatural some of the things we saw you do in those films."

"Ha-ha," Salome snickers. "Momma, maybe if you weren't so prudish in bed with Daddy, he'd stop chasing all the big titty and big butt women at New

Harvest. Just maybe he'd have all his sexual fantasies fulfilled and would not need those other women."

"Girl you have always been the comic in the family."

"Momma, let me think about moving back home. Honestly, I am tired of the business, the backstabbing, and sleazy people out here. And I'm sorry for snapping at you. I didn't mean to take my frustrations with Daddy out on you."

"Oh, praise God, Salome. Please come home. You will find your father has changed for the best. "

"We'll see," Salome responds smugly.

Going Back in time - 9:48pm The Evening Marie fell asleep in N. O.'s Hospital Room (The same evening Chastity exposed herself to Reggie)

"Mrs. Goode. Mrs. Goode," Dr. Hudson says softly awakening her from her long dream about her conversation with Salome.

Yawning, stretching, and aware that due to her trying to get comfortable in the visitors chair her dress has risen several inches above her knees exposing her thick thighs, Marie Antoinette twists her neck and feverishly grabs at the end of her dress trying to make a wasted attempt to conceal what Dr. Hudson has already seen and appreciated, her nice legs.

"I am sorry to awaken you, Mrs. Goode, but the announcement was made over thirty minutes ago for all visitors to leave the hospital before the doors are closed and the alarms were set. I will walk you out because someone with a key must let you out."

"Mrs. Goode, this may be a bad time, but as I indicated earlier, your husband is in a vegetative state from which he will never recover. As a Christian, I can only assume were he able to give his permission, he would gladly give us permission to harvest his vital organs so we might save not a life but lives. Off the record! If you sign the consent form, I am sure that a client of mine who is in desperate need of a heart would provide you with, let me say, more than adequate compensation."

"Are you trying to get me to sell you my husband's heart," Marie Antoinette blurts out loudly, slightly irritated, forgetting it is late and she is in the

Intensive Care Unit.

"Please keep your voice down," Dr. Hudson says as he motions with his finger over his lips for her to be quiet.

"No, I am not trying to get you to sell your husband's heart. I am trying to save several people's lives, given the fact that the way you see your husband now will be the way he'll exist until his body deteriorates and he expires. Is that what you really want for your husband? Do you think that is how he would want to exist, in a vegetative state forever?"

"But he's my husband!"

"Yes, but for how much longer, and again, what you see is what you get. You are certainly too beautiful and too young a woman to be burdened with a living corpse. You need to get on with your life and meet another man who would take good care of you."

"And where would I meet such a man, Dr. Hudson, if I let you take my husband's heart?" Marie Antoinette asks, sensing a mutual attraction between herself and the good Doctor.

Damn, this man is fine. He is a slightly older version of Terrence Howard, green eyes and all, she thinks to herself as she remembers all the turmoil N. O. had taken her through throughout their marriage. The trysts with other women, his controlling ways that led to her being totally financially dependent on him, and his fierce temper that evoked several beatings, followed by the ever so gracious, "Honey, I am so sorry, and I will never do this again."

"Tell you what, Dr. Hudson, let me think about my husband's situation over the weekend, and we can talk early next week."

"I do not mean to sound rude, Mrs. Goode, but given your husband's massive stroke, there is absolutely no guarantee your husband will survive the weekend. A decision will need to be made very soon because, should he expire, and absent a consent form, his organs will be of no use. I want to reiterate, I know a very prominent person who is in need of a heart, and I am sure you would be happy, very happy with the level of financial compensation that would come your way!"

"But you are asking me to let my husband die for profit!" Marie Antoinette whispers, exasperated.

"No, what I am asking you to do is to be pragmatic and realize a financial opportunity. Forgive me for being blunt, but I read the newspaper accounts of your husband's legal case. Again, forgive me, but you are better off without him because of his numerous sexual encounters with other women. Even if he were in perfect health, he would be incarcerated for a very long time, too long for a sophisticated and beautiful woman like you to be waiting for on the outside. If you were my woman, I mean my wife, I would never subject you to the level of scrutiny, embarrassment and ridicule he has subjected you to!"

"Dr Hudson, are you flirting with me?"

"Maybe!"

"Mrs. Goode, may I call you Marie? You are an attractive woman who will shortly become a widow. Even if Pastor Goode were to live another year, he would not know you or anyone else was here. So again, I suggest you sign the organ donor release form, make a small fortune, and move on with your life. I saw where the court seized your husband's domestic and overseas bank accounts so that taxes due would be paid and restitution for monies taken from the church would be paid."

"So what is your point, Dr. Hudson," Marie Antoinette says smugly.

"He left you *BROKE!*" Dr. Hudson retorts, as he looks right into Marie Antoinette's eyes intently.

"Okay, Mrs. Goode, I see you are not swayed by my friends most generous and timely offer. So, I will leave you alone, but you still must exit this facility because visiting hours are *OVER!*"

"You needn't be so rude, Dr. Hudson! You threw a lot at me in such a very short time, and I need to think about what you said. It's true that N. O. was not the best husband and father, but he did have,"

"Did!" Dr. Hudson says, interrupting Marie Antoinette.

"Mrs. Goode, do you realize that you just indicated you know he is gone. It's just a matter of time."

Did I really do that, Marie Antoinette thinks cautiously to herself?

"Well, even if I made a Freudian slip, I still have to think about pulling the plug on my husband for money," Marie Antoinette says defiantly.

"Okay, Mrs. Goode," Dr. Hudson says, his frustration showing.

"Why don't you meet me for dinner and we can discuss this further?"

"Dr. Hudson, I am still a married woman! Besides, we might be seen together, and I do not need or want any more rumors spread about my family."

"If you are not afraid of me, you can come to my sailboat at the Somerset Marina and I could fix you dinner," Dr. Hudson says as he seizes the opportunity to take Marie Antoinette's hands into his and massage them slowly and gently.

Ooh, that feels so good, Marie Antoinette thinks to herself as she sighs, takes a deep breath and closes her eyes.

"Whoa, you are moving too fast," Marie Antoinette says while simultaneously moving her hands from Dr. Hudson's.

"What type of woman do you think I am? I have been through so much this past year, and you probably think that I am very vulnerable, but I am no easy prey for you or any other man!" Marie Antoinette says defiantly as she takes a very deliberate step back from Dr. Hudson, looking at him with great contempt.

"Mrs. Goode, what you need now more than anything is some money for your future and a good man, a professional man who can help you retain your current standard of living," Dr. Hudson says, taking her hands back into his and pulling her close to him.

"Dr. Hudson, what are you doing?" she says as he pulls her to him and wraps his arms around her tightly, then kisses her passionately. She does not resist.

Marie Antoinette is lonely and misses the embrace of a man. She longs for the creature comfort of being made love to by her husband. She has mixed feelings about N. O., but she is still a lovely woman with needs, serious needs!

"So Marie," Dr. Hudson says, taking advantage of this tender moment.

He wants two things from Marie Antoinette, her signature on the organ donor consent form and to make passionate love to her. Even though she is a mother of three, she has taken very good care of herself, and Dr. Hudson can not help to notice her fine brown frame. He is captivated by the outstanding symmetry of her body.

Still holding Marie Antoinette in his arms and tenderly enticing her to give in to his sexual desire by gently kissing her on her ear lobes, Dr Clark Hudson whispers into her left ear,

"Are you going to meet me at my houseboat?"

"Yes, yes, I will go to your house-boat!" Marie Antoinette says as she begins to lose control of herself and starts to kiss Dr. Hudson passionately.

"But if you tell anyone about our one and only encounter, I will not consider the deal!" she says emphatically, her eyes partly closed as she thoroughly enjoys the way he is making her feel.

"Good. I promise you I will not tell anyone and that you will not be sorry," Dr. Hudson says, trying to mask his true desire to only have a one night stand with her.

Dr. Hudson then gives Marie Antoinette the directions to his houseboat but decides to ask her to simply follow him. One has to have a code to enter the marina, so it would be easier if she just followed him, which she does.

Fifteen Minutes Later at the Marina

Dr. Clark Hudson stops a few feet in front of the marina's security gate, gets out of his car, and walks back to Marie Antoinette's car.

"Hey, just pull up as close as you can behind my car, almost bumper to bumper, and follow me through the gate. That way I will not have to come back to your car and give you the code to get into the Marina's compound."

"Okay," she says, a little nervous as she sees another car exiting the marina and thoughts of being seen by someone she knows, especially a New Harvest member, would just drive her crazy. She immediately slides down a little in her car seat and positions her head at an angle where Dr. Hudson's body acts as a shield from the passengers in the other car. Satisfied that she was not recognized by any of the occupants of the other car, Marie Antoinette watches Dr. Hudson re-enter his Lexus 470, and she immediately pulls up behind him and follows him into the marina's parking lot. He signals her to pull into a spot under a covered car port. He gets out of his car and walks over to her and opens her door.

"Thank you," she says, as she slides out of her seat. She notices that he is paying rapt attention to her huge shapely and very exposed thighs.

Damn, he thinks to himself as he is captivated by her beautiful legs.

"Did you get a good look?" she asks jokingly, noticing he has not looked her in the eyes once since he opened her car door.

"Hey, I'm sorry, I do not know what you mean," he responds.

"Oh, you know exactly what I mean!" she retorts.

"Oh, I am sorry for staring, but I just could not help but notice how beautiful your legs are!" Dr. Hudson says, slightly embarrassed. He had not realized just how intent he must have been staring to be caught by Marie Antoinette.

Damn, I am about to get some of that. Maybe I ought to reconsider my position about only doing her once because she is definitely fine! he thinks to himself, trying to conceal his ever increasing lust.

Marie Antoinette is very impressed with all the boats at the marina. She realizes that the marina is well kept and all the boats are well maintained and look new.

"Well, here we are, number 24," Dr. Hudson says, as he stops on the dock by a thirty foot sailboat. He reaches into his overcoat pocket and brings out a remote control that causes the gang plank to extend to the dock like an electronic convertible operates as it is being put up. When the gang plank which has rope handrails is in position, he gently grabs Marie Antoinette's right hand and ushers her across the gang plank onto the deck of his boat.

"So how do you like her?" he asks.

"Her?" she asks.

"Why do you men always refer to your cars and boats as her?" she asks.

"Well, I say her because, like a woman, she s a thing of beauty, just like you!" Dr. Hudson says, escorting Marie Antoinette below deck.

"My Lord! This is like a fancy apartment on water," Marie says, impressed with the boats ambiance.

"Do you mind if I look around?" she asks.

"Oh, go ahead!" he says proudly, loosening his tie in a hurried manner.

Calm down, Clark, he thinks to himself.

We have all night to get that, so slow down and relax.

The first thing Marie Antoinette notices is how neat Dr. Clark Hudson keeps his boat. Everything that has a place is in its place. There is a breakfast nook on the left that would seat four comfortably. To the right of the breakfast nook there is a small stove, sink, refrigerator and overhead microwave. As she goes toward the back of the boat, she sees a small but decent sized full bathroom with a shower stall that could easily accommodate two. She notices that the walls of the sailboat are all well polished teak with white trim. She steps gingerly into the master bedroom and sees a full size bed and all the amenities of a standard motel room; however, this bedroom is classier. There is another room she assumes to be another bedroom, but the door is locked.

"So how many people does this boat sleep?" she asks, still looking around.

"Six, but only two tonight," he responds with a sly smirk.

"This is nice, Clark, I mean, Dr. Hudson." Marie Antoinette says, wishing she had not made the slip and got on a first name basis with him.

"Oh, so it's Clark is it? I am glad you are feeling comfortable, Marie" as he hands her a glass of champagne he just poured. They look at one another intently, click their glasses together, drink the champagne, then disappear into the master bedroom for two hours.

Twenty Minutes Later: The Same Day at Reggie's Apartment

Reggie enters his sparsely furnished apartment. There is a futon with a beige and black mud cloth cover that you automatically see when you enter his apartment. On the right side of the futon there is a pole lamp that has a very noticeable cracked off-white shade. The coffee table is made from a polished piece of marble, about three and one half feet long and two and one half feet wide that is propped on top of three cinder blocks that have been painted black. The marble must have formerly been part of a wall in an office building because if you were to look closely, you can see the remnants of mortar on the edges of the marble slab. The walls, which are painted the standard off white, are bare except for three framed posters, all about six inches apart in a landscape format. The posters are hung directly over the futon. Moving horizontally from left to right there is a framed collage of newspaper clippings from Reggie's college days as the starting point guard on his Division II college basketball team. The second, a Tupac poster. The third, another collage but of family photographs. There is a forty-five inch plasma screen TV to the left of the futon and a burgundy Lazy Boy chair in front the TV.

"Man, it has been a long day," Reggie says out loud before he realizes he is talking to himself in an empty apartment. He walks to the small kitchen, loosens his tie, opens the refrigerator, grabs a beer, and heads for the Lazy Boy. He plops down and opens his book bag that he had dropped on the floor. He rambles through all the things in his book bag until he finds his micro recorder and notepad. He places both on the TV tray and adjusts the handle to recline. He starts to listen to his interview with Ms. Jenkins and tries to focus on how he will put this story of the life and times of N. O. Goode's fall from grace into novel form that will entice people, but more importantly, lead to his story becoming a best seller. But, he is confounded because he can not stay focused. He is still thinking about how sexy and provocative Chastity looked nude.

"Lord, how am I going to get this story finished when I have to go to Ms. Jenkins's house with Chastity being there? I know she only appeals to me physically, but why must I be tempted? Why couldn't she be so unattractive that I wouldn't even look her way? Lord, you have got to help me stay strong! That young girl is something else, and I am not trying to lead her on." Reggie says out loud, spilling beer on his shirt.

Ring, ring, ring, ring!

Leaping from the Lazy Boy, Reggie grabs his cell phone from its holster and says nervously, "Hello,"

"Reggie,"

"Chastity, Is that you? I was just thinking about you," Reggie says, realizing he has made a mistake by making this inadvertent admission.

"Yeah, it's me," she responds a little surprised and pleased to know she is on his mind.

"What do you want? I told you,"

"You told me what, Reggie? That you don't want me? Look Reggie, I want what you want," Chastity says interrupting Reggie.

"And what is that, Chastity?" Reggie says, a little puzzled.

"I just want to hook up with ya a couple of times. I don't want nothing permanent, like a relationship. I just want you to make love to me, and if we get together a couple of times, you won't be sorry!"

"Chastity, I have heard that all before, and I am not looking for a wife, a relationship, or a part-time lover. I just want to focus on my career."

"But Reggie, we can get together on your terms, whenever you say. I just like you, a lot. So you think about it. Don't rush and make the wrong decision because I'm telling you that if you let me make love to you, you won't be sorry. And when you say we stop, then it's over. Please just think about it," Chastity says in her most sexy voice.

"Okay, Chastity,"

"Okay, we can hook up?" Chastity asks excitedly!

"No! Now there you go already. You said you would be cool and for me to think about it. I will think about it, and that's it," Reggie says in a very stern tone.

"Okay, Reggie, I will see you tomorrow at my house."

"Chastity, please don't pull another stunt like you did today, okay?"

"What?"

"You know exactly what I am talking about! Do not try to entice me by being half naked at your grandmother's' house! Okay?"

"Okay Reggie," Chastity says in a disappointed tone.

"Talk to you tomorrow, Chastity," Reggie says hanging up the telephone.

That girl is something else, and I have got to be real cool because my inclination tells me she is trouble, BIG trouble, Reggie thinks to himself as he goes back to the kitchen and drops his now empty beer bottle into a recycle bin, then grabs another beer from the refrigerator. He slowly walks across the living room and sits back in the Lazy Boy and contemplates how he is going to deal with Chastity's interest in him and more importantly how he is going to control his desire to get with Chastity because that one act could lead to dire financial consequences.

On the Other Side of the Country at the Same Moment But Three Hours Earlier

Several months have passed since the Goodes have received the sexually explicit DVD's featuring their daughter, Salome. Salome is still estranged from her father since the time she called the police to quell a domestic disturbance because N. O. Goode had too much Absolut to drink one night and hit his wife because she asked him about his flirtatious attitude toward Sister Goodbody, an usher at New Harvest.

Salome has put the brakes on her porno career and is focusing on legitimate dancing and acting jobs. She returns home this evening tired from the day's routine and decides to take a long, hot shower. Exiting the shower, Salome has wrapped her long weaved hair in a purple towel-like turban. She then wraps a huge towel from a local hotel from her breasts to slightly above her knees. She hears a light thud and notices that the postman has dropped some mail through the mail chute of her front door. She makes sure the towel is snuggly wrapped around her before she bends to pick up the mail.

Hmm, bills, bills, and more bills, and what is this, she asks herself as she looks at an 8 ½ x 11 inch manila envelope with a return address that reads, "County of Los Angeles, Department of Health Services." Nervously and frantically she tries to open the envelope with no success. "Why do they have to use Crazy Glue when they seal these letters!" she says aloud as she enters the kitchen and grabs a butcher knife from a drawer.

Sighing deeply several times, she finally sticks the butcher knife's edge in the right corner of the back of the envelope and with one swift movement cuts the top fold from right to left. She deftly lifts the enclosed letter and reads,

"CONFIDENTIAL:
To: Client Number 730635
This letter is to inform you that the results of your recent HIV/AIDS test were positive. It is the recommendation of this clinic that you either seek immediate care and treatment through the health care professional of your choice or that you return to this clinic for a discussion as to what services and treatment we offer to combat this disease. If you do not have a personal physician, we can offer you state-funded financial assistance as these treatments can be very expensive.

Please be advised that it is our recommendation that you seek treatment for this disease while it is in its early stages because should you procrastinate, the end result could be catastrophic for you and any sexual partners you might have.

We also ask that you supply the clinic with the names of your sex partners for the past year so we might confidentially contact them to recommend that they be tested, and if necessary, treated. The laws of California stipulate that should you knowingly have sex with anyone after having been apprised of your HIV/AIDS diagnosis, then you could be held liable for criminal charges ..."

Salome drops the letter and paces back and forth across her living room. She begins to weep uncontrollably, thrusts her arms skyward and shouts,

"Why me Lord? Why me?"

She runs to the bathroom, gets on her knees, lifts the seat, and throws up violently.

She slumps into the area between the commode and the bath tub. The tears are coming in greater frequency and intensity. She strains to keep from throwing up again.

"Damn girl," she shouts aloud...

"First, you get pregnant by some fool you barely know, and now you have HIV/AIDS?" Salome says aloud, wondering how she might explain these highly detrimental situations to her mother!

Urrgghh! Urrgghh! Urrgghh! Is the sound she makes as she throws up again, and again, and again!

Struggling to get to her feet, Salome washes her face, looks in the mirror and says, "How could you be so stupid, so naïve, to be in such a predicament? I need to talk to Momma; she'll know what to do. I have to figure a way to tell her

I'm pregnant, too! I know she will be very disappointed in me," she says as she heads to her bedroom to get her cellphone. She periodically stops, thinking she might need to make a quick retreat back into the bathroom but makes it into her bedroom.

What are you going to say? How are you going to tell your momma about your problems? You can't just say, Hello Momma, I'm pregnant, and I also have HIV/AID's! What are you going to tell your momma, Salome? What?

She starts to dial her mother's number and stops before entering the final digit. She tries three times until she gets up enough nerve to just tell her mother the simple truth. She lets her mother's cellphone ring, but her call goes to her mother's voice mail. Unbeknownst to her, her mother is with Dr. Hudson.

"Hello, Momma, this is Salome, I've decided to come home. Please call me when you can. I really need to talk to you."

Salome waits thirty minutes, then calls her mother again with the same result. She waits another thirty minutes and calls.

"Momma, where can you be? It's past visiting hours at the hospital! Where are you?"

Reluctant to call the house because she does not want to divulge her troubles to her sister, Delilah, or her brother, Jabez, Salome relents and dials the number to N. O. Goode's residence. She lets the telephone ring a number of times, and when she is about to hang up, her sister, Delilah, answers.

"Hello, Goode residence."

"Hey D, it's me, Salome!"

"Hey girl, where have you been? When you coming home? Daddy's in real bad shape. We need you here now. I know you're mad at Daddy, but we need you here!"

"Whoa, D, I know Daddy's story, and you know how I feel about him. But where's Momma?" Salome says cutting her sister off before she continues talking about their father.

"I don't know!" Delilah responds.

"She's usually home by now, but she has been acting a little strange lately since Daddy's been in a coma."

"But Salome, how are you? How is everything out there in California? Have you met a nice Christian brother yet?"

"D, slow down. You always ask a million questions a minute!"

"Look D, when Momma gets home, have her call me, and tell her it's"

"Hold on Salome, Momma just walked in the door," Delilah says, interrupting her sister.

"Momma, Salome is on the telephone for you," Delilah says excited.

"Salome, I'll talk to you soon. I have got to study for my Biblical Counseling class," Delilah says, handing the telephone to her mother.

"Salome, Baby, I am so happy to hear from you. I know it's been a while. Are you ready to come home?" Marie Antoinette asks without taking a breath.

"Momma, where are Delilah and Jabez right now?"

"Well, Delilah went to her room, and Jabez is in the basement playing some video game because I can hear him shouting like he was at some game from up here. Why?"

"Momma," Salome says, starting to cry.

"Momma, I need to discuss a very private matter with you, so I need you to go into your bedroom, and I'll call you on your cellphone."

"But what's wrong Baby, why can't we just talk now because your sister and brother can not hear us?"

"Momma, I don't want to take the chance that one of them might pick up the house phone and overhear any part of what I am about to tell you. So please, Momma, please go into your bedroom, and I'll call you in five minutes. Please Momma, just do as I ask."

"Okay Baby, I'll go into my bedroom and wait for you to call." Her nerves are on edge because she recognizes a tone of desperation in Salome's voice.

Three and one half minutes pass and Marie Antoinette's cell phone rings. She answers after just one ring.

"Salome, what is wrong? I can tell something is seriously wrong with you."

"Momma, I'm pregnant, and"

"That's okay Baby, a lot of young women make that mistake. Do you want to keep the baby? We can arrange for an adoption, and,...."

"Momma, please let me finish! I am pregnant, and I've been diagnosed with HIV/AIDS!"

"Momma! Momma! Are you there?" Salome asks as she only hears silence on the other end of the telephone.

"I am here, Baby," she says, crying and trying to weep silently so she will not be heard by Delilah, who is in the next bedroom.

"Baby, how did you let this happen? Did this happen because you were rebelling against your father's strict rearing? What can the doctors do about the HIV/AIDS? Are you coming home so I can take care of you?"

"Momma, I am going back to the clinic test for help. They sent me a letter saying the treatments are very expensive! I know some folks out here who have lived for years with the disease, but I am thinking about aborting the Baby because I don't want to bring a child into this world with that kind of load on them from Jump Street!"

"You want to have an abortion? Your father preached about abortion being a sin!"

"Momma, Momma, Daddy ain't got nothing to do with my body and my choices. Besides, for all intent and purposes Daddy's DEAD! I couldn't care less about what Daddy thinks!"

"Baby, that is no way to talk about your father, and"

"Look Momma, are you going to help me or what? What I need to know is, can you get your hands on some money, a large amount of money so I can get an abortion and pay for the HIV/AIDS treatments. If you can do that, I promise once I get stabilized health wise, I'll come home because I know with God's help all things are possible."

"Baby, the court seized all of you father's money, but I may be able to raise some money!"

"How Momma, if Daddy's broke?"

"You just let me worry about that, Salome. I'll make some calls. I still have some influential friends in this community!"

"Are you talking about your Soros's, Momma? Because I don't want them in my business!"

"No Baby," Marie Antoinette responds tearfully.

"I have other friends. Just trust me! We'll work this out. When are you coming home?"

"Well, I'll have to get the abortion, then I assume it takes time to heal, and once I start my treatments and know what drugs they put me on, then I guess I can get my records transferred back home, confidentially. And Momma, please do not talk to Delilah and Jabez about this! Promise!"

"Okay Baby, I promise!"

With both mother and daughter crying on both ends of the line, Salome finally says, "Thank you, Momma! I knew I could count on you. You've always been there for me! I feel so much better now."

"Okay Baby. Let me go so I can start making some arrangements."

"Okay Momma, I love you," Salome says with tears rolling profusely down her cheeks.

"Bye Baby! I love you, too. I'll be in touch!" her chest heaving from her suppressed crying.

Salome finally rolls over on her left side in a fetal position and rereads the letter from the clinic.

"Lord, please forgive me for lying to Salome. I had to lie to her so she would be comfortable about coming home. You know Lord, that I am very upset about her being pregnant, but I had to make her feel at ease so she will not hesitate about coming home and letting me help her," Marie Antoinette says just above a whisper.

Marie Antoinette opens her flip phone and dials a familiar telephone number.

"Hello, this is Dr. Hudson," is the response she gets from the other end of the line.

"Oh, it's you, Marie. Did you enjoy the time we spent together? I know I did! What can I do for you at this hour?" Dr. Hudson says enthusiastically with an over abundance of lust in his voice!

"Clark, you said that someone was eager to pay a lot of money for N. O.'s organs and that I could get that money without anyone knowing if I signed an organ donor release form. Is that still a possibility?"

"Oh, hell yes!" Dr. Clark Hudson responds.

"And how much money am I looking at?" Marie Antoinette asks dejectedly.

"How about 1.5 million?"

"Million?" Marie Antoinette asks.

"Yes! As I said, my client is very wealthy, and I can get you a good faith check for ten percent as soon as you sign the form."

"But Clark, $150,000 in a check will cause some unwarranted attention. I need to get the money without anyone knowing or getting suspicious."

"Not really, because my client has a number of trust funds to shelter his money. He had given money to New Harvest when you were in the storefront. So it could be a donation to you to help pay your husband's medical expenses. Your husband still has his supporters in the community, so I do not see it as a problem. After your husband is gone, the bulk of the funds could be given to you in increments!"

"WHEW! Okay. I will sign the papers in the morning. How much time will you need to raise the funds?" Marie asks.

"I will make a call as soon as we get off the telephone and make the arrangements for you to sign the papers by noon tomorrow and get the check by 4pm that same day. How is that?"

Pausing for about two seconds, Marie Antoinette finally says, "Okay!"

"Okay Marie, I'll talk to you early tomorrow, because like I said, I need to make some calls. Goodnight!"

"Goodnight, Clark," Marie Antoinette says as she stretches across her bed in a fetal position and begins to cry.

"Lord, please forgive me for my making this deal to save my baby girl, but N. O. is not going to make it. It is his life that is ending for Salome's life that is just beginning!" Marie Antoinette says aloud, erupting into tears.

"N.O., I have to let you go so I can save Salome," she says remorsefully as she picks up a family picture from the night stand and clutches it to her chest.

Meanwhile across town

Dr. Clark Hudson calls his contact.

"Hello, Bill, I've got some very good news. I got Pastor Goode's wife to relent, and she is going to sign the release forms for the organ donations tomorrow. I am sure he will not last more than another week and,..."

"How much did you promise to pay her, Clark," Bill Kudneuson asks.

"I told her a million five but,..."

"A million five?" Bill yells.

"Are you crazy?" Bill asks angrily, lowering his voice because he is in bed and his wife is stirring! She opens her eyes, blinks frantically, then falls back asleep.

"Calm down Bill! I said a million five to get her to bite. Greed rules everything. But I told her she would get an initial payment of one hundred fifty thousand. That's all we have to give her because after all she is not in a position to go to the press or the police when we don't pay her the balance. I got with her tonight, if you know what I mean? I think I can string her along until we get what we need from her, and that is her husband's heart! Once she signs the consent form, I will do what I always do, I'll dump her!" Dr. Clark Hudson says erupting into derisive laughter.

"These women out here are so weak, so pliable. It did not take much encouragement to get her to sleep with me, and that was before we talked about the million five!"

"What made her change her mind, Clark?" Bill asks.

"I have no idea, but she called me asking when I could make the deal happen, so I need you to get a check ready for her tomorrow."

"Clark, you never disappoint me. I don't know why I even doubted or questioned you. I'll get the cash from my dad's account and pay her by whatever means you agreed to. But again, we are only talking about one hundred fifty thousand, right? I could not pay her a million five in a million years,..."

"Come on, Bill. If you were to pay her 1.5 million, then where would my cut come from?

"So, since you got a heart for my dad, you still want a half million paid to your account in the Cayman Islands, right?" Bill asks, looking over his shoulder to see if his wife is still asleep.

"Damn straight, Bill! Your dad being in a coma is a good thing for the both of us. And it is a good thing that, against his better judgment, he made you CEO of his company since the Board of Directors wanted to put someone else in the CEO position. So as long as we keep him alive, you will be running things, my friend! But if he dies, then his last will and testament will be read and you may not be in charge anymore. That is a chance we can ill afford to take."

"You are right, Clark," Bill responds.

"Bill, you need time to set up a trust for your father's estate naming your wife and me as joint trustees. Right? That way I'll take care of you and you'll take care of me? I am risking a lot here to get you this man's heart. I have put your dad on the priority list for heart transplant recipients. I could lose my license for violating medical ethics and I have huge debts. If I lose my job helping you out with getting this heart, I would probably become homeless!"

"Clark, you should have gone to Law School instead of Medical School. You'd make one outstanding lawyer," Bill says in an exaggerated tone because he knows he needs Clark to achieve his nefarious financial goals.

"You're right, Clark! You're right!"

"Okay then, Bill. Let's roll with my plan and I need you to *stop playing out of position.* I got this!" Dr. Hudson says as if he were talking to and scolding a subordinate at the hospital.

"Okay, I'll talk to you later, Clark," Bill says.

Turning over and facing Bill, Edna, his wife, asks, "Honey, who was that?"

"No one important. It was just business. A vendor from Seattle who forgot the three hour time difference. Just go back to sleep," Bill says, kissing her on the forehead as she assumes her original position.

I'm getting real tired of everyone thinking I'm some dummy, some fool that needs to be guided through life, Bill says to himself. I am more intelligent than all these people who are constantly implying that I am not as smart as my dad! I am quite capable of running Bill Juniors Appliances, and I have done an excellent job keeping the business afloat during this economic crisis, even to the surprise of the Board of Directors. Yes, I am not as dumb as people think, and I will show them, even Dr. Clark Hudson.

6:45PM the Next Day in front of Ms. Jenkins's House

Reggie pulls up in front of Ms. Jenkins's modest house, turns off the engine and begins to talk to himself.

"Okay man, we've got to get this story completed soon, so when you go in there, don't get distracted by Chastity no matter what she does or says or wears!"

He gets out of his car and buttons his sports coat. He leans over and looks into the driver's side rear view mirror and takes his tongue and wipes the top row of his teeth with his tongue. Satisfied that everything is okay with his appearance, he slings the right strap of his book bag over his left shoulder and makes his way up the thirty foot driveway.

Well I can see how Ms .Jenkins can spend some of her money from the book proceeds. She can get this driveway repaved, he thinks to himself.

Reggie looks around and prepares himself for Chastity's appearance at the door.

Knock! Knock! Knock!

"Who is it? Reggie is that you," Chastity asks from behind the front door.

"Yeah, it's me," Reggie says with a tone of trepidation ringing loud and clear from his response.

Reggie can hear the sound of Chastity frantically removing all the chain locks and dead bolts on the door because after all, Ms. Jenkins does not live in one of the city's better neighborhoods.

When the door finally opens, Chastity, who is dressed in a bathrobe, abruptly rushes into the bathroom and closes the door. Reggie can hear music being played as loud as possible from Chastity's bedroom.

Hmm, she's got the volume of her boom box up to the max, Reggie thinks to himself.

As Reggie walks down the hallway to the kitchen, he sees Ms. Jenkins rustling with her pots and pans. As he passes the bathroom he hears the familiar sound of running water from the shower.

"Hey Baby," Ms. Jenkins says, her hands encrusted with corn meal batter as she kisses Reggie on his left cheek.

"Did Chastity speak to you? That child is getting so disrespectful these days," Ms. Jenkins says, as she slowly lowers a long catfish fillet into a well used cast iron skillet filled with hot popping grease.

"Ah, it doesn't matter, it seems like she is in a hurry," Reggie says, setting his book bag on the floor as he marvels at all the food Ms. Jenkins has prepared.

"Well, I raised her right, and I don't care that she has a date tonight. You're company and she needs to keep her fast fanny here and help me entertain you."

"Oh, that's okay," Reggie says, thinking to himself that it will be a relief that Chastity will not be trying to get him aroused.

Ms. Jenkins might be old, but she isn't too old to catch on to what Chastity is doing, Reggie thinks to himself.

He surveys the stove and counter top again and is awe struck by all the food being prepared.

"Wow, Ms. Jenkins, you always go out of your way to feed me, and this is just too much," he says, as he looks over the array of food which consists of fried catfish, collard greens, candied yams, potato salad, hand squeezed lemonade, and sweet potato pie.

"Ms. Jenkins, I have to watch you because you seem to be trying to get me fat!"

"Heh, heh, heh," she chuckles.

"Reggie, will you go into Chastity's room and turn down that noise! She plays her music so loud, it would not surprise me if she is going deaf. Just go into her room and turn down that noise, please!" Ms. Jenkins says with emphasis.

"But Ms. Jenkins, that is an invasion of her privacy. I should not go into her room without her permission, Reggie says, gulping as he does not want a confrontation with Chastity about being in her room unasked.

"She might get the wrong impression if she comes into her bedroom and I am there knowing she was taking a shower!"

"Reggie, will you do as I say? That girl is going on a date, so she'll be primping in the bathroom for at least another hour."

"Okay, Ms. Jenkins. Okay!" Reggie says reluctantly.

Reggie slowly walks from the kitchen to Chastity's bedroom. He pauses just long enough to check to see if the shower is still running. It is! He slips into Chastity's room like a thief. Once in the room, he sees that Chastity is extremely neat. But what captures his attention the most is the lacy purple Victoria Secret matching bra, panty and thigh high stockings set Chastity has laid neatly across her bed. Reggie pauses for a moment and lustfully reflects, "Wow, I can imagine how good she will look in those!"

He heads across the room to her chest of drawers and turns the volume dial on her boom box to just below the mid range. Nervously, he slowly eases his way out of Chastity's room when he notices a purple mini-dress hanging on the front of her closet door.

Somebody is going to get lucky tonight, Reggie thinks to himself with a slight twinge of jealously. Just as he is about to back out of Chastity's bedroom, she enters, dripping wet, with a towel neatly wrapped around her head and another wrapped around her mid-section. That towel is not sufficient to conceal her bulging cleavage and her shapely legs.

Reggie makes no attempt to conceal his lustful glance.

"What are you doing in my room?" Chastity asks in a very irritated tone.

"Ah, well, your grandmother asked me to come in here and turn down your music. She thinks it is too loud!"

"Okay, well you've done that, so you can leave now," Chastity says, her words still dripping with irritation.

"Sorry! I was just following orders," Reggie says meekly as he tries to divert his eyes from Chastity's outstanding body.

"Okay Reggie, get out! I have a date, and I don't have time to entertain you because you had your chance," Chastity says as she lets the towel covering her mid-section fall to the floor.

"See what you could have had Reggie? This could have been all yours." She slowly turns in a complete circle like a runway model so he can see every inch of her shapely nude and flawless body.

Reggie is temporarily startled by Chastity's moves and surveys her body from head to toe.

If she has any imperfections at all it would be that slight puffiness around her lower abdomen, and any man I know would certainly be able to deal with that, Reggie thinks to himself.

Now having seen Chastity totally naked, Reggie begins to mutter, "Okay, I'm out of here."

Chastity rapidly moves to her dresser and grabs her deodorant which she applies generously and vigorously under both arm pits. Reggie is slowly backing out of her bedroom when Chastity abruptly turns around and twists her head to the right as if to say, "Haven't you seen enough? Now go!"

Reggie takes the nonverbal hint and rushes back into the kitchen.

"Reggie, what's the matter? You look like you done seen a ghost?" Ms. Jenkins asks suspiciously.

"Oh, ah, Chastity came into her bedroom while I was leaving and she seems upset."

"You didn't see her goodies, did you Reggie?" Ms. Jenkins asks, laughing deliriously.

"No ma'am! I did not see anything, ah, she was covered by towels," Reggie says, trying to get his words together.

"It's okay if you did, she likes you and you'd make a good husband for her. She used to be stuck on that fool, Pastor Goode, always telling me how fine he was. Then, here you come along looking like you could pass for his son."

Knock! Knock! Knock!

"That must be her date knocking on the door. He's a might early. Would you go and let him in and tell him to sit in the living room til Chastity's ready?" Ms. Jenkins asks Reggie as she puts the collard greens into a large clear blue glass serving bowl.

"Not a problem," Reggie says.

"Who is it?" Reggie asks through the door.

"It's Tariq Jefferson, and I'm here to see Chastity," the voice on the other side of the door responds, not expecting to hear a man's voice.

"Tariq Jefferson, the basketball player from Northwestern Wesleyan University?" Reggie asks, surprised as he struggles to unlock all the deadbolt and chain locks on the door.

"Yes, that's me'! Tariq responds, chuckling.

Finally getting the door open, Reggie thrusts his right hand toward Tariq and shakes his hand vigorously.

"Hey man, it is really nice to meet you. I am a big fan of your skills on the basketball court, and I hear you are one of the leaders of the college sports Christian Athletes Movement."

"Thanks, and yes! Me and some other guys started CAM three years ago, so if we go to the pros, we won't forget that the Lord made it possible, and we won't get caught up in all the hype about the celebrity, the drugs, partying and the never ending supply of women that will always be around to tempt us," Tariq says proudly.

"By the way, you look familiar to me. Aren't you Reggie Stoddard from Channel 8? "Tariq asks.

"Yes, I am," Reggie says, happy that Tariq knows of him.

"Hey man, I am a fan of your news stories. What are you doing here?" Tariq asks.

"Oh, I am here to interview Ms. Jenkins for a book I am writing about Pastor N. O. Goode of New Harvest Missionary Baptist Church. I know you heard about his legal, and now physical woes," Reggie responds to reassure Tariq that he is not there to see Chastity.

"Oh, that's great!" Tariq says, relieved.

"Yeah, that Pastor Goode was a great preacher, but his personal practices did not line up with what he taught from the pulpit. I visited his church a couple of times, but there was always something missing for me, so I never joined. His sermons always left me with an empty feeling spiritually. He was just like his initials implied just NO GOOD!" Tariq says as he and Reggie both break out into nervous laughter.

"So I guess you are here to take Chastity on a date," Reggie asks, like a proud father.

"Yes sir."

"Well, I do not think she is ready, so why don't I introduce you to her grandmother?"

"Okay," Tariq responds as he follows Reggie down the narrow hallway.

"My, my! Aren't you a very tall and handsome young man!" Ms. Jenkins says, upon laying eyes on Tariq. They shake hands after Ms. Jenkins wipes her hands on her apron. Reggie then introduces them to each other.

"Baby, how tall are you anyway?" Ms. Jenkins asks, straining to look up at Tariq who towers over her by what seems like five feet.

"Ah, I'm six eight ma'am."

"Six eight, Lord you are tall! How'd you meet my grandbaby?"

"We met at the food court at the Olympic Mall, ma'am," Tariq says, hoping he is not about to be the recipient of a third degree.

"Ma'am, your food sure looks and smells good," he continues.

"Well Baby, do you want something to eat? I gots plenty!"

"Ah, no ma'am. Chastity and I are going to a social event on campus and there will be food there," Tariq says reluctantly, knowing fried catfish is his all time favorite dish.

"Well Baby, I bet they ain't got no catfish, especially catfish that is as good as mine,..."

"Oh, I'm sure they don't, ma'am."

"Tariq, trust me. Just try a piece of her catfish. It's outstanding," Reggie says as he sits pointing to a seat for Tariq to sit in while Ms. Jenkins puts an overloaded plate of food in front of him.

Looking around as if he expects Chastity to rush into the room, Tariq slowly and sheepishly says, "Okay, you've convinced me. Ma'am, I'll have just one small piece of catfish while I wait on Chastity."

Ms. Jenkins smiles as she loves to be complimented on her food, and Tariq will be just another confirmation of her cooking skills. Besides she knows that Chastity is primping to look her best for Tariq and will be busy long enough for Tariq to eat an entire meal if he wanted to.

Tariq looks eagerly at the huge lightly breaded golden catfish fillet Ms. Jenkins has placed on a plate in front of him. Breaking off a piece of the fillet with his fork, he looks up from his plate to see both Ms. Jenkins and Reggie staring at him. He takes a bite and it is more than obvious he enjoyed the first bite. It's quickly followed by several other bites until there is no evidence there was ever any catfish on his plate.

"That was very good. I mean that was some of the best catfish I've ever had in my life," Tariq says enthusiastically.

"Want another piece, or better yet do you want a whole plate? No telling when Chastity will be ready," Ms. Jenkins says unabashedly and proud of the fact that she has gained the favor of another man.

"Ma'am, truthfully, I could sit here and eat your food until it was all gone, but Chastity and I must get going because I'm on the program tonight. I've got to do the benediction."

At that moment Chastity enters the kitchen.

"Oh, I see you met Big Momma and her friend, Reggie," Chastity says sarcastically.

"Well Big Momma, Reggie! Me and Tariq have to go, don't wait up."

"What do you mean, young lady? As long as you live under my roof you'll be in by eleven! Do you understand me, Chastity? You too young man," Ms. Jenkins says sternly.

"Yes ma'am," Chastity and Tariq respond in unison.

"Do you want another piece of catfish for the road?" Ms. Jenkins asks proudly.

"Oh, no ma'am," Tariq responds, looking at Chastity as if he does not want to offend her.

"Man, if I were you, I would grab a piece of paper towel and get a piece of that catfish, to go." Reggie says, slowly lifting his head up from his plate where he is tearing into his meal.

"Okay," Tariq says without any hesitation.

Reggie rises from his seat and walks Tariq and Chastity to the front door, peeking out the window too see what kind of car Tariq has. It's a late model Volvo.

"Hmm, the boy's got class," Reggie says to himself.

Reggie walks back to his seat in the kitchen and dives back into his meal.

"He seems like a nice enough young man," Ms. Jenkins says with a puzzled look on her face.

"You know Reggie, he kinda reminds me of you and Pastor Goode. Y'all got some of the same features!"

"Ms. Jenkins, I might favor Tariq, but I don't look anything like Pastor Goode, other than our hair texture and complexion, Reggie says, trying to be polite.

"Well, there's something similar bout all three of y'all," Ms. Jenkins says, as if she is in deep thought.

After Reggie finishes his dinner, he volunteers to help Ms. Jenkins clean up the kitchen, but she refuses.

"Well, we'd better get back to the story," Ms. Jenkins says from the sink.

"Reggie, you write and I'll talk while I clean up the kitchen,…"

"Okay, "Reggie says, as he gets his notepad and micro recorder out of his book bag.

About two hours into her rehashing parts of the N. O. Goode saga there is a loud commotion at the front door.

"What is going on? It sounds like somebody's trying to break in," Ms. Jenkins says as she slowly walks to the front door. Someone is trying to hastily get into the house but they obviously have keys. Reggie rises from his seat, grabs a butcher knife from the kitchen counter, and accompanies Ms. Jenkins to the door.

"Chastity, is that you?" Ms. Jenkins asks as the person on the other side of the door seems to be frantically trying to get into the house.

"Yes, Big Momma," Chastity says, sobbing loudly.

Chastity is finally able to unlock all the locks and rushes into the house past her grandmother and Reggie. She runs like a track star to her room with tears profusely pouring out of her eyes.

Ms. Jenkins hobbles down the hallway shouting,

"Chastity, what's the matter, Baby? Did that young man do something to you?"

Reggie looks out the storm door and sees that Tariq is still sitting in his car with the engine running, but he looks sorely disappointed and dejected."

I better check into this, Reggie says to himself, his reporter instincts telling him there is a story worthy of his curiosity and interest. He steps onto the porch and realizes he still has the butcher knife in hand, so he reenters the house and lays the butcher knife on the coffee table.

Approaching Tariq's car he says, "Hey Tariq, what's up? Why did you bring Chastity home so early? And why is she crying?"

"I don't know, man. We went to the event on campus. We were having a good time, or at least I thought so, when she insisted we leave and go to my place after I did my talk. So I told her we could but that as a Christian Athlete we couldn't do anything sexual. She said okay, that she just wanted to be alone with me so we could talk. I take her to my place and we're watching a DVD and she starts getting undressed right in front of me. When I told her I was serious about being celibate, she took off all her clothes but her underwear and started giving me a lap dance. I ain't going to lie and say I didn't enjoy seeing her like that, but I must remain true to my faith. I was getting excited, so I jumped up from the sofa and told her I was serious about not doing anything and that I thought it best that I take her home. It was about that time she fell on the floor and started crying and asking me why nobody really loved her, why every man she liked didn't want her! What was wrong with her?"

"So what did you do then?" Reggie asks.

"I told her we needed time to get to know each other. I told her that if we were going to ever be a couple, she'd have to understand my beliefs and wait until we got married before we did anything. That just seemed to make the situation worse, so I held her and rocked her in my arms until she finally saw I was dead serious and put her clothes back on. Man, I watched her and wanted to get with her, but, I was strong, real strong!"

Sighing, Tariq continues, "On the ride back here all she did was look out the window and cry, mumbling something about she was going to be in trouble with her grandmother."

Damn, man, you mean you turned THAT down? Reggie thinks to himself, envying Tariq.

"Wow! I feel sorry for you man! I know you do not want to be a hypocrite. I know it had to be real hard to turn her down. She is FINE though!" Reggie says as Tariq nods his head shamefully in agreement.

"I know she had to be hard to resist," Reggie says.

"She's a beautiful girl, man. Too young for me, but she's definitely an attractive woman," Reggie says trying to conceal a twinge of envy and an over abundance of lust still focused on what Chastity must have looked like in her purple underwear!

"Well, when I pulled up in front of the house, she asked me again why nobody wanted her, why nobody loved her. I told her again it takes time to fall in love. Anybody can fall into bed together, but the best relationships are based on what people have in common and how they follow the word of God. She then looked at me, never said another word and ran up on the porch trying to get into the house as quick as she could. That's when you and her grandmother came to the door."

"Okay Tariq. I'll talk to her grandmother and try to square things for you. Here, take my card and call me tomorrow about 2PM, and I'll let you know where you stand with Chastity. You do like her, don't you?" Reggie says in a fatherly tone.

"Oh definitely, but I'm just trying to get to know her, and she wants me to be her man on our first date? You have no idea how many girls try to get with me since I play ball," Tariq says, as he puts Reggie's card in his shirt pocket.

"Oh, I know, I definitely know how it is," Reggie says, reflecting back on his experiences with Chastity.

"Okay, wait here a few minutes and let me talk to Chastity and her grandmother. Hopefully, everything can be worked out if that's what you want,

Tariq."

"Yeah man, like I said, she's a nice girl, one I'd like to get to know better, but we just need time. When we met, all she talked about was her faith and belief in God and how disappointed she was with Pastor Goode. I was thinking I had just met a winner, but now man, I don't know. I just don't know what to think!" Tariq says shaking his head vigorously in disgust.

"So can you wait for me to check things out for you Tariq?" Reggie asks solemnly.

"Yeah man, I can wait a few."

"Okay, just give me about ten minutes."

Reggie reenters Ms. Jenkins's house and hears the muffled conversation between Ms. Jenkins and Chastity. One word rings out loud and clear with no chance of him misunderstanding it, the word is PREGNANT!

Reggie creeps down the hallway trying to get closer to Chastity's bedroom without being noticed and sees her door is closed. He gets close enough to the door and hears Ms. Jenkins ask, "But Chastity, how could you let that man of all mens get you to lay with him?"

"Big Momma, I don't know! Maybe because I never had a father in my life. Maybe because he is such a persuasive talker. Or maybe I just wanted to have a Baby so I'd know that I had someone who'd definitely loved me." Chastity says still crying.

"But Chastity how could you, a child that I raised and took to church every time the doors were open, get pregnant by such a deceitful, greedy and arrogant man?"

"I don't know, Big Momma. I was weak! You see I was in the mall at closing one evening about two months ago and he approached me in a very friendly manner. He asked me how I was getting home. I told him the bus. He asked if I wanted a ride, so I said yeah if it wasn't a problem. But on the way home he asked if I was hungry, and I said yeah, I could use a bite. So, we stopped at the little restaurant in the back of the Short Stay Motel on Twelfth and Main. He was a perfect gentleman. He opened my door for me and told me I could order anything on the menu. He told me how upset everybody in his family was getting about the trial and that he'd be glad when it was all over. After we ate, he showed me a key card to a room he must keep at the motel. He asked if I was in a hurry to get home. I said not really because I looked up to him because he was such a nice dresser and was always so polite, and I knew he was unhappy in his marriage."

"How'd you know that, chile? Maybe he's unhappy with his marriage because it prevents him from chasing all the women in the church both single and married!" Ms. Jenkins says compassionately.

"Well, he asked me if I liked him enough to go to his room and spend some time with him. And without thinking, I said yes. Big Momma, I just needed to feel like someone loved me. I just needed to be held by a man and just needed to feel like a woman, so I said okay."

"Umm, Umm, Umm," Ms. Jenkins sighs. "So what else happened?"

"Well Big Momma, he had some orange juice and vodka and made me a drink. I can't remember how many drinks I had and truthfully don't remember if he was any good in bed or not! I think he must've put some of that date rape stuff in my drinks because," Chastity says pausing, looking down at the floor knowing her grandmother will get highly upset with what she is about to reveal.

"Promise you won't get mad," Chastity says, leaning back from her grandmother who had been holding and rocking her in her arms.

"I won't chile. I promise," Ms. Jenkins responds, fearing the worse.

"Well, when I came to, Pastor was getting dressed, and he and his cousin, Trustee Theo Lane, were laughing about how they been running this game on so many women at church. I remember Pastor saying something about needing a stress reliever and having sex with me was right on time! Pastor thanked Theo for calling him and letting him know that I was unconscious and ready to be taken advantage of. Pastor also said how nice my body looked naked and how I wouldn't say anything because I would look like a slut and who would believe me anyway over them. The Pastor of one of the biggest churches in the city and the Co-Chair of the Trustee Board? Honestly, Big Momma, I was attracted to Theo. That's why I went to the room with him, but I'd never planned to get with Pastor, even though I used to think he was fine!"

"Baby, why didn't you tell me about this sooner? I would have taken you to the police. Those men need to be dealt with! They raped you!"

"No, Big Momma, only Pastor raped me cause I went with Theo willingly!"

Taking a deep breath and sighing, Ms. Jenkins begins to weep.

"But Big Momma, it was my fault! I did go into the motel room willingly with Theo. I never expected it was a setup, and now I'm pregnant and don't know which one of them is the father. How would that make me look? Just look at how you are looking at me. How could I deal with the ridicule of the whole congregation if this gets out?" Chastity says abruptly, standing up and pacing back and forth across her room.

Reggie makes a sound to let them know he is outside so they will not think he was snooping.

"That must be Reggie. I'll tell him we'll have to talk another day, we have some things to work out about this here situation," Ms. Jenkins says crying.

"Big Momma, will you help me get an abortion?" Chastity whispers.

"Ah, we'll have to talk about that, Baby. I ain't for taking an innocent life because you made an innocent mistake," Ms. Jenkins says. Chastity stands straight and checks her appearance in the full length mirror. She nods her head to her grandmother, letting her know she is ready to be seen by Reggie.

Ms. Jenkins slowly opens the bedroom door. Reggie stands as if he had not heard a word. "Is everything all right?" he asks.

"Yes Baby. Everything is all right! Me and Chastity just had some girl talk about you men folk. Hey, is it okay if I call you and let you know when to come back over? Chastity and I have to work a few things out."

"Sure, sure," Reggie responds.

"How about I call you over the weekend?" Reggie asks.

"That'd be fine." Ms. Jenkins says.

"Well, I will just get my stuff and call you over the weekend. Are you sure everything is okay? Is there anything I can do?" Reggie asks.

"No we'll be just fine, Baby. You go on now, and let us women finish our little conversation."

Reggie walks to the front door and lets himself out. He then realizes that Tariq is still waiting for him, and he knows he can not reveal the conversation he just overheard.

Damn, if I tell Tariq what I heard and he tells Chastity, Ms. Jenkins might get upset and there goes my Pulitzer. Okay Reggie, you are good thinking on your feet, think of something he will believe.

"Hey look, Tariq, Chastity really likes you, but she is a little misguided, a little out of sorts right now. You know, she just finished that time of the month," Reggie says, waiting for Tariq to respond or at least nod in agreement.

"Oh yeah, that time of the month. So that's why she was,"

"A little emotional? Yeah, Tariq, she is a nice girl. Just give her some time. She feels like she made a fool of herself with you, so I told her I would talk to you. I also told her you would wait about a week or two before you called her just so she could have some space. Was I okay in saying that?" Reggie says thinking Tariq is a naive in the ways of love.

"Yeah, that's definitely okay! I could use a little space, too!" Tariq says, relieved.

Well Reggie, I gotta go. I'll give you a call in a few weeks to see how she's doing,"

"Yeah, that's cool," Reggie says, thinking that he needs to adjust his very proper way of speaking to sound like he is from the hood.

Driving off, Tariq thinks to himself, like that old school singer, Keith Sweat, sings, sumthin sumthin, sumthin just ain't right!

Reggie drives home wondering how Ms. Jenkins will deal with Chastity's pregnancy. He does not have to worry long. Entering his apartment, he notices he has three messages on his answering machine. One from his editor at Channel Eight. One from a buddy asking him if he can borrow a few dollars until the weekend, and one from Ms. Jenkins. Reggie listens to the messages and is taken aback by the one from Ms. Jenkins.

"Hello Reggie, this is Ms. Jenkins. I needs to talk to you about a little problem Chastity is having. I knows you are the only person we can trust because if you was to tell someone, we'd stop working on the book. So please call me when ya get home."

"Damn! That was a little cold," Reggie says aloud as he reflects on how Ms. Jenkins went straight to the jugular about him keeping his mouth shut about Chastity's pregnancy.

"So you would stop helping me with the book, huh?" Reggie muses, a little angry with Ms. Jenkins demanding retort.

I would have never thought that Ms. Jenkins would confide in me on this issue, but it is a lucky break for me because if she trusts me, and I keep my mouth shut, she will not hesitate to help me finish the book, Reggie thinks to himself, his anger dissipating. He dials Ms. Jenkins house with no reservation after listening to her message.

The telephone at Ms. Jenkins only rings once before Ms. Jenkins picks up and, seeing Reggie's name on her caller-id, says with a sigh of exasperation, "Hello Reggie. Thanks so much for calling. I need a big favor and you gotta promise me you will not tell anyone what I'm about to tell ya! Ok?"

"Yes ma'am, you can count on me. I promise," Reggie responds trying to present a simultaneous tone of surprise and concern.

"Okay Reggie," Ms. Jenkins says with a deep sigh.

"Chastity done got herself pregnant and,"

"Pregnant?" Reggie shouts into the telephone, pretending to be more than surprised.

"Yes, pregnant, and I want you to help her get an abortion!"

"Me? You want me to help her get an abortion?" Reggie asks in an acting job deserving of an Academy Award.

The wheels of intrigue and suspense are going into over-drive in Reggie's mind. How does she want me to handle this? Does she expect me to arrange an abortion for Chastity here in town? Does she want me to take her somewhere out of town? How does this sweet old lady want me to handle this delicate situation?

"Look Reggie, I don't want nobody at the church or in this town to know my Baby is pregnant, so this is what I wants you to do. Find some clinic where they do that sorta thing in another state. I knows you got connections or can look up a story were this type of situation was handled somewhere out of this state. I will pay for your time and transportation and whatever they charge to get rid of this baby. Do you understand?"

"Yes ma'am, and you do not have to pay me," Reggie eagerly interjects trying to play the role of a hero.

"Nah, that would not be right for you to pay for all that's involved," Ms. Jenkins retorts in a very demanding tone.

"We carry our own load around here! You just find the place and tell me how much it's gonna cost, and I'll handle that end of this deal, okay Reggie?"

"Yes ma'am," Reggie responds.

"Okay then, find a place and tell me how much it's gonna cost me. Chastity will call in sick saying she got the flu bug, and that will give her a couple of days to get her herself back together. Lord knows I don't want her to go through, this, but I don't see no other way out."

"I understand Ms. Jenkins. I will get on it right now and will call you tomorrow morning with a place. How about I drive Chastity to whatever place I find so we won't be seen at the airport or bus terminal? It could arouse suspicion in this city since she is so well known at the mall and is so popular!"

"That's a good idea," Ms. Jenkins says.

"Okay, Ms. Jenkins. Leave everything to me and I will work it out so Chastity has the abortion and gets her rest, and no one will be the wiser!" Reggie says, feeling proud of himself. After all, he needs Ms. Jenkins's support on the book deal, and by helping her, she will not be able to deny him anything. Reggie can hear the Ka-ching of the cash register in his mind and dreams of being wealthy beyond belief.

I just hit the lottery for big money, he thinks to himself.

"Okay, goodnight Baby," Ms. Jenkins says in a tone that lets Reggie know just how deeply hurt she is and tired as a result of this recent turn of events.

"Good night, Ms. Jenkins. We will talk in the morning."

Reggie pulls out his laptop and searches Channel 8's archive for stories about abortion clinics near their city. He finds one in a neighboring state and decides to check it out early the next morning.

10:22AM the Next Morning

Reggie has been up most of the night and has found an obscure rural health clinic only about an hour across the state line where Chastity can get an abortion. Since she is over twenty-one, she will not need to be accompanied by an adult. To protect their clients confidentiality, they accept walk-in patients.

"Thank God for that," Reggie says out loud as he stretches and yawns at his kitchen table. He has only slept about two hours. He reaches for his cell phone, but before he can even open his flip phone, it vibrates. He looks at the caller-id, and it's Ms. Jenkins.

"Good morning, Ms. Jenkins. I was just about to call you," Reggie says, sensing something is wrong.

"Reggie, we have a problem! "Ms. Jenkins says loudly.

"A problem?" Reggie asks.

"Yes, Chastity done fixed it in her mind that she wants to keep the baby and blackmail the Pastor and his worthless cousin, Theo, and make them pay her to keep quiet about who the baby's daddy is!"

"What?" Reggie shouts into the telephone, not realizing just how loud he has gotten with Ms. Jenkins.

"Ms. Jenkins, she can not do that. Theo is not one to be played with. He hangs around some pretty tough characters who have been linked with but never proven drug related murders. One of his buddies has been arrested many times and has been more successful at staying out of jail than John Gotti. We have got to change her mind!"

"I know Reggie. I know! " Ms. Jenkins says sighing.

"Maybe I can reason with her, Ms. Jenkins," Reggie says in a sincere and pleading tone.

"Okay Baby, I sure hope you can talk some sense into that girl. We stayed up all night, and she told me she was determined to make them pay!"

"May I speak to her now?" Reggie asks in a respectful tone, realizing what is at stake here. If Chastity attempts to blackmail N. O. and Theo, she might come up missing and Ms. Jenkins might become so depressed she would at the very least want to stop work on the book for some lengthy time. That certainly was not part of Reggie's Get-rich-quick off the book scheme.

"Chastity, Chastity," come to the phone! Reggie wants to talk to you," Ms. Jenkins shouts so loud that Reggie has to remove the telephone from his ear.

"What does he want?" Chastity yells back sarcastically.

"Baby, just come to the phone and talk to Reggie," Ms. Jenkins pleads.

"Why, Big Momma? What can Reggie say to help my situation?"

"Chastity, please come to the phone and talk to Reggie," Ms. Jenkins now says in a demanding tone.

"Okay, Big Momma!" Chastity slips on her house shoes and stomps into the kitchen from her bedroom.

"What!" she yells into the phone so loud that Reggie again has to move the phone some distance from his ear.

"What!" Reggie yells back.

"Look Chastity, your grandmother asked me to help you, and that is what I am going to do!"

"Help me? Help me how?" Chastity snaps back.

"Look, get a couple of casual outfits together as if you were going away for the weekend, because you are. I am taking Thursday and Friday off so I can take you out of town to have an abortion."

"But,...."

"There are no buts, Chastity. Get up right now, go to your room, and get an overnight bag together like I said!"

"But Reggie, how am I going to get to the place to have an abortion, and didn't my grandmother tell you I plan to have the Baby and make Pastor and Theo pay me BIG TIME?"

"Chastity, I don't think, no, I "know" that is not a good idea because Theo is no joke, and he would have you and your grandmother killed to protect his loot!"

"Are you serious?" Chastity asks.

"YES, I have done several new stories about organized crime in this city and Theo's name is frequently mentioned by a lot of the criminal element. He's definitely a slippery character. I would not put it past him to harm you and your grandmother in an attempt to maintain a pious image. He is riding on your pastor's coat tails, so no, I would not expect him to take your accusations lightly."

"But Reggie, you do not understand."

"What is there to understand, Chastity?" Reggie asks, cutting Chastity off.

"They took full advantage of me when they raped me!"

"What do you mean?" Reggie asks, slightly confused.

"They did things to me that are forbidden in the Bible," Chastity blurts out hysterically.

"Are you saying they sodomized you?" Reggie asks incredulously.

"Yes," Chastity responds tearfully, her chest heaving as she tries to catch her breath.

"I know I was wrong for going to that motel with Theo, but I didn't deserve to be treated like a piece of trash! And they laughed at me and said I was dumb."

"Damn!" Reggie responds with a high degree of real compassion.

"Chastity, I do not know how or when, but we will make them pay for what they did to you but not by making it public knowledge right now! I want you to trust me! Will you trust me and get ready so you have an abortion?"

"Okay Reggie! I'll trust you."

"Okay, please get ready and I will be there in about a half hour," Reggie says, looking at his watch.

"Thanks Reggie, and Reggie,…"

"Yes Chastity."

"Do you think someone will ever want me if they find out what Pastor and Theo did to me?"

"Sure, Chastity. You are a beautiful and talented young woman. I am sure that one day you will meet the man of your dreams," Reggie says in a sincere and reassuring tone.

"Reggie, I love you. I love you so much and wish that man could be you,…"

"Slow down, Chastity. Let's take one step at a time. We need to get on the road and take care of your little problem."

"So are you saying we could make it one day?" Chastity asks, sitting upright on her bed and wiping the tears from her eyes.

"Chastity, all I am saying is, let's take one step at a time. Okay! Now will you please get ready so I can pick you up?"

"Okay, I'll be ready in thirty minutes," Chastity says uncrossing her legs from her yoga like position. She could not be more enthused about going on this trip with Reggie than if they were about to elope. She daydreams about one day being his wife.

"Chastity! Chastity, are you getting ready so Reggie can pick you up and take you out of town? " Ms. Jenkins yells, standing just outside Chastity's bedroom door.

"Ah, yes ma'am," Chastity responds.

Across Town at Reggie's Apartment

Reggie is already packed. Since he works for a TV station, he knows that he could be called upon to travel for a special assignment at a moment's notice, so he keeps a small carry-on bag packed for such occasions. He decides to throw in a couple of casual outfits, then heads over to Ms. Jenkins.

On the ride over to Ms. Jenkins he talks out loud to himself saying, "I certainly hope that Chastity does not go off, once the reality of the abortion sinks in. This is a major step in her and any woman's life, but she has to get it done!"

Reggie finally arrives at Ms. Jenkins's, and with a quick and deliberate pace, races to her door.

Knock! Knock! Knock!

Without asking who it is or looking out the peep hole, Chastity opens the door. She is dressed in a grey jogging suit with pink stripes down both the sleeves and pants. Reggie is happy with her choice of clothing because he did not want her to wear something tight because he might construe that she is flirting with him, and the very last thing he wants is to get emotionally involved with a young lady less educated than him, and most importantly what he used to classify as a "soiled dove": A woman who loses her virtue to multiple men then tries to regain it by hooking up with a respectable man. A man with a promising career. A man of means.

"I'm ready," Chastity says as she hands Reggie her well used and stuffed overnight bag."

Straining to lift the bag, Reggie asks, "Hey girl, what do you have in this thing? It's heavy as hell!"

"Well, since we are staying overnight, I thought I'd bring some music, so I've got my small boom box and some CD's."

Ms. Jenkins has now positioned herself near the door. "Reggie, I know you will take care of my baby, and Chastity, don't you cause Reggie any problems while y'all are gone!" she says sternly but smiling at the person she loves more than anything.

"Ah Big Momma, I'm gonna be good! What kind of problems can I cause Reggie because I read that after the abortion they'll give me something to sleep and,..."

"Well you just be on your best behavior, young lady, and don't talk Reggie's head off on the road or in the hotel room!"

Chastity's face lights up as she is thrilled by the prospect of sleeping in the same bed with Reggie even though she will not be able to do anything because of the abortion.

With a tear in her eye, Ms. Jenkins leans over and kisses Chastity on her cheek, then tenderly puts her right hand on the nape of Reggie's neck pulling his head down so she might kiss him, too.

She whispers, "I knows you're gonna take good care, real good care of my baby. Just hurry back home as soon as you can."

"Do not worry, Ms. Jenkins. I will handle this, and everything will be all right."

Ms. Jenkins hands Chastity a large brown paper shopping bag that has a small grease stain on both sides.

"I know what that is," Reggie says in a delighted tone, knowing it is one of Ms. Jenkins excellent dinners for the trip.

The trip to the abortion clinic only takes about one and a half hours. Reggie covered the seventy-three miles without making any stops. Chastity slept all the way as she was up all night worried about the procedure and its possible impact of denying her any children. She wants children desperately, especially if she had them by a man like Reggie.

Arriving at the abortion clinic, Reggie looks around and decides not to park his car in the lot adjacent to the small storefront clinic. As a newsman he has heard the stories of how Right to Life protesters try to harass anyone going into an abortion clinic, and he certainly does not want to exit the clinic after Chastity's abortion to find his tires slashed or windows broken. Chastity is still asleep as he pulls into the small strip mall parking lot about a half block from the clinic. When Reggie turns off the engine, he looks over at Chastity and thinks to himself, "She looks so beautiful when she is asleep. I hate to wake her because she looks so peaceful!

"Chastity! Chastity, wake up! We're here," Reggie says, gently rubbing Chastity's left arm to awaken her.

"Oh, we're here?" she says, stretching in her seat.

"So where is the abortion clinic?"

"Oh, it's down the street, a few feet down the street," Reggie responds not wanting to divulge his reason for parking away from the clinic.

Stretching again and taking a deep breath, Chastity says, "well, let's get this over with."

"Reggie!"

"Yes, Chastity," Reggie responds, hoping she is not about to change her mind.

"Are you sure that a good man, a nice man will still want me if he found out I had an abortion?"

"Look Chastity, I know you know you are a beautiful woman. You can not let this incident affect your future. This is a chapter in your life that is about to be closed. So yes, any man in his right mind would want a beautiful woman like you," Reggie says, his twofold intent to build her self esteem and encourage her to get this over with so he can make Ms. Jenkins further indebted to him.

"Thanks Reggie," Chastity says, in a voice filled with sexual desire and thankfulness.

"Thanks Reggie, for having my back!" she says trying to open the door.

"Hold on, Chastity, I will get that for you," Reggie says with his gentlemanly charm. "Let me get that door for you."

Chastity smiles and waits for Reggie to come around to the passenger side of his car to open the door for her. She thinks he is interested while all he is thinking of is making points with her grandmother, the walking/talking repository of the Pastor N. O Goode story.

Reggie extends his left hand to help Chastity out of the car and locks the door as soon as she gets out. She grabs his hand and asks, "It's okay if I hold your hand since I'm so nervous, right?"

Aware that his response could hurt her feelings, he says, "not a problem."

They walk down the street toward the clinic holding hands. Chastity is as happy as she has ever been in her life. She is so happy, she wishes that someone would recognize them.

Reggie's feelings are opposite. He hopes she does not read more into his holding her hands, and the very last thing he hopes would happen would be to be seen by someone they know.

Reggie thinks, man, if we were seen together like this in front of an abortion clinic, I would have a difficult time explaining this to even my most trusted friends.

"May I help you?" the petite Asian nurse says as they reach the counter.

"Yes, my name is Reggie Stoddard, and I made an appointment for my cousin to have an abortion," Reggie says, fumbling in his back pack for a folder that he has placed an appointment slip he got on-line.

"Your cousin?" the nurse says sarcastically looking at the two of them.

Oh, I have heard that line before, she thinks to herself as she checks the computer for Chastity's appointment.

"All right Mr. Stoddard, I've found her appointment. Since she is within the first twelve weeks of her pregnancy, she is scheduled for a suction aspiration procedure at 11:30am. It's a good thing you got here a couple hours early because we will have to prep her by giving her some general anesthesia. You do know that our website stipulates that you must stay on the premises during the entire procedure, right Mr. Stoddard?"

"Yes, I'm aware of that rule," Reggie says, trying not to be noticed. After all, he is a TV personality and his station is probably within this remote town's reception area.

"May I ask a question?" Chastity asks, a twinge of nervousness oozing from her voice.

"Certainly," the nurse says, looking at Reggie's obvious discomfort, then at Chastity.

"What is a suction aspiration?"

Startled, Reggie thinks about answering, but the nurse beats him to the punch.

"A suction aspiration is one of the most common abortion procedures. First we dilate your cervix, then a tube is inserted into your womb. This tube is attached to a vacuum cleaner-like machine that sucks the placenta and fetus into a jar that is disposed at the end of the procedure. It's quick, clean and very efficient!"

The nurse says in an encouraging tone.

"Will it hurt?" Chastity asks nervously.

"Not at all. We will put you out, and you will not feel a thing, okay?"

"Okay," Chastity says, reassured.

"Okay, Mr. Stoddard, you may take a seat in the waiting room, and you can expect to see your *COUSIN* in about an hour and fifteen minutes," the nurse says, pointing to a small and virtually empty waiting room.

The nurse gently places her right hand in the center of Chastity's back and escorts her down a long and narrow hallway. Chastity walks with deliberate steps as if she were being led to an execution chamber. She quickly looks over her left shoulder to see if Reggie looks concerned. He does! At the end of the hallway there is a set of double automatic doors, and Reggie watches as they disappear into the prep room. He takes a seat, pulls out his laptop, and starts to proofread his entries about the Pastor Goode story.

An Hour and a Half Later

"Mr. Stoddard, you many come back. We need to go over some after-procedure do's and don'ts with you and your cousin," the nurse says, her sarcasm still evident. She escorts Reggie to a small room down the corridor.

Chastity is sitting in a huge burgundy recliner and looks as if she just awoke from a very deep sleep.

"Chastity, are you okay?" Reggie asks, noticing how lethargic Chastity looks.

"Yeah, I'm okay!" she says, trying to sit up because she is eager to go.

"Okay Mr. Stoddard, I notice you two live in the next state, and even though you might return to your home in a couple of hours, we recommend that you two spend the night here in Goldsburgh. That's just a safety precaution in case there are any adverse reactions to the abortion," the nurse says, rubbing Chastity's right hand.

"That's fine! I have reservations in a motel here because I did my research and it led me to believe that we would be ill-advised to take a two hour ride with her being jostled by the highway."

"Oh that was thoughtful of you," the nurse says.

"Please read over this list of do's and don'ts. And make sure she gets plenty of rest tonight and the next day or so. She should be able to resume her normal activities in two to three days."

"Okay, great," Reggie says, taking the paperwork and placing it in a folder in his book bag.

"Chastity, are you ready to go?" Reggie asks.

"Yes," she responds, trying to stand on her own. She is a little shaky, so both the nurse and Reggie gently grab her and help her out of the recliner. The nurse brings a wheelchair for Chastity and she is wheeled to the front door.

Then Reggie and Chastity walk out of the abortion clinic arm in arm. She takes advantage of her delicate condition to clutch his right arm so she doesn't fall flat on her face. She has just endured a procedure she never imagined would happen to her, she is glad it is over, and more than glad that she is with Reggie.

He must really care about me to be here with me like this! Chastity thinks to herself.

Man, I can not wait until tomorrow so we can get back on the road and I can get back to my normal routine, Reggie thinks to himself. Their thoughts for each other are at polar opposites.

Fifteen Minutes Later at the Easy Rest Motel

Reggie has driven the short three blocks to the Easy Rest Motel. He has a foldable travel dolly that he places Chastity's and his over night bags on. Like a gentleman, he goes around to the passenger's side of his car, opens it, then gently assists Chastity onto the sidewalk. She feigns weakness, so he grabs her to prevent her from falling.

"Chastity, can you lean on the car for a second?"

"Sure."

Reggie goes to the rear of the car, grabs the travel dolly, then positions it on the sidewalk so he might pull it with his left hand and walk arm in arm with Chastity with his right. They walk about twenty feet and enter the lobby of the motel.

"May I help you folks?" the heavyset woman says in a thick German accent.

"Yes, my name is Reggie Stoddard and you are holding a reservation for two connecting rooms in my name."

"Okay. Let me see here, Stoddard, Stoddard! Oh, yes, here it is. Mr. Stoddard we have a slight problem."

"Problem?" Reggie asks in a very quizzical tone.

"Ah yes. The wing of the motel with the connecting rooms is controlled by a separate fuse box than the rest of the motel. We have no electricity in that wing. All we have are singles that do not connect, but I can give you the largest single we have at half the usual rate." Feeling uncomfortable with the prospect of having to sleep in the same room with Chastity, he is now concerned about having to either sleep on the floor or in the same bed with her.

"Do you have two non-connecting singles next to each other?" Reggie asks in a pleading tone.

"Not a one. We are pretty full because of a local archery competition. The closest I could put you would be five doors apart on the same side of the hallway or across the hallway but two doors down from each other," the clerk responds.

"By the way, the largest room has a king sized bed and a love seat, so you two should be comfortable!"

"What are you afraid of, Reggie? I won't bother you. I'm too tired anyway," Chastity says smiling, yawning and grimacing in pain.

"Are you okay, Chastity?" he asks.

"Yes, but I just need to lay down. I mean like, as soon as possible. I'm so tired," she says.

"Okay, we will take the large room, and you did say at half the normal rate right?" Reggie says reluctantly.

"Fine, that will be sixty-four dollars. Will that be cash or credit card?" the clerk asks.

"Cash!" Reggie quips, knowing that he will not leave a paper trail.

Okay, Mr. Stoddard, here is your receipt and the key to your room which is room 79. Go out the door, turn right, then at the end of building take the stairs. Room 79 will be the third room on your right."

"Thanks," Reggie says. He grabs the luggage dolly and goes arm in arm with Chastity as they make their way to their room. They have to take it easy as Chastity's post abortion instructions were for her not to do any heavy lifting or climb a lot of steps.

Reggie opens the door and assists Chastity to the bed. When he turns his back to get the luggage, she lays on the bed and pulls the comforter over her. Once in the room, Reggie observes she is about to fall asleep in the comforter cocoon she has made when he yells, "Chastity, what are you doing? Don't you know better that to wrap yourself in that comforter? Do you know that is one of the last things they change, so you have no idea if it's clean or not?"

"Sorry, Reggie! I'm not the big time traveler like you. I didn't know that."

"I'm sorry I yelled, but I just do not want you to get any type of germs on you, especially after what you just went through."

"Okay Reggie, I know you are just trying to look after me." She grabs her overnight bag and heads to the bathroom.

"Is there anything else I should know?" she asks.

"Yes. Take this can of disinfectant and this roll of paper towels, and spray and wipe down everything in the bathroom you might touch," he says.

Chastity follows Reggie's instructions, thinking him to be a little anal about cleanliness. The room seems perfectly clean to her. She combs her hair into a pony tail, then uses a scrunchy to hold the pony tail in place. She washes up, brushes her teeth, and puts on some sheer lavender pajamas. Her matching bra and panties are a deep purple, and they make a sharp contrast to the sheer top and bottoms. After getting ready for bed, she walks out of the bathroom slowly, as if she were a drunken runway model. She brought this particular pair of pajamas to get Reggie's attention, and it worked. She is still feeling the effects of the anesthesia. She is no where near being graceful as she moves to the bed, but she is ever so provocative in her sexy outfit, too sexy for a woman who just had an abortion. Too sexy for a woman who knows she can not get intimate on this particular night. Too sexy to sleep with a man who has no real interest in her, no matter how much she and Reggie might want to become intimate for a booty call.

Damn! What does she think she is doing? Reggie asks himself looking at every curve of Chastity's outstanding body.

He goes over to the bed and pulls the comforter and top sheet back, then inspects the linen for any stains. Satisfied that the linen is clean, he gestures to Chastity to get under the sheet. Then he pulls the comforter far enough back so it will not touch her face. Chastity leans upward in a feeble attempt to kiss Reggie on his cheek, but he avoids the kiss and politely says, "Good night, Chastity."

"But Reggie, aren't you coming to bed, too?"

"Not right now. It is still early, plus I have a few work related things I need to get completed before I come to bed."

"Okay," she responds, tired and dejected. She drifts off to sleep in less than ten minutes.

Reggie goes across the room, plugs in his laptop, and starts to edit his notes for a story he is working on. He periodically gets up, walks across the room and looks at Chastity as she sleeps. She seems to be purring, so he goes back to what he is working on. Yawning and stretching, he looks at his watch and discovers it is 10:23PM. He retreats to the bathroom, and sprays everything in sight except Chastity's makeup kit and other feminine items she left on the sink counter. He takes a shower and puts on a red t-shirt and some grey pajama bottoms, then slowly walks over to the bed in a concerted attempt to not awaken Chastity. She is sleeping soundly on her side, so he pulls the covers up just enough to slide into bed beside her. While pulling the covers up, he can not help but notice the beautiful symmetry of her body. Her perfect butt and hips. Her well rounded shoulders and her devastatingly beautiful legs.

"Lord help me," he says in a whisper as Chastity rolls over in her sleep and displays via the sheer pajamas her small but shapely breasts and **almost** flat stomach.

"If she had some education and was a little older, I could see myself with her, but as it stands, she is just another hood rat looking for a sugar daddy."

Reggie does not fall asleep immediately because he is in total awe of Chastity's physique. He finally starts to doze off but not before he kisses her on the cheek. Chastity smiles but does not awaken. She got to sleep with Reggie in the same bed, but they were not intimate. They get up the next morning, have breakfast in a small diner down the street from the motel, then make the short trip back to reality, Ms. Jenkins's house.

Two Weeks Later

Since Chastity's abortion, Reggie has been on a special assignment dealing with the economic devastation of the city's economic base as a direct result of the high foreclosure rates. While he is still very focused on his book about the rise and fall of Pastor Goode, he sees equal opportunity to achieve his goal of being a national household name through this assignment. The station manager gave Reggie this assignment because of the number of e-mails Reggie received for how well he consistently handles himself on the air. His popularity in the community has grown tremendously. Although extremely busy, he just can not get Chastity off his mind. He calls Ms. Jenkins daily to check on Chastity and asks her not to tell Chastity that he is concerned because secretly he does not want to get anything started with Chastity. When Ms. Jenkins asks why he does not want Chastity to know that he asks about her, he just plays it off by saying, "You know how these young kids are, Ms. Jenkins! I do not want her to think she owes me anything because I helped her."

    His feelings for her, however, have increased, and he has to ask himself daily what the attraction is. She is, in his mind, too young for him because he is seven years older. She does not have his same level of education, and she certainly does not have his same level of sophistication, not by a long shot. But there is something beyond her physical beauty and her exquisite body that, at the very least, fascinates the hell out of him!

7:20PM Channel Eight's Editing Room

Reggie and Cliff (the video editor) look at the final product.
    "Damn, Reg, you've done an outstanding job on this puppy! It's going to get you nominated for an award this year."
    "You think so, Cliff?" Reggie says trying to sound and appear modest.
    "Oh for sure. You are a definite nominee, and if the awards committee has any sense at all, you'll win an Emmy for this story. It's thorough, sensitive, and gives people in this community a ray of hope," Cliff says as he hands Reggie a copy of the DVD with the finalized news story on it.
    "Thanks man," Reggie says as he gently places the DVD in his book bag, stands, hugs Cliff and shakes his hand as he makes his way out of the editing room.
    Reaching the parking lot, Reggie thinks to himself, You are on your way, Reggie! You are definitely on your way to the top.
    Reggie pulls his Blackberry out of his left inside suit jacket pocket, locates Ms. Jenkins's number and presses the screen to dial.
    It only rings twice before Chastity answers, "Hello!"
    "Hey Chastity, where's your Grandmother?" Reggie asks, going out of

his way to be rude.

"What about a, Hello Chastity, how are you doing?" Chastity says sharply in retaliation to Reggie's rudeness.

"Oh, was I being rude?" Reggie asks knowing he has Chastity's attention.

"Well, I'm sorry Chastity if I forgot my manners, but I need to talk to your grandmother. Is she available?"

"No," Chastity shouts into the telephone.

"She has not been feeling well the last couple of days and she's asleep now."

"Okay, Chastity, tell her I will call tomorrow about starting back on the book, and ..."

"Reggie, why you being so mean to me? I thought we had an understanding? I ain't gonna bother you no mo', so you can at least be a little pleasant with me when you call this house," Chastity says, interrupting Reggie.

"So you are not going to try to hook up with me when I come by?" Reggie asks.

"Yes, Reggie! I am so tired of you lame ass brothers. I don't care if you like me or not. I just want you to show me some respect. I would have been the best thing that ever happened to you. I would have made you a very happy man with the things I would have done for you. You could have had it anyway you wanted it!" Chastity says emphatically.

Anyway I want it, Reggie says to himself. He is turned on by Chastity but realizes that to be with her could diminish his standing with his peers and other professionals in the community.

"Well Chastity, I'm sorry if I hurt your feelings, but like I said sometime ago, we are not on the same level and you do not look or act like a woman who would be content to be the other woman, a kept woman, right?" Reggie asks, wondering if the potential is there for Chastity to be his outside woman.

"Chastity, who's that you're talking to," Ms. Jenkins shouts from behind her bedroom door.

"Oh it's **nobody,** just Reggie," Chastity shouts back sternly standing with her hand on her hip.

"Is he coming by tonight?" Ms. Jenkins asks, sitting up in her circa 1940's bed.

"No ma'am! He said he'll call you tomorrow. I told him you're not feeling well."

"Okay then," Ms. Jenkins responds as she slowly pulls the covers back over her and returns to a fetal position in her bed.

"Okay Reggie. Are we clear? If you want me to, "I'll arrange to be gone when you come by to see Big Momma!"

"No, that will not be necessary, "Reggie says, unable to get over Chastity's statement that he could have her anyway he wanted out of his mind.

"Okay then! Call Big Momma back tomorrow around ten to see if she will be up to seeing you, okay?"

"Okay. I will, Reggie says.

"Reggie, aren't you even gonna say, bye? Chastity says exasperated.

"Sure, bye Chastity."

"Bye Reggie!" Chastity says loudly, slamming the telephone into its cradle.

She loves me, that is for sure. I have to be real careful how I play this situation! When I make it, she could be a nice little lay toy on the side. The question is, will she keep her mouth shut like she keeps saying?

Meanwhile, across town at Ms. Dorothy's Diner – The Clandestine Rendezvous

Dr. Clark Hudson has secured the appropriate organ donor forms for Marie Antoinette's signature. He has agreed to meet her in an out of the way diner on the outskirts of town to finalize this transaction. He is sitting in a booth on the east side of the diner that is in the shape of a 50s style mobile home. He chose Ms. Dorothy's Diner because its clientele usually consists of the working class poor. Not a place where your upscale professionals would be caught dead! He feels, therefore, this is a very safe place for him and Marie to meet.

"What is the likelihood that either of us would be recognized here?" he says aloud.

His constant staring out the window attracts the attention of the cook who is continually putting orders up on the widow ledge that separates the kitchen from the counter area and the waitresses.

"Barb, keep an eye on that dude sitting at table six. He's a little nervous acting if you ask me! Just let me know if he starts acting stranger. Ya know I got my sawed off back here," Donnie, the cook says slightly above a whisper in an aggressive tone.

Just as Barb turns around to see who Donnie is talking about, in walks Marie Antoinette Goode. There is not one speck of makeup on her face, and she has her long natural hair pulled back into a ponytail. She is wearing a red and white jogging suit and some running shoes. Her face is almost completely covered by some sunglasses, the type that people usually get after having eye surgery.

"Excuse me, is this seat taken?" she says as she swivels her shapely hips and sits in the booth with Dr. Hudson.

Damn, she is just as beautiful without her makeup, he thinks to himself, never taking his eyes off her.

"Certainly, certainly," he says, making a feeble attempt to be a gentleman by trying to stand up since that is what he knows she expects.

Barb leans into the window as if she were about to place a customer's order and whispers, "Donnie, you can calm down. The guy at table six must be cool cause he was just joined by my Pastor's, I mean my ex-Pastor's wife. So everything must be cool!" She then chuckles and smiles as she grabs an order pad and briskly walks to table six.

Marie Antoinette is tugging on this huge straw hat she is wearing in an attempt to tilt it in an angle to hide the left side of her face.

She looks up and sees Barb staring right into her face, but since New Harvest is a mega church, she does not recognize Barb. Barb plays along and acts as if she has no idea who Marie Antoinette is.

"And what would you folks like to order?" Barb asks, her head down and her ink pen firmly perched at the top line of her receipt pad. She is popping her gum to the irritation of Dr. Clark Hudson. He shakes his head in disgust.

When she does not get an immediate response from Marie Antoinette and Dr. Hudson, Barb then looks at them as if to say, "Did y'all come here to eat or to conversate?"

Finally, after looking at Marie Antoinette with sustained lust, Dr. Hudson blurts out, "You may have anything you want. Everything is on me!" He continues to stare at her with his obvious lust apparent to Barb.

"I am not really hungry, so I will have a Greek salad," Marie Antoinette says softly, not making eye contact with anyone in the diner. She never diverts her eyes from the well used plastic covered and slightly greasy menu.

"I will have a dressed hamburger with fries," Dr. Hudson says "Well Marie, you certainly are stunning in your incognito attire. No one would recognize you."

"Thanks Dr. Hudson,"

"Dr. Hudson? Why so formal? I thought we were on our way to being great friends," Clark Hudson says, reaching across the table trying to hold both of Marie Antoinette's hands in his.

Stunned and looking around the diner, Marie Antoinette says in a barely audible voice, "Dr. Hudson! Remember, I am still a married woman, a Pastor's wife. What happened between us was a once in a lifetime situation, one I regret tremendously!"

Feeling rebuffed, Clark pulls his hands back across the table and says, "Well I guess we had better get down to business."

"Yes, that is what I would prefer we do. Now I have decided that since you need me to sign these documents, I need a good faith payment of, let's say, twenty-five thousand dollars up front. If that is not agreeable to you, I will just wait until my husband passes and collect on an insurance policy that I recently discovered he had taken out on himself."

"How much is the policy worth?" Clark responds tersely, then remembers he is in a public place.

"That, Clark, is none of your business. Do we have a deal or not? I promise if I get the twenty-five thousand up front, that I will deliver by signing the documents. Oh, by the way, I want the twenty-five thousand dollars NOW!"

"Where do you expect me to get twenty-five thousand at this time of day, at an ATM?" Clark says sarcastically.

"No, I will take a check," Marie Antoinette responds with an equal amount of sarcasm.

"But Marie, even if I wrote you a check, how could you cash it without arousing undue suspicion?"

I thought about that. You can make the check out to The M. A. Goode Foundation for Unwed mothers, a foundation I founded over five years ago. Do we have a deal or not?" she says, making movements as if she is about to leave.

"Hold on, Marie. Let me think about this for a minute."

"What is there to think about?" Marie Antoinette asks impatiently.

"Okay, okay! We have a deal. We will have to go across town to my office so I can get my business checkbook out of my safe."

"Okay, but I will wait in my car because like I said earlier, what happened between us is in the past and will never, ever happen again."

"Okay Marie! I understand! Let's leave so we can transact this business, but before we leave, when will you sign the papers?"

"Tomorrow, if that is okay with you, after I am sure your check is good!" Marie Antoinette says calmly.

"Okay, let's go." Clark says, disgusted.

"What about the food we ordered?" Marie Antoinette says, seeing Barb headed their way with their order.

"I will take care of it."

"Here's your order, Miss. You had the,..."

Clark interrupts Barb and says, "That's okay. We have to go, so take this and have a good evening."

"Oh, thank you sir! Thank you very much," Barb says as she takes the fifty dollar bill from Clark Hudson's hand.

Barb stands mute and even goes so far as to hold the bill up to the light to see if it is real. It is.

Marie Antoinette and Clark Hudson leave the diner, and Marie follows Clark to his office building. She sits patiently in the attached parking structure until Clark comes to her car with an envelope in hand containing the check.

"I hope I will not have a problem cashing this," Marie Antoinette says as she removes the check from the envelope and makes sure it is made out as she instructed and that it is for twenty-five thousand dollars. Satisfied, she starts her car and drives home. Reaching her residence, Marie Antoinette takes the check out of her purse and reviews it carefully from one edge to the other.

Okay, he might think me a fool, but we will see if Dr. Clark Hudson is as reputable as he wants me to believe, she thinks to herself."

She retires for the night, satisfied that she is at the very least on an even playing field with Dr. Hudson.

"I am so tired of men, especially N. O. thinking that I have no street smarts," she says, as she looks at the check written on Dr. Hudson's account at the Physicians and Nurses Credit Union.

She is tired, and after changing into a sexy night gown, falls asleep.

Back at the parking structure, Clark Hudson sits in his car thinking
I'll get my twenty-five grand back from Bill when I make the final payment, Clark thinks to himself. He hastily drives away shaking his head in disbelief as he thought he was working Marie, and she turned the tables on him.

"Why did she ask for a check up front? I wonder if she is suspicious of me? I hate smart women!"

8:50AM the Next Morning

Marie Antoinette sits parked in front of the Physicians and Nurses Credit Union. She is well dressed because she hopes a teller will recognize her. She sits, impatiently tapping the steering wheel of her ruby red fully accessorized Cadillac Escalade with her right hand. She watches as one of the Credit Union's guards opens a deadbolt lock slightly over his head, then one near the base of the door.

She hastily exits her car and briskly walks into the door which is being held open by the security guard who is checking her out from head to toe.

She sho is fine, the guard thinks to himself as he watches her walk past him. He continues to stare at her as she gets in the cattle line leading to the teller stations.

"I can help the next member," the twenty something Asian female teller says.

She smiles and moves up to the counter and digs into her purse to get the check.

"Good morning. I would like to open a checking and savings account."

"Okay, we require a minimum daily balance of one hundred dollars in our saving accounts and a minimum balance of fifty dollars in our checking accounts. We also offer overdraft protection, which I highly recommend," the teller responds as she hands Marie Antoinette a form to fill out.

"So how much will you be depositing to start your accounts today?"

"I want to deposit fifteen thousand in the savings and ten thousand into the checking."

"That's a total of twenty five thousand," the teller says, surprised at the amount.

"Yes, and I would like to start my accounts here with this check."

"Aren't you the First Lady of New Harvest?"

"Yes, will there be a problem?" Marie Antoinette **says,** thinking that the well-publicized seizure of N. O.'s accounts will haunt her."

"Oh no! No problem at all! I loved your husband's ministry, and I am sorry to hear about his troubles. I am a big fan and I'd like to do whatever I can to help you. People are so cruel these days," the teller says sympathetically.

"Thank you so much! How soon will the funds be available?" Marie Antoinette asks with her head bowed, embarrassed by the teller's concern.

"Oh, since this check was written by Dr. Hudson and I know you are legit, I will assign a VFC to this account so your funds will be available in twenty-four hours instead of the usual three days,..."

"A VFC? What is a VFC?" Marie Antoinette asks.

"Oh, I'm sorry! A VFC means Validated Funds Code. We usually enter this code to expedite funds transfers between two businesses that we have dealt with for years and especially those who maintain accounts with us or a sister Credit Union. Since you are not cashing the check, I can push this money into your account faster. I know Dr. Hudson, and I've been to your church many times, so I trust you," the teller says with a reassuring smile.

"Thank you so much! I am a little nervous handling a check for such a large amount, but the young ladies I help need so much, you know?" Marie Antoinette says trying to play on the sympathy of the teller.

"Oh, I truly understand. Is there anything else I can do for you?" the teller asks with a smile of contentment and pride on her face, handing Marie Antoinette her receipt.

"No, I cannot think of anything else. You have been so helpful. I really appreciate what you have done for me. Thank you," she says as she reaches across the counter to shake the teller's hand.

Marie Antoinette exits the credit union more pleased with herself than she was the night before.

"Thank you JESUS!" she shouts proudly, turning the ignition key. She looks into her side and rear view mirrors and pulls off.

"Now I can call Salome and tell her she can come home, since Clark will not be able to do a stop payment because today is the day he is scheduled for surgery all day. So who's the dummy?" Marie Antoinette gleefully shouts aloud as she drives to her house laughing and singing her praises to God.

Meanwhile on the West Coast

Salome sits dejectedly in her apartment. She is lounging in her living room in a bright red sweat suit completely oblivious to the fact that RED is the color always associated with a harlot!

Her telephone answering machine is busy recording her numerous messages. She is so depressed, she does not want to talk to anyone, especially her new agent. He has called three times about some roles he wants her to audition for in some low budget porno films.

She sits alone on the sofa crying.

Her telephone rings again. She has no intention of answering until she hears a very familiar voice.

"Salome, this is Mommy! Please pick up. Please Baby, pick up!"

"Mommy, what's wrong? You sound like something's wrong!"

"Oh no, Baby. I have some good news! You know how you have always told me I need to stand up for myself? Well, I did just that! You are going to be so proud of me! I have some money and will be getting a lot more, so you can make plans to come home!"

"But Mommy, how did you get some money? I thought most of Daddy's money is all tied up for a while, so where did the money come from? Mommy what did you do to get a lot of money?" Salome asks frantically.

"Baby, we can talk about that when you get here. When are you coming home?"

"Well I have a few things I need to get situated out here, so let me say about a month, Salome says, breathing deeply.

A month? Why so long?"

"Mommy, just trust me. There are some things I need to pursue and close out before I can come home. Please do not forget I have an apartment out here with furniture and..."

"Baby you can leave all that stuff. You will not need it, so try and come home sooner."

"Okay Mommy! Okay! I will try to get home soon," Salome says softly caving in to her mother's request.

"Okay Baby, we will talk in a few days. You be good and hurry home."

"Okay Mommy, Goodbye."

Laying the telephone into its cradle, Salome resumes her position on the sofa.

"What am I going to do? I have HIV, and I'm pregnant. WHEW! What am I going to do?

6:30PM the Next Day at Ms. Jenkins's House

Reggie has called Ms. Jenkins and set up an appointment to continue with the book. He is concerned that Ms. Jenkins's health is failing and about what would happen if she were to die? Who would or could provide him with all the information about the life and times of N. O. Goode if she were to pass away? He could offer Chastity a slice of the book proceeds if she were to help by telling her story. No, she probably does not know much about the real deal on N.O. Goode. No, he is in a coma, and it is assumed he will not recover. Reggie could ask Marie Antoinette Goode? Hmm! Maybe she would be agreeable to telling her husband's story for a small fee. But how much of N. O.'s devious lifestyle would he have confided to his wife? No, his only recourse was to get Ms. Jenkins to go into overdrive and finish sharing the story of Pastor N. O. Goode's fall from grace!

Reggie finally pulls up in front of Ms. Jenkins's house because he was stuck in traffic for over an hour due to a semi-tractor trailer accident on the freeway. Grabbing his book bag and micro recorder, he bolts from his car. He looks toward Ms. Jenkins's front door and sees her peering through her curtains. He rushes to the house hoping Chastity is not home.

"Hey Ms. Jenkins, I hope you are feeling better. Where is Chastity?" Reggie asks as he enters and gives Ms. Jenkins a long, tender, grandmotherly hug.

"Oh, that girl done decided to get a part time job at the Lathan Mall. Said she needed to make some money so she could move out, get her own place."

"Get a place of her own?" Reggie exclaims, surprised.

"Yes, she thinks I am too old fashion and don't give her no space. What she really means is that I ain't gonna let her bring no mens up in here to lay up with her, eating my food and sucking up all my heat in the winter and air conditioning in the summer," Ms. Jenkins says chuckling.

"Don't worry, Ms. Jenkins. When she gets out there and the bills start piling up, she will run back to your house like an Olympic sprinter. Trust me, she's not going anywhere."

Releasing her from his embrace, they walk to the kitchen where, as usual, Ms. Jenkins has cooked another sumptuous meal.

"Wow!" Reggie exclaims as he sits down to eat. Thirty minutes after gorging himself, Reggie uses the heels on both feet to scoot back from the table. His heels make an eerie noise as they are dragged across the linoleum floor.

"Ms. Jenkins, if I were just a few years older, I would ask you to marry me. Man, your cooking skills are outstanding."

"Chastity can cook as good as I do, and she would make you a better, younger and prettier wife if you'd just give her a chance," Ms. Jenkins responds, halfway joking, halfway serious.

"Okay,"Reggie exclaims in an attempt to change the subject.

"Ms. Jenkins, I have three areas I feel we need to cover to complete this book, but before we address those areas, I just want you to help me understand why a man, a very proud and disgraced man like Pastor Goode, would confide all the sordid details about his life to you? That just puzzles me!" Reggie says.

"Well, like I said the last time you asked me," Ms. Jenkins starts a little sarcastically. "When he came to the church, I was one of the first ones to reach out and help him adjust to New Harvest. I was the first one to invite him and his family over for dinner on Sunday after church, and I'm probably the only person who kept inviting him and his family to Sunday dinner up til the time of the shootings."

"But Ms. Jenkins,...."

"Look Reggie, everybody needs a friend, and I was his best friend! He had so much on him, that stuck up wife! Them bad ass chillren, and most of the deacons had turned on him. Early on he tested me by telling me something he said was a secret just to see if it would come back to him. It didn't! So he knew what he told me wouldn't go nowhere. That's why he always trusted me."

Sighing deeply, Reggie says, "Okay, let's get on with the story if you're up to it."

"Oh don't you fret about me. I know Chastity told you I was down and out, but I ain't as sick as people make out. I love the Lord, but I ain't ready just yet to meet Him."

Both Ms. Jenkins and Reggie burst into derisive laughter .and it takes them about thirty seconds to get to a point where they can contain themselves and start her reminiscing about the life and times of N. O. Goode.

"Where do you want me to start? With the part about Pastor Goode beating his wife and going to jail? Or the part about his daughter being in them dirty movies? Or the part about the shooting on that Saturday in May at New Harvest?"

"Let's start with the beating of Minister Marie Antoinette Goode," Reggie says, turning on his micro recorder.

"Well, it all started bout seven years ago when Pastor was seeing Sister Goodbody on the side. You see, him and his cousin, Theo Lane, had this little apartment where they would take womens to do their dirt. Well, Deacon H. O. Monger found out about the apartment because he and Pastor had started to get a little close. So one day Pastor and Theo asked Deacon Monger if he wanted to use the place, but he'd have to pay a third of the rent. They also agreed that they'd each have reserved nights so they wouldn't bump into each other with their womens. Deacon Monger said yes. Well, one evening, Deacon Monger and Pastor got their wires crossed cause Pastor said he had some Pastor's meeting to attend and they met at the apartment with their girlfriends. Pastor got there first and he and Sister Goodbody was already going to town in the bedroom when Deacon Monger walks in with guess who, Pastor's wife. Sister Reverend Goode knew Pastor was cheating on her, but she had no idea with who! And of course, Sister Goodbody wasn't the only New Harvest woman Pastor had on the side. Deacon Monger always had his eyes on Sister Goode, and he never thought that the Pastor would find out that he'd been flirting with Sister Goode who just had a weak moment and decided to get revenge on Pastor. Since Pastor wasn't expecting company, he left the bedroom door wide open.

"Baby, what are you doing here with Deacon Monger?" N. O. asks angrily, his nostrils flaring as he leaps from the bed. Sister Goodbody also jumps up from the bed, shielding her body with the top bed sheet. She scrambles to get her bra and panties on which she had thrown into a chair near the bed.

"What am I doing here?" Marie Antoinette yells at the top of her lungs. She lunges toward Sister Goodbody, who is dressing like the room is on fire.

N. O. also tries to dress hastily, but he struggles to get his pants on. He is glaring at Deacon Monger with his hatred being very obvious.

"Deac, how could you? How could you have the audacity to bring my wife here to have sex with?"

Before he can respond, Marie Antoinette has grabbed Sister Goodbody by her fake ponytail, spins her around, and yells, "I knew you would do whatever it would take to get with my husband, you heifer. I am going to kill you right here, right now!"

"Marie," N. O. yells as he tries to decide whether to knock out Deacon Monger or go to the aid of his girlfriend, Sister Goodbody.

Marie Antoinette has grabbed Sister Goodbody by her shoulder, spun her around, then immediately takes her fist and hits her in the nose. Sister Goodbody begins to yell and scream as blood pours profusely from her nose.

"You broke my nose! You broke my nose," Sister Goodbody yells. Marie Antoinette is in such a rage that both N. O. and Deacon Monger have to pull her off Sister Goodbody.

"Marie! Marie," N. O. yells as he and Deacon Monger finally pull her off Sister Goodbody.

"You'll pay for this! Both of you will pay for this! I'm going to ruin you both at New Harvest. I'm going to make you pay dearly for breaking my nose," Sister Goodbody yells as she finally is able to get all her clothes on even though they are in disarray. She is bleeding so bad that the blood from her nose has virtually saturated her white linen blouse and her perfectly white tight jeans. She grabs her purse and keys and exits the apartment saying,

"I knew I never should have hooked up with you, Pastor. I knew in my heart that something like his was going to happen, but I promise you, I'm going to make you both pay me for this," Sister Goodbody says as she slams the door hard behind her.

"N. O., how could you do this to me? How could you do this with someone right under my nose at the church? And why did you have to do it with her, of all people?"

N. O. is slightly distracted because he is peering out of the second story apartment window watching Sister Goodbody hastily and angrily get into her late model Corvette convertible.

Damn, what am I going to do now? I might lose the church behind this, he thinks to himself.

"N. O., how could you do this to me?" Marie Antoinette asks again as she slumps down on the bed crying uncontrollably.

"How could you do this to me?" N. O. retorts.

"The question is how could you do this to me with a Deacon in my church?" N. O. says angrily as he slowly approaches Deacon Monger.

"Pastor, I know you're upset, but you better think about what you're going to do because I'm from the Eastside and I'm no pushover. I don't want to hurt you, and if you think **about it,** if you were taking care of business on the home front, your woman wouldn't even consider being with me this evening or any other evening," Deacon Monger says as he makes his move toward the door and leaves the apartment.

"He had better leave before I get more upset than I already am," N. O. says, breathing deeply.

"N. O. I want a divorce," Marie Antoinette yells hysterically, sobbing so much she can barely catch her breath.

"Look Baby, we'll talk about this later at home."

"N. O., I do not want you to come home tonight. You will have to go and stay with one of your women!" Marie Antoinette says curtly.

"Marie, we will talk about this at home, and by the way, how do you plan to get home because Deacon is gone!"

"Well, you can drop me off at my car which is parked at the airport short term lot," she retorts.

"No, Marie, I will take you to your car and you WILL follow me home!"

Without uttering a word Marie Antoinette abruptly leaps to her feet and, staring at N. O., says, "Okay, but I still do not want you to stay in the house tonight with me and the children."

"Hmm," N. O. sighs as he opens the door to the apartment and lets her walk to the car.

All he can think about is the potential repercussions of Sister Goodbody's anger.

The ride to the airport only takes about fifteen minutes, but given the hostility between them and the fact that neither of them said a word, the trip seemed like it took hours. N. O. drives into the lot and drops Marie Antoinette by her car. He then follows her out of the garage as they head home. He then pulls out his cell phone and calls Theo Lane, his cousin.

Ring, Ring, Ring!
"Hello Cuz, what is up?"

"Theo, we have got a BIG problem! I was with Sister Goodbody at the apartment when Deacon Monger waltzes in with Marie Antoinette."

"Are you serious?" Theo asks in disbelief.

"So what are you going to do? What do you need me to do, Cuz? You know I've got your back!"

"I know, Theo, but that is the lesser of my problems."

"Why Cuz! What's up?"

"I think Marie Antoinette broke Sister Goodbody's nose, and she was so upset that I just don't think she is rational."

"So what do you think she'll do?" Theo asks. "Well, she said she was going to get even with Marie and I at the church."

"Hold up, Cuz! We've got a good thing going at New Harvest. You got me on the Board of Trustees, and I moved up to co-chair. We've got Chairman Bass in our pocket! He won't take a spilt, but he's scared of me cause he knows me from back in the day. Life can't be sweeter. We've been very successful at skimming a little off the top of all the tithes, offerings and money raised by all the ministries. And Cuz, when its your anniversary we dip into all the ministry accounts for a *special* Pastor's Anniversary assessment. We've got a real good thing going since I am in charge of the count every Sunday. It's as sweet as the mob being in the count room in a Vegas casino, and we can't let her mess that up for me, I mean us."

"Hold on, Theo, everything is not about money. I just want you to talk to her for me. Make sure she gets medical attention, and give her enough money to go somewhere like Miami for a couple of weeks to recuperate. We can cover any losses she will incur from being off her job."

"I don't know, Cuz! I could have someone take care of her for less money and,..."

"Theo," N. O. yells, disappointed, interrupting Theo's violent suggestion.

"Look Theo, I do not want anything to happen to her. I love her. She has no inhibitions and will do whatever I ask of her sexually. Here's her number, "N. O. says, as he recites the telephone number three times and asks Theo to read the number back to him twice.

"Okay Cuz, but I think my plan is better. I know someone who could handle our business with no muss and no fuss. But you're the man. I'll do it your way until she becomes a problem. Cuz, I just don't want to lose the fifty to sixty grand a year that we've been putting in our pockets with the game we got going on at New Harvest."

"Thanks Theo. I know my way is the best way."

By this time Marie Antoinette has used her garage door opener and quickly drives into their four car garage. She starts to close the garage door, then notices that N. O. is right behind her. She exits her car, rushes into the house, and heads straight for their bedroom. She locks the door and begins to cry again hysterically. She cries so loud that all the children can hear her and rush to the door, knocking and yelling in unison, "Momma, what is wrong? Let us in, Momma."

N. O. enters the house with a fierce expression on his face. Noticing the commotion stemming from the children outside his bedroom door, he shouts loudly, "Go to bed! All of you, go to bed right now!"

The children all fold their arms and stand like guards at Fort Knox until Salome shouts, "Daddy, what did you do to make Momma Cry?"

"I told all of you to go to bed! So do like I told you before I take my belt off and whip all of you."

"Daddy, what did you do to Momma to make her cry like that?" Salome asks defiantly. Neither she nor Delilah and Jabez have budged from their positions in front of the bedroom door.

"Hmmm," N. O. sighs loudly as he bullishly pushes the children aside and leans heavily on the door and yells, "Open this door Marie. Open this damn door before I break it down!"

"Go away N. O., just go away."

Without waiting a second, N. O. uses his broad right shoulder to push open the door. He used so much force that he tears the lock off the door.

"Get out of here," N. O., Marie yells crawling across their bed, recognizing the crazed look of a mad scientist in N. O.'s eyes.

"Daddy, leave Momma alone," the children all shout.

N. O. rushes across the room and grabs his wife who is sitting on their bed. He roughly grabs her by her upper arms and squeezes them so hard she screams in excruciating pain.

The children all plead with their father over and over to stop. He ignores them, then with the force of an offensive lineman, pushes her onto the bed with her head hitting the head board. That act makes a loud sound like a homerun off a baseball bat! He then slaps her repeatedly, as she tries to cover up. She is able to thwart most of the vicious blows to her head, absorbing the onslaught with her forearms. Still enraged, he then places his massive hands around her petite neck and starts to choke her. She gags and struggles to both hit him and to catch her breath! Her eyes are bulging. She is violently tossing and turning, trying to break N. O.'s stranglehold. She begins to turn red and is about to lose consciousness when she knees N. O. in the groin, causing him great pain, but he persists in choking her. Tears are streaming down both Marie Antoinette's and N. O.'s cheeks. He looks like a vicious killer intent on ending his wife's life. Suddenly the children all shout, "Daddy, **PLEASE** leave Momma alone!"

Jabez jumps on his father's back and takes both hands and pulls his father's head back by his forehead. This causes N. O. to cough, and his grip on Marie Antoinette's neck is loosened, albeit for a brief moment.

Salome rushes into the kitchen and dials 9-1-1.

"Hello police, please hurry to 47280 Ridgeway Terrace. My daddy is trying to hurt my mother. I think he is going to kill her if you do not get here soon!"

"We have a squad car already on the way because one of your neighbors has called us and..."

"Hurry, please hurry, my daddy is choking my momma," Salome shouts into the telephone.

Delilah and Jabez see their mother is about to pass out from asphyxiation, so they both began to pound their father's head with their fist.

They each then grab one of his arms and drag him to the floor, forcing him to loosen the grip he has around their mother's neck.

At that moment two police officers rush into the bedroom and restrain N. O. They put him in handcuffs after a fierce but brief struggle. They drag him out of the house, and like a scene from COPS, push his head down with no real concern for him or his head as they sit him on the back seat of the squad car. N. O. looks around in a panic and simply slides to his left and lies on the back seat. The Goode's live in a well diversified neighborhood, so it could have been anyone who called the police. Most of their neighbors mind their own business! It is so dark that the neighbors can not make out who was thrust into the back seat of the squad car. Was it an intruder intent on a home invasion? Was it a burglar? Was it the renowned Pastor of New Harvest, the mega church, N. O. Goode?

"Ma'am, are you okay?" Sergeant Wilson asks as he stands over Marie Antoinette who is still gasping for breath.

"Yes, "Marie Antoinette responds in a barely audible, raspy voice.

"Ma'am, I need to look at your neck for a moment," Sergeant Wilson says, shaking his head feverishly from side to side.

"Ma'am, there is a serious bruise on your neck. I am going to call EMS so they can check you out."

"That is not necessary. Believe me, I am fine," Marie Antoinette says, grimacing.

"Ma'am, I'm sorry, but state law requires me to do two things in this situation. One, I must arrest your husband for domestic violence, and,..."

"Is that really necessary? All married couples argue, and my husband and I were just..."

"Two, I must determine if I should call EMS based upon my perception of how bruised you are. Ma'am, I'm sorry, but I'm taking your husband to jail, and I'm calling EMS."

"But my husband is an important man, and what will our neighbors think?"

"Well, hopefully this experience will lead to my never having to come to this house again to arrest your husband. Personally ma'am, I have no regard for any man who'd hit a woman. And it appears to me that your husband has both hit and attempted to strangle you," Sergeant Wilson says sternly.

"But he did not mean it, I can assure you," she replies.

Officer Wilson ignores Marie Antoinette's pleadings and calls for the EMS. They arrive on the scene in less than five minutes, and the paramedics attend to Marie Antoinette's bruised neck and back where N. O. had slammed her head against the bed's head board.

Marie Antoinette erupts into tears, and Salome and Jabez sit on both sides of her, comforting her. Delilah sneaks into the kitchen where there is a cork board on the refrigerator with a list of the telephone numbers of all the Officers of New Harvest. She locates the number of Deacon Isa Crooke and goes over to the corner of the kitchen, dials his number, and whispers into the telephone when he answers, "Hello,..."

"Deacon Crooke, this is Delilah. My daddy is getting arrested for fighting my momma, and we need you to get him out of jail."

"Where is Pastor Goode now?" Deacon Crooke asks in an irritated tone.

"The policemen have him sitting in the back seat of their car and they called an ambulance to see if Momma is okay." Delilah responds excitedly.

"Well, you can go out and tell your father that I'm gonna get my attorney and we'll post bail for him within the hour. Can I speak to your mother?"

"I'll see if she can come to the phone," Delilah says as she scampers into the bedroom where her mother is being attended to by the paramedics.

"Momma, Deacon Crooke wants to talk to you,"

"Deacon Crooke? How did he know to call our house at this particular time?"

"Well Momma, I thought we needed someone to get Daddy out of jail and he's Daddy's friend, so I called him because I don't want to see my daddy go to jail."

"Hand me that telephone, girl," Marie Antoinette says, disgusted with her daughter's actions.

"Excuse me," she says to the paramedics, who have completed their evaluation of her bruises.

She stands and walks toward the other side of the bedroom and whispers into the telephone,

"Deacon Crooke, I am so sorry that my child disturbed you. Everything here is under control. So we will not need your assistance."

Abruptly cutting her off, Deacon Isa Crooke responds, "My sister, with all due respect, you may think that you have everything under control, but I know how situations like this here can get blown way out of proportion, so please let me help y'all. I'll get my attorney and meet you down at the precinct station to post bail for Pastor. It is very important that we keep situations like this out of the press. Do you think any of your neighbors know what happened?"

"I am not sure, but obviously some have peered out of **their** windows since there are both police and EMS here at the house."

"Okay, here's what I need you to do, my sister. I need you to pack your and the children's clothes and be ready to leave town for a couple of weeks."

"A couple of weeks?" Marie Antoinette shouts into the telephone, losing sight of the fact that the police and EMS personnel are still within earshot.

"Please let me finish, my sister! That way your bruises will have time to heal. I'm assuming that if the EMS is there, you are bruised, right?"

"Right," Marie Antoinette responds sheepishly.

"We'll tell the people at New Harvest you had a family emergency and had to leave town."

"But Deacon, what about my children's school work?" Marie Antoinette asks.

"Not a problem! You type up a letter to the school saying that you had a very private personal family emergency and that you will be out of town with the children for about two weeks and you'd like to have their homework sent to your house so Pastor can send it to you out of town."

"But Deacon," Marie tries to interject.

"Listen to me, Sister Goode! Just listen to me. Just do like I say! If you do what I'm telling you, it'll look like you and Pastor are not having problems, and Sister Goode, now is the time you really need to forgive him and stand by your man. We all got faults, but think about how this could hurt the church. We are becoming one of the largest mega churches in town, and if there is a hint of scandal, we all could lose everything we've worked for so long."

"But Deacon,..."

"Look, my sister, I know what I'm talking about, so please do like I say and get everything together and let me handle everything. I'll even get my cousin to bring his limo over and pick you and the children up. I'll have him take you to my vacation home along the Ohio River in Newport, Kentucky. As soon as your bruises are healed then you and the children can return. Okay? Understood?"

"But what about N. O.?" Marie Antoinette inquires, a little confused with her stance in this situation.

"Don't you worry about that. I got that covered. You need to trust me!" Deacon Crooke says with authority.

Meanwhile, Theo Lane Is Calling Sister Goodbody's cell phone incessantly

After dialing the number five or six times and not getting an answer, Theo tries one more time to reach Sister Goodbody.

"Answer the phone, damnit!" Theo yells into his telephone, impatiently waiting for a human voice.

"Hello," Sister Goodbody says, as if she has cotton stuffed up both nostrils.

"Sister Goodbody, this is Theo Lane from New Harvest. Hey, I want to apologize for what happened tonight, and I just wanted to talk to you before you did anything brash like call the cops or,..."

"How dare you call me and try to fast-talk me. Like I told Pastor Goode and his wife, she is going to cost all y'all for beating me, so,..."

"Hold on my sister! That's why I'm calling you. I know you are a sensible woman, so I am calling to offer you five thousand dollars to make this little problem go away," Theo says in his best playa voice.

"Five thousand dollars! Are you insane? I have my cousin who is in med school over here looking at my nose and you'd better get down on your knees and thank God that my nose isn't broken. Because if it was broken, you'd be watching me on the 11 o'clock news! All channels! So five thousand dollars ain't nearly enough because I know the church got plenty of money. And by the way, Pastor told me how you are dipping into the collection baskets. Nah, five thousand ain't nearly enough for my pain and suffering and knowledge of your wrong doing! I want twenty-five thousand dollars now!"

"Twenty-five thousand dollars!" Theo yells bitterly and aggressively into the telephone.

"You heard me, twenty-five thousand dollars or I go to the TV stations and the papers and before the church. I can certainly lose my reputation for that kind of money, Brother Lane," Sister Goodbody says sarcastically, her head moving from side to side.

"Look, my sister, let's be reasonable. How about Eight grand?"

"Eight thousand dollars, HELL NO!"

Sighing deeply, Theo continues, "Okay, fifteen thousand and that's my final offer," Theo says in a tone that more than suggests he knows she will accept.

"I'll take twenty-thousand and not a penny less," Sister Goodbody says, her voice and tone lacking a degree of confidence in her demand.

"My sister, maybe you've got me confused with somebody who is in the habit of repeating themselves. My best and final offer is fifteen thousand dollars! Do we have a deal or what? Remember, if you go on TV, you'd have to tell folks just how you were sleeping with the Pastor and his wife gave you a serious beat down. I think my offer is more than fair because most women would see you as a gold digger who got what she deserved," Theo says, believing he has her on the ropes.

There is dead silence on her end of the telephone. Then suddenly Sister Goodbody blurts out. "Okay, okay, I'll take the fifteen thousand dollars, and I want it in cash, and I'll give you to Monday of next week to get my money."

"Monday's cool. I'll get the cash and meet you somewhere public, so you'll feel comfortable. Okay my sister?"

"Okay, and I'll pick the place!" Sister Goodbody says.

"Great! You have my number because all the deacons and trustees are listed in the church bulletin. I'll talk to you at church on Sunday, okay?"

"Tell you what Theo, let's meet at Momma's Skillet on the Boulevard for lunch on Monday, let's say around 11:30am," Sister Goodbody says.

"Okay, I'll be there, and please come alone since we are meeting in a public place. I'll have your money wrapped like a gift, so it won't cause any suspicion. Okay? And remember, come alone," Theo responds.

"Right! Goodbye Theo," Sister Goodbody says slamming the telephone into its cradle.

Hmm, obviously she don't know who she messing with, Theo says to himself.

He dials another number with a nefarious grin on his face.

"Hey, Tommy, what up? I'm gonna call in a favor, and you'll get to make some change on this deal. I need some trash taken out for five grand. Are you interested?"

"Five grand! Yeah Theo, I'm always interested in making some money," Tommy says, elated.

"Okay then, we'll meet and discuss the details on tomorrow morning. You got any plans for breakfast?" Theo asks.

"I do now!" Tommy says laughing.
Okay, later Tommy,..."
"Later Theo," Tommy says with a Cheshire-like grin on his face.
"Five grand will come in handy right about now!" Tommy says to himself as he returns to watching COPS reruns on TV.

The next morning Theo and Tommy meet at Marty's Waffles and Chicken Shack.

Theo lays out his plan for dealing with Sister Angela Goodbody. The place is crowded, so they sit in the very rear.
"Okay, Tommy, here is my deal. On Monday at 10:30AM I need you to meet me at Momma's Skillet on the Boulevard, but you can't be seen sitting with me."
"Why?" Tommy asks puzzled."
"Because I want you to see the lady I'm gonna meet. She's the target. So it would be good if you could bring a kid or two with you and treat them to lunch. Like, a father and son deal. Who would expect you sizing up a target with some kids in tow?" Theo says, chuckling with Tommy joining in.
"Okay, but what is it that you want me to do to her," Tommy asks, knowing already the answer to his own question. He has known Theo for a long time and has taken on other assignments like this. He is fully knowledgeable that Theo is not the one to be messed with.
"I want her to disappear forever. I don't want any traces of her to be found anywhere," Theo whispers because people are being seated by a hostess in the seats near them.
"So, Tommy, can you handle that? Can you make her disappear permanently?"
"Sure," Tommy says, leaning in closer.
"Yeah Theo, I can handle that. I don't like taking out women, but I can handle that, this one time."
"Deal?" Theo asks as he slides an envelope with money in it across the table in a folded newspaper."

"Deal!" Tommy responds.

"Remember, Tommy, no muss, no fuss. Gone, never to be seen or heard from again."

"Not a problem!" Tommy says casually.

The following Monday Tommy appears at Momma's Skillet. He gets there a little earlier than planned. He is dressed in a delivery man's uniform to blend in with the other customers. He did not bring a child like Theo asked, thinking it may lead to an innocent being involved indirectly in a heinous crime.

That is just not Tommy's style. He is a true professional.

May I help you, sir?" the grandmotherly waitress behind the counter asks.

"Yes ma'am. I'll have the lunch special."

"Okay. That'll be the meat loaf with mashed potatoes and gravy and turnip greens. Do you want soup or salad?"

"I'll have the salad with ranch dressing."

"We're all out of ranch, what else would you like?"

"I'll take blue cheese then," Tommy says, handing the plastic covered menu back to the waitress. He looks around and sees Sister Goodbody come in with a man who looks like a pro lineman. She is dressed in a tight fitting outfit that looks like she bought it at Maaco's. Thinking they are just a couple, Tommy thinks to himself, Damn she's fine! What's she doing with him?

Tommy then notices something strange. Sister Goodbody looks over the diner and points to a table where the big dude might sit alone and have an excellent vantage point when she has her meeting with Theo. She touches her escort on his bulging right bicep, he nods his head in agreement, then she sits on the stool right next to Tommy.

Not trying to be obvious, Tommy turns around, takes a sip of his soft drink, and starts to read a newspaper.

"Excuse me, is this seat taken?" Sister Goodbody asks Tommy in a hurried and somewhat fearful tone.

"Not at all," he responds.

"Okay, great," she says, throwing her huge purse on the counter and digging through it. She looks over her shoulder toward the guy Tommy has now sized up as her bodyguard.

"And what can I get for you? My, those are some pretty earrings!" The waitress **tells** Angela Goodbody who is looking at her small mirror.

"Thank you. I'm waiting on someone to join me, then I'll order. I hope there is no problem with me sitting here until my friend comes," Angela says, smiling. She is appreciative of the compliment.

"Not a problem," the waitress responds.

At that moment Theo Lane enters the diner. He is carrying a paper grocery store shopping bag. He looks around and sees Angela Goodbody sitting at the counter next to Tommy. Theo smiles, walks over to Angela, kisses her on her left cheek, and says, "Hey Baby, I'm glad you could meet me here. Let's find a booth in the back where we can talk."

Angela is trying to conceal her nervousness, swings her legs around to get off the stool, and accidentally kicks Tommy on his ankle.

"Oh I'm terribly sorry," she says putting her well manicured hand on Tommy's forearm.

"It was my pleasure," Tommy says, laughing. Angela also laughs, and she follows Theo to the rear of the diner and slides into a U-shaped booth.

"Look Theo. I don't know why you called me Baby, but I'm not your Baby!"

"Hey, chill! I was just trying not to cause any suspicion up in here. We got business to conduct and what I don't want is a bunch of nosey people in our business. Nuff said?" Theo says, rolling his eyes at Angela Goodbody.

"Okay, where's my cash?" Angela whispers tersely, extending her hands across the table.

"My sister, why don't you slide your pretty self around and sit next to me. That way I can hand you your loot under the table without drawing suspicion."

"Okay, but you'd better not be trying to pull anything. I ain't nobody's fool."

"My sister, are we here to conduct some business or not?" Theo asks impatiently.

"Yes, we are here to conduct business," Angela responds reluctantly.

Damn I hate to let this piece get away without tasting it first. I guess I'll have to ask N. O. just how good she was in bed. But she's gonna be a problem, Theo says to himself. He looks over at the counter at Tommy while Angela looks toward the other side of the diner and checks on her bodyguard. Everyone seems comfortable and satisfied with what is transpiring.

"Okay, Angela. I'm gonna do like they do in the movies. I'm gonna leave this shopping bag with you, and I'm gonna get up and leave and pretend like I forgot something and need to leave right now. Your money, and before you get started, all your money we agreed to is in an envelope at the bottom of the shopping bag. Cool?"

"It better be," Angela responds.

"It's there! All of it, like we agreed!" Theo says, rising from the booth.

To act out his scene he looks at his watch and says loud enough for those in a booth two booths down to hear, "I'm sorry Baby, but I forgot another appointment with my accountant, so I'll have to run. Can we do this again soon?"

"Sure!" Angela says, playing along.

Theo walks out of the diner and drives off into the distance. Angela's bodyguard signals her by tilting his head to the right that Theo is gone. Angela gets up and goes hurriedly into the diner's Ladies room. She finds an empty stall and enters.

"I better check and see if all my money's here! I don't trust Theo or Pastor anymore!" she says, rifling through the brown paper grocery store shopping bag. She notices that there are fifteen stacks of twenty dollar bills with a bank band around each stack indicating that each stack contains one thousand dollars each. She fans through each stack like they do in a gangster movie to ensure herself that there are no pieces of dollar bill sized paper in any of the stacks. She then pulls one bill from the middle of each stack and holds it up to the light trying to determine if they are counterfeit.

"My God! The little thief kept his word! Fifteen thousand dollars! I've got fifteen thousand dollars!"

Just then two women, laughing and talking real loud, enter the Ladies room, so Angela quickly arranges the money in the bottom of the shopping bag, flushes the toilet, then exits the Ladies room.

She walks out of the diner followed by her bodyguard who waits about forty-five seconds trying not to be conspicuous. He follows Angela to her house on the west side of town. They are followed by Tommy who is driving a 20 foot rented moving truck. He is wearing a uniform similar to that of a local Delivery Truck company to avoid suspicion.

Angela pulls into her driveway and parks her car in her detached garage. Walter, her bodyguard, follows her and parks in the driveway near the back door of the house. Angela enters the house through the back door and turns off her burglar alarm. She empties the contents of the shopping bag on her kitchen table and begins to count the money again. She and Walter are interrupted by a knock on the front door.

Gathering the money, which she had not finished counting, and stuffing it into the grocery bag, Angela asks Walter to see who is at the door.

"Was this Theo trying to get his money back?" she thinks to herself.

"Who is it? Walter shouts from behind the door. He peeks through the peephole and sees Tommy in his work uniform. Tommy has his head turned in a profile position.

"Capitol Delivery Service," Tommy yells back.

"Angie, are you expecting a delivery," Walter yells back in the direction of the kitchen.

"It looks legit because the guy is in a uniform and his truck is parked out front.

"What kind of delivery?" she asks, still worrying about what to do with the money she was counting. She is so nervous she drops a couple of bills on the kitchen floor.

"Is this the residence of Ms. Angela Goodbody?" Tommy asks through the door.

"Yes," Walter responds.

"Then I have a delivery for a home stereo system for Ms. Goodbody from All American Book Club Sweepstakes."

"Angie, the guy says you've won some sweepstakes prize. Should I let him in?"

"I do remember entering a bunch of sweepstakes, but I didn't get a notice I won anything," Angela says as she approaches the front door. She looks through the peephole and sees the truck and the delivery man placing two large cardboard boxes on a hand truck to bring his load up her driveway.

"Okay, let him in," she says with great anticipation.

Walter opens the door and holds the storm door open just wide enough for Tommy to start backing his hand truck into Angela's living room.

"Whew," Tommy says, dropping his load onto the floor reaching for the metal clipboard receipt box which is lying on top of box.

"I'll need a signature, Ms. Goodbody."

"Okay," Angela says happily.

With her head down and Walter looking at the boxes, Tommy pulls a small .380 automatic pistol from the receipt box. It has a silencer on it.

Psst! Psst! is the sound the two shots make that hit Walter directly in his heart.

Too shocked to even scream, Angela starts walking backwards, holding her hands up as if she is able to block the bullets she expects to be fired at her.

"No! Please, no," she begs Tommy as she begins to crouch in her posture.

"I've got money. I'll give it all to you, but please, don't kill me. I promise I won't tell anyone. I'll leave town tonight. Please just take the money and go," Angela pleads. Tears are running down her face, and her fear is causing her voice to be very raspy and slightly above a whisper.

"How much money?" Tommy asks.

"Fifteen thousand," she responds.

"Okay, we got a deal, but you must get out of town tonight because you don't want to see me again, right?" Tommy says, waving the pistol so Angela will walk toward the kitchen.

She walks slowly down the hallway constantly looking over her shoulder praying that Tommy will not shoot.

Just as she arrives at the edge of the kitchen doorway she turns around and looks Tommy directly in the eyes. A feeling of peace and calm come over her.

Psst! Psst! Tommy fires two shots into her heart.

She drops to the floor, blocking his way to the kitchen and the shopping bag containing the money.

"Damn, what a waste. She was beautiful!" Tommy says as he takes the silencer off the pistol and places the pistol in his right pocket and the silencer in his left.

Tommy calmly pushes her body aside, collects the money, then returns to the living room and opens the boxes where he has stored some masking tape and plastic drop clothes. He wraps Angela's and Walter's bodies in the drop clothes and ties the ends and middle of the plastic with the masking tape. He places Angela's body into one of the boxes and takes it out to the truck. He goes back into the house with an empty refrigerator box and puts Walter's body in it. He meticulously cleans up the evidence of his being there. He walks back through the house and makes sure he has all his shell casings and his roll of masking tape. Satisfied, he takes the bodies to the funeral home he works for and waits until two hours after they close. As an employee, he has keys. He fires up the cremation furnace and disposes of the bodies.

Man, that was a hard one. I got a thing about taking out women. But a contract is a contract, Tommy says, with remorse as he turns off the lights and locks up.

Reaching his modest but well appointed home, Tommy takes an extra long shower. He puts on his pajamas and sits on the sofa in his family room. He pours a three fingers deep drink of Makers Mark Kentucky Bourbon. He then dials a number from a throwaway cellphone.

"Yeah, Theo, the trash was taken out today with no problem. Well there was one problem! There were two piles of trash as opposed to one, like you said. So it's going to cost you a little more than what we agreed on. Okay. Holla at me tomorrow."

Two Hours Later at the Police Precinct Station

Deacon Isa Crooke and his attorney, Ms. Imma Shyster, arrive at the 13th Precinct Police station and inquire about N. O.'s bail. They are told it is five thousand dollars cash bond. Deacon Crooke, who is carrying an old school satchel, opens the belt-like lock on the satchel, looks around to see who is looking, then pulls out one of three envelopes stuffed with one hundred dollar bills. He hastily moves the other contents in the satchel around to cover the two .38 pistols he has for protection. He motions to Attorney Shyster to shield his actions and counts out fifty bills, folds them, and hands them to Imma Shyster who goes to the bullet proof window. The police clerk takes the money, counts it, and generates a computerized receipt. Deacon Crooke knows the deal, so he walks over to the seats arranged like a hospital waiting area and using his cane, slowly descends into a seat.

When Imma Shyster approaches, he says, "You might as well have a seat because we're gonna be here for a little while!"

"Really? I did not like the way they treated me at the window. You would think that I was a criminal the way the clerk talked to me. She was so discourteous! "Imma says, highly irritated.

"You'd better get used to it. No matter the offense, no matter what job you hold, no matter how proper you speak or how well dressed you are, those people who probably make minimum wage see you as an extension of the person you're bailing out. They're criminals; therefore you're a criminal," Deacon Crooke says with a smirk on his face.

"Well I don't like it, and I might write a letter to the mayor," Imma says, staring at the clerk behind the bullet proof glass.

"I should report her to her supervisor. After all, I am an officer of the court, and there was no call for me to be treated in such a fashion," Imma grumbles.

"I tell ya, it won't do no good. Like I said, just get used to it," Deacon Crooke says like a father chastising his child.

Imma sits down, dejected, and opens her briefcase to get a copy of *O magazine* and starts to read an article on the best spas for women in the country.

The two of them wait for slightly over an hour before they see the huge heavy door of the lockup open and N. O. walk through it.

N. O. looks like he has slept in his clothes. He is carrying a large manila envelope that contains his personal effects.

"Deacon, thanks so much for getting me out of that horrible place. I was beginning to think that I was going to have to fight a couple of guys off me because they were looking at me as if I were a woman. I had to use the bathroom so bad but held it, so I need to go someplace close so I can relieve myself."

"Oh, I am sorry, Miss. I did not mean to talk so vulgar in front of you," N. O. says extending his right hand to shake Imma's. He then looks at Imma from head to toe with lust in his eye. She reminds him of Marie Antoinette, but she is a plus size shapely woman. He knows he has nothing coming when he gets home.

"Deacon, can we get out of here now! Like I said, I need to relieve myself, and I refuse to do it in here. We can talk about what we need to do about this situation while we are riding!" N. O. says, showing the strain of holding a bowel movement. The pain is displayed widely across his face.

"Sure, Pastor. Let's go. I know a little restaurant near here that is small, clean and private," Deacon Crooke says, knowing that N. O. owes him big time! Deacon Crooke also notices N. O.'s obvious attraction to Imma Shyster.

He's got enough problems as it is, but he just can't keep his thing in his pants. I'm surprised that we ain't had any sexual harassment cases filed against him the way he done run through some of the women at New Harvest. But there's gotta be something about being a Pastor that causes women, usually sensible women, to chase a Pastor! It's the damnedest thing. That's probably why he and his wife were fighting! Deacon Crooke thinks to himself as he tries to hide his extraordinary contempt for N. O. who is still trying to be extra attentive and flirtatious with Imma Shyster.

Deacon Crooke takes a few shortcuts through the city. He drives through alleys and down streets most reasonable people wouldn't go down even if they were being chased by a lynch mob. Finally, they arrive at a quaint out-of-the-way hangout. Actually it is an old 1920's speakeasy.

"Deacon, where are you taking us?" N.O. asks, still having to use the restroom but afraid to get out of the car. The expression on her face betrays the fact that Imma is not to happy to be at this location either.

Deacon Crooke uses a key card to enter the establishment.

"Hey everybody, it's Isa Crooke," the bartender shouts to the twenty or so patrons in the dimly lit but spacious bar. The patrons are scattered across the room, some sitting at the bar, others sitting at tables playing poker and Bid Whist.

"Pastor, the men's room is all the way to the back and the first door on the right."

N. O. is desperate to use the bathroom but does not want to be discovered in such a place even though it looks well maintained and very clean.

He walks in obvious discomfort as he tries not to walk to fast to attract attention and not too slow because he needs to use the bathroom bad, real bad!

"I certainly hope we do not have to stay here long," Imma says, looking around checking the place out but avoiding making eye contact with the mostly male patrons.

A tall, very dark, muscular guy with a menacing and penetrating gaze catches Imma's attention. She notices that he is staring directly at her.

I wonder how tall he is standing? Six feet six, or six feet eight? Imma wonders. She had observed him staring at her, and he then rises from his table where he and three others were drinking beers. He moves across the room in Imma's and Deacon Crooke's direction.

"Oh my God, that behemoth is coming our way," Imma whispers in a distressed tone to Deacon Crooke, her head down.

"Deacon Crooke, please do not let that man talk to me." she says nervously.

When the man is about eight feet away, he makes a slight change in direction and walks over to the huge ornate jukebox. Imma sighs in relief but keeps her eyes on him.

"Lord, please do not let him bother me. He is very scary looking," she says, still trying to use Deacon Crooke as a shield due to his girth.

The man inserts a five dollar bill into the jukebox and selects twelve songs, the first of which is an up-tempo song that people ballroom to. He then makes his way over to where Imma and Deacon Crooke are waiting for N. O. and extends his hand out to Imma and says, "Lovely lady, would you like to dance?"

Imma's initial reaction is to freeze. She looks at Deacon Crooke for support, to defend her, but to her surprise he says, "Sure, she'd love to dance with you, Tommy."

Tommy gently pulls Imma by her right hand, and she instantly feels how tender he is toward her. A chill goes up and down her spine because the tender way he touches her excites her almost to the point of arousal. They dance. To her surprise, Tommy is a very good dancer for a man of his stature. She loves to dance and is very impressed, so much so that they dance to the next two records.

N. O. finally exits the bathroom straightening his clothes and pretends he does not see any of the patrons. He joins Deacon Crooke who has been joined by Imma and her new friend, Tommy, at the table.

"What did you say your name was?" Imma asks.

"My name is Tommy, Tommy Bryant."

"So Tommy, what is it that you do?" Imma asks, her eyelashes fluttering and her heart pounding from the ballroom dancing with this powerful but gentle man.

"You wouldn't believe me if told you," Tommy responds sheepishly.

"Try me," Imma says, puzzled.

"Well, I'm a contract killer," Tommy says softly, exposing a toothy grin.

Momentarily stunned, Imma looks at Tommy, then says, "Okay, I get it. You are a comedian, right?"

Looking over his left shoulder to see if his buddies are paying attention, Tommy responds, chuckling, "Yeah, that's it, I'm a comedian."

N. O., Deacon Crooke, and Imma all burst into unified laughter, but only Deacon Crooke knows that Tommy is not joking because he has used Tommy's services in the past to collect gambling debts owed to him. Tommy never killed anyone for him, but he did break several arms and legs for those who did not pay their debts to Deacon Crooke on time. But that was back in the day. Back before Deacon Isa Crooke got saved!

"Okay Tommy, what is it that you really do?"

"Promise you won't be turned off?" Tommy asks, gently taking Imma's hands into his.

"Promise!" Imma responds.

"I'm a mortician's assistant, and I do work for all the major funeral directors in the city. I also have a trash hauling business where I contract to people on an as-needed basis to take out large amounts of trash when other contractors can't handle the job," Tommy says, again looking over his shoulder at his friends who appear to be getting either jealous or impatient. After all, Imma is a beautiful well-manicured and well-dressed full-figured woman. They all want her, sexually!

"Look Imma, I got to get back to my crew. I hope this won't be the last time I see you. Can I have your number?"

Reaching into her purse, Imma pulls out a business card and writes her home telephone number on the back.

"I'll look forward to your call. The best time to reach me is after 7p.m."

Tommy rejoins his friends, and N. O, Imma, and Deacon Crooke make their exit, too.

"Pastor, we'll need to conversate about this evening's events cause we don't want this situation to get out of hand. We've got a lot to lose if this gets out. I've already made arrangements for your wife and kids to be out of town as a cover-up."

"Thanks, Deacon. I'll always be indebted to you," N. O. says as he opens the front passenger door of Deacon Crooke's car and let's Imma in. He is such a dog that he doesn't disguise looking at her stout legs and behind as she sits in the car. She is not aware of his lustful glances because she is focused on meeting Tommy. It's been a while since she has been with a man. Deacon Crooke takes Imma to her home, and he and N. O., who has now jumped into the front passenger seat, follow her to her high rise apartment. They watch impatiently as she uses her key card to enter the underground garage.

Back at Ms. Jenkins's

Reggie is so enthralled with Ms. Jenkins's story telling that he is not aware of how late it is. He barely hears Chastity open the multiple dead bolt locks and enter her bedroom.

"Chastity, is that you?" Ms. Jenkins shouts, knowing that it could not be anyone else.

"Yes Ma'am,"

"Well why don't you come in here and say hi to Reggie? We've been working on the story again."

"Ahh, that's okay, Big Momma. I am sure Reggie doesn't want to see me, and I'm tired anyway."

"That's not true, Chastity," Reggie shouts back.

"Well, you always act like you don't want me around, so why you changing up on me now?" Chastity says in a very nasty tone.

"Reggie, why don't you and Chastity go and sit down in the living room and talk. Y'all seem to have some problems, and I would like for you two to work it out. I need peace in my house, and I don't want Chastity to be moping and stomping around here like a spoiled brat. It's late and I'm ready to go to bed anyway," Ms. Jenkins says, stretching in her chair. She braces herself with her cane and rises from her seat and says, "Go on now, and talk to my grand baby."

Reggie packs up his stuff, throwing everything into his book bag. He is of the mind that he does not want to irritate Ms. Jenkins. Getting everything situated, he rises from the kitchen table and follows her orders.

Reggie looks back over his shoulder and watches Ms. Jenkins slowly enter her bedroom, yawning every step of the way. He knocks on Chastity's door, but she does not answer immediately.

"Chastity, open the door, we need to talk. You heard your grandmother, so open up!"

When she does not respond, Reggie starts walking down the hallway towards Ms. Jenkins's bedroom, but he stops abruptly when he hears her snoring so loud the pictures on the wall are rattling.

Damn, what should I do? I better not wake up Ms. Jenkins. It's ten minutes to ten.

Reggie sighs, then walks back down the hallway to Chastity's room and knocks on her door one more time and says, "Okay Chastity, I tried to do what your grandmother asked, but we can not talk if you will not open the door. Besides, I can hear you breathing from this side of the door, so I know you can hear me. Goodnight Chastity. Don't forget to lock the door when I leave."

Reggie starts to walk away and Chastity's door opens, but it is only cracked open.

"Okay Reggie, so you want to talk to me now?" Chastity asks rudely.

Trying to peer through the crack of the slightly open door, Reggie says, "Yes, I honestly want to talk to you!"

Chastity slowly opens the door and Reggie takes a deep breath because Chastity is standing completely naked with a tube of KY Jelly in one hand and an accordion like roll of condoms in the other.

"So if you want to talk, let's talk," Chastity says, moving to the side as an obvious invitation for Reggie to enter her bedroom.

"Girl, you are too crazy! We can't do this! What happens if your grandmother wakes up while we,"

"I can keep quiet. Can you?" Chastity says coyly, closing the door behind Reggie who is already taking off his sports jacket.

"Oh yeah, I can keep quiet," Reggie says, tenderly grabbing Chastity and kissing her passionately.

With Chastity's help, Reggie finishes undressing, then picks her up and slowly lays her on her bed. It's 10:02p.m. He leaves quietly at 2:06a.m.

"Wow! She was fantastic! I hope I will not live to regret tonight, but whew! The girl is something else!"

9:10AM The next Day in N. O.'s Hospital Room

"Mrs. Goode, I was just about to call you," Dr. Mendoza says.

"Oh, has my husband taken a turn for the worse?" Marie Antoinette asks nervously.

"No! No! Quite the contrary. "Dr. Mendoza says happily and enthusiastically.

"Mrs. Goode, it's a miracle. Your husband has opened his eyes and is alert. Now I do not want to suggest that he has completely turned the corner, but for a man who was on a death watch yesterday, he has made some miraculous improvement. It is possible he could make a complete recovery."

"A complete recovery?" Marie Antoinette asks, covering her mouth with both hands, tears streaming down her cheeks.

"A complete recovery?" she shouts incredulously.

"Well, he will have some rehabilitation to go through, but he could be up and walking in six to nine months."

"Thank you JESUS! Marie Antoinette shouts, her hands stretched upward to heaven, turning around in a circle."

Dr. Mendoza hugs her, which brings her back to reality. She is in the hallway of a busy hospital and is making a spectacle of herself. Most of those observing her are happy for her.

"Well, I have to write up my shift report, and the day shift doctor should be here, so I'll let you go, Mrs. Goode. Mrs. Goode, did you hear me?"

"Oh yes, I heard you. I am just happy, thankful, and stunned," Marie Antoinette says reaching into her purse for a handkerchief.

"Oh, Mrs. Goode, here comes the dayshift doctor, Dr. Duncan. I am sure you have met him," Dr. Mendoza says, reaching into his inside jacket pocket to retrieve his Blackberry.

"I have to take this call," Dr. Mendoza says, waving and walking away from Mare Antoinette.

"Well, how are we today, Mrs. Goode?" Dr. Clark Duncan says in a menacing tone. He is still smarting about having to give up on the twenty-five thousand dollars.

Marie Antoinette just ignores him and walks into N. O.'s room.

"Well, are we ready to sign the organ donation papers?" Dr. Duncan asks sarcastically.

"I will not be signing any papers anytime soon," Marie Antoinette responds tersely.

"What do you mean?" Dr. Duncan says, stepping up to Marie Antoinette like she were a man that he is about to fight.

"Did you not hear? N. O. has had a turn for the better. He is going to survive!"

"Survive?" Dr. Duncan says loudly, then remembers he is in N. O.'s room.

"Yes, SURVIVE!" she says, making her way to N. O.'s bed. He is asleep or so she thinks. She caresses his right hand as she sits down in a chair adjacent to his bed.

"But we had a deal! I gave you an advance of twenty-five thousand dollars, so I need either his organs or my money back," Dr. Hudson says in a mean spirited tone, looking around to make sure they are the only ones in the room.

"Well, he is not going to die. My prayers have been answered, so you can not have his organs."

"Well, you need to,..."

"Please do not presume to tell me what I had better do DR. DUNCAN! And let me assure you I am not going to give you your money back. It is too late for you to do a stop payment. The money is already in my account!"

"Why you b ..."

"No, you are not getting your money back because you tried to play me and "you" wound up getting played, right?" Marie Antoinette says, gloating.

"And go ahead, Dr. Duncan. Go to the authorities and tell them how you offered me money for my husband's organs. There is a law about trafficking in human organs. I know because I checked! So my advice to you is to write off the twenty-five thousand dollars as a loss. And now, if you do not mind, I would like to spend some quality time with my husband. Have a good day, Dr. Hudson," Marie Antoinette says, pointing to the door.

Dr. Hudson abruptly walks out of the room bumping into a nurse who has come to check N. O.'s vitals.

Marie Antoinette sits back in the chair and reflects about her guile and the fact that as long as N. O. is alive, she will be taken care of by the church. It is the best of times for her: N. O. will survive. Salome will be moving home, and Delilah and Jabez will not have to move to another home with fewer amenities.

"God is good," she says.

"Ahhh, ahhh". N. O. whispers, smacking his lips.

"Honey, do you need something?" Marie Antoinette asks frantically as N. O. exits his coma.

"I would like some water," N. O. says in a raspy voice.

She reaches over to the portable hospital food tray, grabs a plastic cup, and fills it with water from the small brown plastic pitcher. She inserts a straw, then places the straw near N. O.'s lips.

He struggles to crane his neck to reach the straw, so she slips her right hand under his neck to lift his head. He is now able to take in the water. N. O. slowly raises his left hand to signal Marie Antoinette that he has had enough water. She lets his head slip back onto the pillow, and he looks over at her and says, "Baby, I am so sorry that I am taking you through all this. All I ever wanted was to be a successful pastor, and things just got out of hand. I let Theo convince me to put him on the Board of Trustees so we could steal money from the Lord. I let my selfishness and arrogance come between you and me and the children. I let all the women who wanted to sleep with the pastor have a turn, well not all, just the pretty ones," N. O. says, laughing. He gets choked up momentarily from the water and his jokes. He then continues, "Baby, if you want a divorce, I will understand. Even though my attorney said they will probably send me to a country club prison, I don't want you sitting home alone waiting on me, and ..."

"N. O." Marie Antoinette says loudly, interrupting,...

"The District Attorney has asked the judge to send you to a maximum security prison, alleging that you and Theo were part of a criminal enterprise. He said that since you were ultimately responsible for the shooting at the church's quarterly business meeting last year, plus all the money you and Theo stole, you deserved the harshest penalty possible. Your attorney thinks the DA will get his motion approved."

Dead silence permeates the room. Neither N. O. nor Marie Antoinette can hear the incessant beeping and whining of the life monitors attached to N. O. He was scared before thinking about doing time in a minimum security prison, but to be sent to a maximum security prison with hardened criminals was a nightmare of magnificent proportions.

"So Baby, do you think I'll do time in a maximum security prison? I have been in jail for social protest before but never for a felony," N. O. says with tears in his eyes.

"Yes, N. O., and truthfully, I hope you do go to a prison far away for all that you have done to your family. You were supposed to be a man of God, but you turned out to be a man who used God to get rich and to get women. If

I knew that your ministry that started in that little storefront church would have led to this point in our lives, I would have fought you tooth-and-nail to not let the church grow so big and so fast. We were happy then, but look at us now. Your children distrust you, and Salome hates you. You let your own cousin pimp you. Theo made a small fortune stealing the churches money, and if it weren't for the shootout at the quarterly business meeting, he would be living in the Cayman Islands. The Deacon Board despises you but realizes that you carried the church a very long way from that old storefront. And me, I will never stop loving you, but I do not want to live with you anymore. Deacon Crooke has made a deal with me that he will make sure I get your pension as long as I do not do anything like writing a tell-all book that would discredit the church. I took the deal! Is that what you would do?"

"But Baby, like I said, everything just got out of hand! I never meant to hurt you and the kids, never..."

"Too late, BABY!" Marie Antoinette says loudly and sarcastically.

"Do not worry N. O. As long as the church takes care of me, I will play the role of the doting wife and mother while you are in prison. By the way, I tore the house up looking for the combination to the wall safe you had installed. I thought it very clever of you to highlight passages in your Bible for the combination! Ruth 4; Lamentations 5; Revelations 20! Right 4, left 5, right 20. The blue highlights on those passages while you highlighted everything else in yellow was a dead giveaway. Remember, I am your wife, so I know blue is your favorite color. I have cashed the 70 thousand dollars in Bearer Bonds and the 280 thousand dollars in cash will be deposited into my account in small amounts over the next few years. And BABY, I had a new wall safe installed just in case you got some criminal friends that might try and break in and take what is mine," she says, leaving N. O. speechless.

At that moment two US marshals enter the room with Dr. Clark Hudson.

Dr. Hudson has a vengeful smirk on his face.

"Reverend Goode? Hi, I am Deputy US Marshall Karl Madowski. This is Deputy Marshall Brian Dobson. We've been apprised by the hospital staff that your condition has improved dramatically. We are here to inform you that as soon as your condition improves well enough for you to travel, we'll transport you to the Federal Maximum Security Prison in Lewiston."

"Can't this wait?" Marie Antoinette asks, angered by what she feels is the rude treatment by the Marshals.

"No Ma'am! We're only doing our job. Dr. Hudson here called us and told us Reverend Goode has improved, and while we were originally told he was near death, we still have a job to do and that is to take your husband when he is well enough to the Federal prison to serve out his sentence," Deputy Marshall Madowski says sternly.

"Oh, so it was Dr. Hudson who could not wait to tell you my husband's condition had improved. Now, that "is" a surprise!!" Marie Antoinette walks right up to Dr. Hudson and slaps him as hard as she can across his face.

Instantly, both Marshals separate Marie Antoinette, from Dr. Hudson who is so stunned that all he can do is stand there rubbing the left side of his face.

"Ma'am, we need you to calm down, or we will be forced to put you under arrest. Dr. Hudson was only doing what is required by law," Marshall Dobson says.

"I am sorry," Marie Antoinette says, retaking her seat by N. O.'s bed.

"Reverend Goode, since your condition has improved, we'll have to put you in restraints to keep you from escaping."

N.O. just lays there. He has yet to utter a word because he can not fathom what has just transpired. First, he has to marinate on what his wife had just said. Now he is dealing with the reality of doing serious time in a serious prison. He is still speechless.

He remains speechless while the marshals attach the leather bound straps attached to handcuffs to his bed. The scene is reminiscent of a death row prisoner being readied for a lethal injection.

Crying, Marie Antoinette says, "Oh Baby! Oh Baby!"

Assured that the restraints are secure, the marshals make a hasty exit with Dr. Hudson straddled between them. He looks back like a little spoiled brat kid, taunting Marie Antoinette. He might as well have stuck out his tongue.

The three vanish from the room. Marie Antoinette walks over to the door and peers down the hallway to ensure they are out of earshot. Assured that they are, she goes over to N. O.'s bed and whispers, "How did you like the show, BABY? Was it worthy of an Academy Award?"

"Marie, why are you tormenting me like this? I thought you said you loved me?"

"I do love you, but payback is a dog, isn't it? When they ship you off to that maximum security prison, I want you to think about all the pain and misery you have caused me. Do I love you? Yes I do! But do I want revenge? YES I DO!! Well N. O., I will plan to see you in prison at least once a month. I hear they search the visitors to ensure they are not bringing drugs in for the convicts. I do not know how long I will be able to tolerate such treatment being fondled by a female guard just to see YOU!"

"But Marie!"

"Bye N. O., What is it they always say in those comedy prison movies? Oh yes. Do not bend over for the soap!" Marie Antoinette says as she flings her huge designer purse over her right shoulder and walks out of the room smiling as if she just won a lottery jackpot.

N. O. is so angry that he pulls against the restraints. If he could only reach her he would finish the job of choking her that he had started years before.

"Lord, why have you forsaken me?" N. O. shouts so loud one of the attendants stops in to check up on him.

The attendant does not hear a word, but N. O. hears the Lord's response, "The real question is why did you forsake me?"

6:45PM Later that Same Day at Ms. Jenkins's House

Reggie has just arrived in front of Ms. Jenkins's house. He has developed a sincere love and respect for Ms. Jenkins because she is a sweet old lady. He also is growing concerned about her health. He is so near to the end of the story, but what happens if she were to pass away before the story is complete. After all, he could finish the interviews but have questions about points he simply forgot as he recorded his notes.

"I have got to get her to finish this story in the next two or three sessions," Reggie says out loud sitting in his car.

He has another concern, Chastity!

Reggie bounds out of his car and presses the doorbell feverishly.

"Who is it?"

"It's me, Ms. Jenkins. Reggie."

"Oh, hi Baby, you're a little early today," she responds.

Reggie waits impatiently as Ms. Jenkins goes through the process of unlocking the series of deadbolt locks.

I could get into Fort Knox quicker, Reggie thinks to himself.

"Hi Baby," Ms. Jenkins says as she stretches upward to hug Reggie.

"Hi Ms. Jenkins. Hey, do you really feel like working on the book today? You look a little tired."

"Naw Baby, I've cooked as usual, so come on in and let's get started after you eat."

Reggie walks down the hallway behind Ms. Jenkins.

She is something else. I can tell she is not feeling well, but she likes me so much she wants to help me get this book done. Well, if she is up to it, who am I to stop her, Reggie thinks to himself.

"Ms. Jenkins, you have got to stop setting it out like this. There is too much food here again."

He fixes his plate with turkey and dressing, candied yams, macaroni and cheese, ham, and potato salad.

"Hey, where is Chastity?" Reggie asks, a little fearful of her answer.

"Oh, she got a job at the mall, working in some dress shop. You know the girl makes most of her clothes. She wants to be a designer one day, and the girl can sew! She'll be home directly," Ms. Jenkins says as she sits down grimacing in pain at the table. She looks up at Reggie and nods her head as a signal that she is about to bless the meal. She does!

After the meal, Reggie sets up his note pad and micro recorder and says, "Okay Ms. Jenkins, I think if we can cover two or three other areas of Pastor Goode's fall from grace, we can finish up the first draft of the story. I'll probably finish it in two weeks, and I'll have to do at least one rewrite. Are you sure you feel well enough to continue tonight?"

"Sure, Baby," she responds.

Thank God, She is not looking well to me. I just hope she can hold on for another couple of months, Reggie thinks to himself.

"Okay then. I know we talked about how under Pastor Goode's leadership New Harvest grew from a storefront church of about seventy-five members to a mega church of over six thousand members in less than five years."

"Wait a minute, Baby," Ms. Jenkins says, straining to lean forward in her seat.

"Most folk's give Pastor Goode credit for New Harvest's growth, but the plain truth is God has a special anointment on New Harvest. When other churches were struggling to get members and stay financially afloat, New Harvest always had members who gave until it hurt to build the sanctuary we are in now. Pastor Goode was a good preacher, but it was the generosity of the members that led to New Harvest getting as big as we are now. We'd be the same church with or without Pastor Goode. That must be made plain in this story, okay?"

"Yes ma'am," Reggie responds.

"Ms. Jenkins, I really understand what you are saying, so I would like to explore two major issues about Pastor Goode's life. First, what happened after Pastor Goode received the blackmail threat? And secondly, what led to the shooting and murders at New Harvest?"

"Now there is where we need to go so we can finish this here story," Ms. Jenkins says, seeming to be focused and having more energy for this line of discussion.

"Well let me tell you something about that blackmail thing. Pastor Goode was in for a big surprise when he finally found out who was behind it.

Real surprised!" Ms. Jenkins says as she begins to reminisce.

Back to the Day that N. O. met Theo to Discuss the blackmail threat

After meeting Theo at the car dealership, N. O. goes into his basement and checks his wall safe to determine just how much money he has.

"Okay, I got about $360 thousand in cash. Whew! I did not realize I had that much," he thinks to himself proudly, smelling the stacks of crisp one hundred dollar bills.

"I've got another $144 four thousand in Bearer Bonds and let's say about $45 thousand dollars in Krugerand gold coins." N. O. says. He reads his total gold coin value from an ordinary piece of notebook paper in the first of six large freezer bags which contain the gold coins. This piece of notebook paper is his ledger of sorts, and he simply wrote down the new total values every time he bought more coins.

Sighing deeply because he knows he will have to make a deal to get the DVD's of Salome in the porno movies, he comes to grips with the undeniable fact that the blackmail transaction will put a serious dent into his ill-gotten stash! Tears well up in his eyes.

"Damn it. I have built an empire only to see it dissipate right in front of my very eyes because of one of my own offspring! Damn it, Salome! Why couldn't you just stay here and go to school where we could know what you were doing instead of going all the way to LA to be corrupted by some greedy, immoral user and exploiter of women!"

At that moment the telephone in the Goode's residence rings.

"Hello," N. O. says tersely, still consumed with anger about his potential monetary loss.

"Hey, Cuz, it's me, Theo. I made contact with the people with the DVD of Salome. Hold on. You didn't talk to the cops, did you?"

"No, Theo. I did like you asked and have not gotten the police or FBI involved. That would only make matters worse."

"Good! Like I said, I'm trying to help you. I owe you a lot cause you got me on the Trustee Board, and we both have made gains from my being there, right?"

Right," N. O. says.

"Look Cuz, here's the deal. They want fo hunid grand."

"You mean they want **$400 thousand** dollars? Are they insane?" N. O. says, pacing frantically.

"Yeah Cuz. It's fo hunid grand or they spill it. And Cuz, they seem to be real serious about the loot. They say they'll give us the master DVD, and they want a yes or no answer by tomorrow midnight; otherwise, they'll drop a copy off at every TV and radio station in town."

"Theo, can you contact them and see if they will take less money?"

"I'll try Cuz, but I ain't thinking they'll take less. By the way, did you figure out how much loot you have?"

Feeling he needs to protect himself even from his own cousin, N. O. says, "Yeah. I did not have as much as I originally thought. I have about **$100 thousand** in cash and Bearer Bonds combined."

"I don't know, Cuz. We might have to figure a way to get some more loot through the church. Like I said, I'm thinking they won't take that much less than the fo hunid grand. Do you think you could put pressure on Trustee Bass for a loan of about, hmm, let's say another one hunid fifty grand?" Theo asks earnestly.

"Cuz, we really need to come up with the extra cash or everything we've worked for at New Harvest will go up in smoke, and I ain't having that. We've got a sweet deal going at the church, and I ain't ready to walk away from it. Not now Cuz. Not now!"

"Theo, I can not approach Trustee Bass with a request for a loan and expect him to just rubber stamp it before tomorrow night. To get that kind of money could raise some red flags at the church with some of the deacons especially Deacons Fellowes and Haran. Also, we need to be careful because that kind of transaction could even draw the attention of the IRS, and we certainly do not need that, right?" N O. says, exhibiting his street smarts and his business sense.

"Yeah Cuz, you're right. Tell you what, I'll kick in a hunid and fifty grand of my own money and you can pay me back later. Deal? I'll contact them again and tell them a quarter mill is all you can raise in the short time frame and it is a take it or leave it offer! Okay?"

"Thanks, Theo. Man, you have always been there for me. I know if anyone can get them to take less, it's you."

"Right Cuz! Right!" Theo responds, gloating.

"I'll get back with you after I've gotten back with them. They have a system where they call me about every two hours and have me call them from a disposable cell phone they left for me in a trash bag behind Mr. Lucky's barbershop. I'll wait for their next call which should be in about forty-five minutes. Later Cuz."

"Thanks Theo," N. O. says, hanging up the telephone.

"What next Lord? What next?" N. O. shouts, knowing that he is alone in the house.

Quarter Past Midnight. That Same Day

The throwaway cellphone that was left for Theo rings. He has been waiting on the call because he has wanted to go to bed but must deal with the blackmailer. He has not gotten into his pajamas but is sitting up in the same clothes he has had on all day.

"Hello," Theo says gruffly. He then responds to the voice on the other end of the telephone.

"Do I have the money? No, not all of what you asked for. I've only got $250 thousand. That's all my man can raise on short notice."

The voice on the other end of the line has been altered by some audio device that makes the caller sound like a person who has had a tracheotomy and uses a microphone to talk.

"Well, the deal is off, fool!" the caller says angrily.

"Wait a minute, wait a minute," Theo yells into the phone. I am ready to make the drop, but like I said, my man can't give you what he ain't GOT! It's a quarter mill, dude, and that is all he can get right now!" Theo yells into the phone, jumping to his feet and pacing across the room.

"C'mon, don't try to play me. Pastor Goode has more than that. We know he has way more than that. So call us when you get the other 1.5 mill, and not a cent less!"

"Look, it's all my man got right now. He can't get any more loot without raising suspicion at the church or with the IRS. So do we have a deal or what?" "Besides, the question you should be asking yo'self is whether or not a quarter mill is more than zero?" Theo says in his most reasoning voice.

"Okay we'll take the quarter million, but it has to all be in cash and unmarked bills. Any deviation from our terms, and we go on TV with the DVD. You got me?"

"Ah, we might have a slight problem cause some of the money is in Bearer Bonds. Is that a problem?"

The caller pauses, then responds by saying, "Are they legit? Because if they ain't, we know where you live."

They know where I live? Theo says to himself. "Damn!"

"Look fool, we're gonna call you in about a half hour to tell you about the drop. Stay by the phone, and do not call the cops or the FBI! Ya feel me?"

"Yeah, I feel ya," Theo responds sarcastically.

"Okay then. Talk to ya in a half hour." ***Click!***

"Damn! There is something familiar, very familiar about that voice, even though they obviously used some kind of machine to disguise it," Theo says as he rubs his chin with his right hand.

Theo sits in his lazy boy and impatiently taps the armrest with the remote to his big screen TV. The phone rings and he is instructed to make the drop at an unusual place: the homeless shelter operated by New Harvest.

Theo's instructions are very simple. He is to drive to New Harvest's homeless shelter where a homeless man with a cane will be standing in front of the bin used by people to do a drive-by drop-off of items of clothing. It is past 7PM, so the shelter has closed for the evening. The drop off bin is easily accessible for people to drop off clothes like they could drop off a DVD at a video store. It also makes it easy for a clothing donor to make their donation without coming into direct contact with a homeless person.

Theo drives down the narrow one way street and looks for the bin, which is basically a three feet high, four feet wide, and six feet long dumpster with no lid. He parks alongside the bin, then pops his trunk. He looks around and notices there are a lot of cars parked on the street near the shelter.

"I guess there must be a lot of working poor in there," he thinks to himself.

There is a huge parking lot across the street from the shelter and it's also packed with cars, most of which are old, very old.

Per instructions, Theo looks for a homeless man with a cane. He is looking toward the curb when a shadowy figure dressed in a big floppy hat, dark glasses and an overcoat that is too heavy for such a warm morning approaches his car on the driver's side. It is obvious to Theo that the man is wearing a disguise.

Startled by the sudden appearance of the tall man, Theo shouts, "Damn, you scared me!"

The homeless man points to the bin with his cane as if to say throw the money in the bin.

With a puzzled look on his face, Theo shrugs his shoulders as if to say, "What?"

Again, the homeless man points to the bin and raises his cane once again to signal, "Put the money in the cloths bin!"

Finally, Theo catches on and places the money and Bearer Bonds, which he has placed in a book bag, into the bin.

Suddenly, a car pulls out of the parking lot across the street from the homeless shelter and blocks Theo's car in. Then another car pulls out of the lot and the homeless man, who has grabbed the book bag, jumps into the back seat. The driver of the car blocking Theo's gets out, turns off the ignition and throws the keys under Theo's car. He then jumps into the front passenger seat of the second car. The second car speeds down the one way street in the wrong direction and turns sharply at the corner. Since it is early in the morning there is no traffic so the blackmailers plan paid off big time. They drive off into the distance, before Theo had time to react. Helpless Theo sits in his car, trapped.

"Damn it," he yells, pounding his steering wheel with both fists.

"Ain't nobody supposed to get over on me like that!" Theo says, as he goes to the trunk of his car and opens it.

"Okay Milt, I guess I won't need you as backup now."

"What happened?" Milt, a short, wiry man says, as he carefully climbs out of Theo's trunk with a sawed-off shotgun.

"They got over on me!" Theo says, shaking his head in disbelief.

"They got over on ME!"

"It wasn't supposed to go down like this. I was gonna give them the money, then you'd pop out of the trunk after my signal and we'd get my money back. Damn!" Theo says, pounding the trunk of the car blocking him in.

Milt retrieves the keys under Theo's car. Theo then pulls the car that was used to block his car into the parking lot and parks it in a far corner. He has Milt put the sawed-off in the trunk of his car, and they drive off with Theo cursing every inch of the way.

Back at the Home of Ms. Jenkins

As Ms. Jenkins continues to relate the story about the rise and fall N. O. Goode, Reggie looks over at her and notices she looks very flushed, very faint.

"Ms. Jenkins, are you okay?" Reggie asks as he takes his right hand to keep her from falling out of her chair.

Ms. Jenkins's eyes seem to be rolling around in their sockets as she struggles to breathe.

"Ms. Jenkins, Ms. Jenkins," Reggie shouts nervously as he continues to prop her up in his arms. He grabs his cellphone to call EMS.

The EMS crew arrives in less than five minutes, but Reggie has to lay Ms. Jenkins on the kitchen floor to open all the locks on Ms. Jenkins's front door.

The EMS technicians enter the kitchen and check Ms. Jenkins's vital signs.

Reggie stands to the side and is hovering over the EMS folks to the point where one of them says, "Excuse me, sir, but we need you to go into the other room! Please move now!"

Reggie moves slowly and starts to pray in earnest. "Lord, please don't let Ms. Jenkins die. I am asking that you restore her because she is a wonderful person and doesn't deserve to die on her kitchen floor. What would happen to Chastity, Lord, if Ms. Jenkins dies?"

It was at this moment that Reggie realizes that he has come to truly love Ms. Jenkins, and he is genuinely concerned about her well being as opposed to her surviving just so he might finish his book.

The lead EMS technician calls the emergency room and informs them that they are bringing Ms. Jenkins in because they believe she has had a stroke.

"A stroke," Reggie gasps in disbelief.

Reggie stands stunned as the EMS technicians put Ms. Jenkins on a gurney and struggle to get down the narrow hallway and out the front door.

One of her neighbors must have called Chastity because she has just arrived in a cab and frantically goes over to the gurney just as the EMS personnel are lifting it up into the ambulance.

"Big Momma! Big Momma," she screams as Reggie comes over and holds her with both arms. They both watch helplessly as the rear door to the ambulance closes.

Reggie has the presence of mind to ask what hospital they are taking Ms. Jenkins to.

"St. Julian's," the EMS driver shouts as he closes his door and turns on the siren.

"Chastity, let me go into the house and get my stuff, and I will take you to the hospital, okay? You will need to lock up, and I will be ready to go."

Chastity just barely heard Reggie but nods in agreement. She slowly walks into the house and watches Reggie as he hastily packs his book bag. He just throws everything in with reckless abandon.

Ten minutes later they arrive at St. Julian's.

Reggie uses valet parking so he and Chastity can get a quick status on Ms. Jenkins. They rush into the wide revolving doors and stop at the front desk where Reggie inquires about Ms. Jenkins. They are told to go to the third floor **ER** waiting room. They take the elevator with neither of them uttering a word. They find seats together in the crowded waiting room. They wait for well over three hours.

"The family of Louabelle Jenkins," a nurse shouts just after having pulled her surgical mask down.

"That's us," Reggie says as he pulls Chastity up from her chair. Obviously he is contemplating the worst and so must Chastity as she begins to cry.

"How's my grandmother?" Chastity asks, sobbing uncontrollably.

"She's going to be fine. We're going to keep her overnight and when we release her, she'll need plenty of bed rest!"

"Are you sure she is okay?" Reggie asks, shaking nervously due to his genuine concern.

"Yes. I'm sure she's okay! We thought she had a stroke, but her sugar was elevated."

"Can I go back and see her?" Chastity asks, sighing with a sense of relief. She then begins to chant, "Thank you, Jesus! Thank you, Jesus!"

"Sure, but you can only stay a few minutes. Like I said, she needs her rest. Is this your husband? He looks familiar?"

The nurse says, looking at Reggie with that "I know you from somewhere gaze."

"No, he's not my husband, he's,..."

"I am a good friend of the family," Reggie blurts out, interrupting Chastity.

Following the direction of the nurse, Chastity and Reggie stay about ten minutes because Ms. Jenkins is asleep and snoring loudly. Chastity kisses her grandmother on the forehead and turns to Reggie and says, "Thanks for being there. She could have died if she was alone."

She then hugs Reggie, but he does not feel the same type of sensuality as he felt from previous hugs. The gentle, tender sexual feeling is totally absent. This hug Reggie feels is totally based on gratitude. Gratitude, and nothing else.

The next day, just as the nurse had indicated, Ms. Jenkins was released from the hospital. Reggie was so grateful to God that she survived that he did not bother her about the story for over two months. He did, however, go visit her and sent her monetary gifts in cards and kept her in fresh flowers. The feeling of urgency of her staying alive so he might finish his story is no longer present. He has taken a sharp turn in a positive direction on the curve of his priorities. He now has his priorities straight.

Two Months Later at Ms. Jenkins's House

"Ms. Jenkins, I truly hope you are feeling better. I thank you for your call telling me you are ready to continue working on the book, but we can wait if you are not feeling well. I do not want to rush you. And I certainly do not want you to get sick trying to help me."

"Boy, hush up and come on in my kitchen. I'se feel fine! Don't you worry about me. I want to help you cause you helped me and Chastity so much."

"By the way Ms. Jenkins, where is Chastity?"

"Oh, she's at Bible Study. She has really gotten into going to church lately. She comes home from work, checks on me, then off she goes to church.

New Harvest is interviewing for a new Pastor, so they got the candidates preaching at two services on Sunday and teaching Bible Study on Wednesdays for two weeks."

"Good for her, Ms. Jenkins," Reggie says, relieved that Chastity is not home.

"So where did we leave off?" Ms. Jenkins asks.

"Ah, we were talking about how the blackmailers got away with a quarter million dollars from Trustee Theo Lane," Reggie says, as he adjusts his micro recorder's volume control.

"Oh yeah! Theo Lane burned with hatred over that issue for a long time, according to Pastor Goode. Theo was such a con man he never thought he'd get conned, not him!" Ms. Jenkins says, laughing heartily. "You see what was happening at New Harvest was that Theo had convinced his cousin, Pastor Goode, to have Trustee Bass let him be some type of business manager. I think his title was Investment Manager. And that was the beginning of the end for Pastor. Theo was ordinary looking, so you wouldn't think he was crooked. He was always at the church helping out anybody and everybody. He made fast friends with most folks, but Chastity used to always say there was something not quite right about him. I don't know nothing about handling big money, so I didn't care."

"But what did he do that led to the shooting?" Reggie asks, puzzled.

"Baby, be patient! What I was about to say was that Theo was smart enough to make sure that the lights, gas, air conditioning and such was always on. People on the church payroll got paid, and from the outside it looked like the church was prospering. But what he was doing was running, what did the judge call it, oh, a Ponzi Scheme, whatever that is.

"So are you saying that Theo Lane was cooking the books at New Harvest?" Reggie asks with a surprised look on his face.

"What does cooking the books mean, Reggie?"

"Cooking the books means that, as Co-chairman and financial planner of the church's trustee board, he led the members of New Harvest to believe that the church had more money in the bank or in investments than you actually had. He probably used your quarterly financial statements to do this. he had to do was print up some false reports and share them with the church at your business meetings. So, unless the church had an independent financial audit, you all would think you had a million dollars when you only had, let's say, two hundred thousand. I am just using those figures as an example."

"Well all I knows is that he made the members believe we had all this money in the bank, but he was taking a lot of the money and cutting Pastor in for a little. When Pastor found out how much Theo was stealing and how much of the stolen money he got, he was real mad at Theo."

"But Ms. Jenkins, there are a lot of intelligent, well educated people at New Harvest. How could Theo Lane get away with such thievery for so long and no one caught on?"

"Baby, some of smartest people in the church are some of the **DUMBEST!** They believe everything the pastors and deacons says without investigating it. They are spoon fed Christians! Good at their jobs but failures in knowing the true word of God when they hear it and whose who and what is what in God's house!"

"But thank God it was two deacons who discovered what was really happening, Deacon Fellowes who always hated Pastor and Deacon Haran who was the smartest man at New Harvest."

"Why did Deacon Fellowes hate Pastor Goode?"

"Well, it seems that back in the day before Pastor got saved he used to deal a little drugs on the side. He dabbled in some of his stash and one night got so high he ran a red light and hit the car driven by Deacon Fellowes. It seems that Deacon Fellowes was taking his wife to the hospital because she was about to have a baby."

2:37AM. Back in the Day at the Scene of the Accident

N. O. struggles to get out of his Bonneville after running the red light at the intersection of 16th and George Washington Carver Boulevard. He has slammed into the car driven by John Fellowes. His head spinning, N. O. checks the damage to his car and realizes he only has minor damage to the left front bumper. He slowly limps across the street to where the Fellowes car is resting on the curb. N. O. looks around and is thankful that no one is out on the street in this business section of town, due to it being the wee hours of the morning. He looks into the front seat and sees that John Fellowes is moaning in intense pain. He obviously has a head injury because there is blood dripping down from the top of his head and streaming down his nose and across both eyes. His hair is long and braided and the massive amount of blood cascading down his face makes him unrecognizable. There is so much blood that N. O suspects John Fellowes will bleed out in a few minutes if he does not get immediate medical attention! N. O. looks into the back seat where he sees Deidre Fellowes lying perfectly still. She is lying on a blanket and looks as if she were asleep. N. O. notices that she is bleeding profusely, but her blood trail is coming from between her legs. He grabs her right wrist to check for a pulse and there is none. Immediately dropping her limp arm, he looks in her eyes that are wide open and gasps!

"She's dead! Damn, what have I done?" N. O. says as he again looks around to see if there are any witnesses to his crime. He is not feeling much pain, but that is probably because he is so high from the cocaine and the cognac he had taken earlier.

Satisfied that no one is around, N. O. slowly starts walking backwards from the car. He gets midway through the intersection and now has his back to the car when He hears John Fellowes moan and say in a weakened voice, "Hey man, where you going? Come back and help my wife! Please help my wife!" John Fellowes shouts, in obvious serious pain.

N. O. turns to look back at the car and shakes his head as if to say, Naw man, you are on your own!

John Fellowes continues to shout at N. O. to no avail. N. O. quickly walks back to his car, and after it stalls for a few seconds, which seemed like hours to him, it starts.

"With all the blood he is losing he'll probably die, too," N. O. says, putting the car in gear, thinking that he has gotten away with murder. He has!

Back to the present day at Ms. Jenkins's House

"So Ms. Jenkins, if Pastor Goode killed Deacon Fellowes's wife in a car accident, why didn't Pastor Goode do time?" Reggie asks.

"Well, Pastor and Theo got together and paid this guy a lot of money to take the blame for the accident. By the way, the Fellowes's Baby boy was also killed in the accident. Pastor set his car on fire to burn up any evidence he was in the car, and the fall guy said he stole Pastor's car and had the crash. By the time Deacon Fellowes got out of the hospital cause he was really banged up, there was nothing he could do to Pastor. It was shortly after that, that Pastor got saved."

"But Ms. Jenkins, why would some guy go to prison for Pastor Goode?" Reggie asks in disbelief.

"Oh, that's simple! The guy owed Theo a lot of money for drugs and gambling debts. Besides, the guy, I think his name was Richard Turner, was used to doing time. Theo promised the guy they'd get him a good lawyer so he'd be back on the street in about seven years. He also told the guy he'd put money on his books in prison and take care of his family while he was locked up! The guy felt that seven years in prison would be better than being DEAD! Because no one ever got over on Theo but the blackmailers."

"Well, did Theo keep his word?"

"Yeah, I've got to give him credit. He kept his word and took care of the man's family until he got stabbed to death in prison after being locked up for a couple of years," Ms. Jenkins says with conviction.

"But Ms. Jenkins, don't you think it a little suspicious that the guy got murdered in prison? He was the only link to the truth about Pastor Goode being the culprit and the murderer of Deacon Fellowes's wife and baby son. Theo impresses me as someone who would go to great lengths to protect his interest, and keeping Pastor Goode out of prison was definitely in his best interest!. Seems to me Theo and Pastor Goode were cleaning up all loose ends."

"Well, you got a point, Reggie. I guess since Pastor told me this story like he was confessing to a priest, I believed him. I still don't think that he had anything to do with the shooting at the church or Richard Turner getting killed in prison. That was all Theo's doing!"

"Another question, Ms. Jenkins. Why didn't Deacon Fellowes go after Pastor in court for murdering his wife and unborn son?"

"Well Reggie, the word on the street was that Deacon Fellowes remembered Pastor's face but did not know his name. He then searched for him all across the city, but the accident was what made Pastor try and turn his life around. So while Deacon Fellowes was looking for Pastor Goode in all the hole-in-the-wall bars, Pastor was going to church and even started taking bible classes. He followed that up with going to a Bible Teaching College. Deacon Fellowes was looking for Pastor in all the wrong places."

"Well before we get to the shooting, did Theo and Pastor ever find out who the blackmailer was?"

"Naw, Baby, they didn't, and I bet Theo steamed about losing his big money because he never got it back. Pastor always felt Theo was behind it, but he could tell by how Theo kept whining about losing his money that he finally believed that he and Theo both got ripped off. And Theo ain't the kind a man that walks away from that kinda money easily. He was known to have people's arms and legs broken for a few dollars they owed but did not pay."

"Oh Ms. Jenkins, what ever happened with Salome after she got the letter from the California Department of Health saying she had HIV/AIDS?"

"Well, she didn't tell nobody out there in California, and she eventually came home. Her momma convinced her to get a second opinion, and she went to a doctor here who her momma trusted who said she was okay. No AIDS no where!"

"Wow! That is amazing," Reggie says, shaking his head rigorously.

"That is simply amazing!"

"That's right, Baby. Only God can work miracles like that. Reggie, I want you to promise me something!"

"Sure, Ms. Jenkins, what is it you want me to do? I will do anything for you."

"Good! If anything happens to me, I want you to make sure Chastity is taken care of. I want you to help her get situated with a house and a good job. Will you do that for me, Reggie?"

"Yes ma'am. I promise," Reggie says as he takes Ms. Jenkins hands into his as an act of reassurance.

"I'm trusting in you, Baby, to keep your word, okay!"

"Yes ma'am, I promise. I do not have to marry her, do I?" Reggie says, generating a laugh from Ms. Jenkins.

"Okay Ms. Jenkins, let's talk about the shooting at New Harvest. After we go over that part of the story, I should be able to complete the first draft of my book, and then you can read it and,..."

"Baby, I can't read."

"Oh you mean your sight is bad?"

"No Baby, I never learned to read! Why not let Chastity read it, or you can read it to me and I can tell you if it sounds like the story the way I told it to you,..."

"Okay Ms. Jenkins."

"Well, this is what happened with the shootout at New Harvest. What you got to understand is this: Deacon Haran and Deacon Fellowes started asking for the church to approve someone to come into the church and check the church's books."

"So they were calling for an audit," "Yeah Reggie, that's what they called it, an audit. You see, both them deacons had a lot of respect in the church, but Pastor Goode was always downing them from the pulpit. He always attacked his enemies from the pulpit, and that got on most people's nerves at New Harvest. He even tried to embarrass them one Sunday during the Lord's

Supper. The Lord's Supper! He's going to Hell for that one, because the Word says, "do this in remembrance of me,... not in remembrance of PASTOR N. O. GOODE!" Once, during the Lord's Supper he tried to show the congregation they opposed him. He never called them by name, but everyone knew who he was talking about. Pastor would say something like, 'yeah some people who attack me think they know more than I do, but the Lord put ME here, not YOU, as Pastor of this church.' Or he'd also criticize Deacon Haran by saying, 'I remember when some of you came to this church with your gang banger clothes on, then all of a sudden you started taking a few Bible classes and teaching Sunday School, and now you got people running into my office telling me they learned more from you in Sunday School than they do listening to my sermons.'"

"Sounds like Pastor Goode was very insecure," Reggie says.

"Well, he always had issues about wanting to always be viewed as the best in everything by the deacons, trustees and the rest of the members. We had a lot of people who left the church because he treated some of them like they were nobodies when they made more money, had more education, and were much smarter than him. And I mean to tell you Deacon Haran was the smartest man at New Harvest. And he was three times smarter about the Word than Pastor, and everybody, especially Pastor, knew it."

"So are you saying that Pastor felt inferior to Deacon Haran?" Reggie asks.

"Ah, Baby, Pastor was so insecure (and I didn't notice this at first) that he only wanted yes men and women around him. He'd put people in charge of ministries that were his friends who really couldn't do the job, but if you were capable and seemed to be as smart as Pastor, you didn't get a chance to lead at New Harvest."

"Hmm," Reggie mumbles.

Ms. Jenkins begins to reminisce about the events that led to the shootout at New Harvest a few months ago.

12:46PM The First Saturday of the Month

The telephone at Theo's house rings incessantly. Theo hears it ring but ignores it. He is lounging at home, sitting in his recliner, a Montecristo Open Eagle Cuban cigar in his left hand and a double shot of Patron in his right hand. The TV is on, but he is completely oblivious to anything on the screen. He is in a self-induced state of unconsciousness.

"Theo, this is N. O. We have to talk! The Church Quarterly Business Meeting is tonight at 6PM, and the church is up in arms about the report that Deacons Fellowes and Haran have put together and sent at their own expense to the congregation. Look Theo, it's your fault that I am in this bind, so the least you could do is return my calls and tell me what we should do to stop this madness. You have always come through for me in the past, so I need you now more than ever before. PLEASE CALL ME SOON! We both have a lot to lose if the deacons get their way and make a presentation tonight."

Theo sits forward in his chair. He has heard the previous messages from N. O., but this one got his attention. The words, "we both got something to lose" resonate, and he is now paying attention.

"Yeah Theo, you're the man! Think! You've always been able to figure a way to get out of situations like this. Who are Deacon Haran and Fellowes to you? You're Theo Lane!"

Theo leaps from his seat and decides to get dressed. He's got a church business meeting to go to and show the church who's running things. But first he must make two telephone calls.

He dials N. O.'s number. "Hey N. O., what's up?"

"Theo, where you been? I have been calling you all day today. Look, the deacons have got an independent auditor to look at the books! We are in trouble when they find out that you have been cooking the books, and..."

"Look N. O., everything I did, I did with you having full knowledge, so don't play me like it's all on me to get through this. We've got to work together. You have control of most of the members, so all we got to do is discredit Deacon Haran, and what has Fellowes got against you? He's been on your back since day one."

"I don't know, Theo. He always looks at me like he knows me from somewhere and I did something to him. I can't figure him out."

"Well, he scares me more than Deacon Haran. Haran is nothing. He's just a book smart dude, not a street smart dude like me," Theo says in a very superior and arrogant tone.

"Hey, he is a nothing in my book either," N. O. responds to Theo's rant.

"Okay, here's what we're going to do. You're going to call Trustee Bass and tell him to object to everything the deacons are trying to do. Have him tell the members of New Harvest that he assures them that there is nothing wrong with the church's financial standing and that we'll get them some statements from the bank next week. That'll give us enough time to put some money back into the bank, and I'll get my computer geek to roll out some fake bank statements that'll show the members we are in good shape. Then I'll need you to attack Deacon Fellowes and Haran in front of everybody."

"No problem," N. O. says, happy that there is a plan.

"When you attack them, you need to say that they want to take over the church and that they are trying to get rid of you after all you've done to build New Harvest. Ya feel me, Cuz?" Theo says.

"Okay then. I got another call to make, Cuz, so don't worry, I'll be there, and I got your back. We've come too far and made too much money to let this good thing go. Besides, the people at the church are just like sheep. They believe everything you say. They never questioned anything until these two troublemakers come along, and I'm gonna get rid of the troublemakers."

"Theo, promise me that you won't hurt them. Even though you told me Angela took the money and moved out of town, I am not saying I do not trust you, but I do feel she is dead!"

"How many times we gotta go over this N. O? I gave her twenty-five grand to leave town and told her if she ever came back this way that I'd mess her up. But have you heard about any missing women's bodies being found on the news? Look N.O., she's gone, and as long as she doesn't make her way back here, I really don't care where she is or what she's doing!"

"You're right, Theo, you're right! Please remember that we need to make sure we don't do anything that will further exacerbate the situation"

"Ex-acer what? Speak English, Cuz!" Theo jokingly shouts into the telephone.

"I am just saying we don't want to make matters worse by bringing the wrong people or forces into this situation," N. O says nervously.

"Okay Cuz. I gotta go. I've got other calls to make before we meet at the church. We need to get there about 5PM to make sure we got everything covered. Now make sure you talk to Trustee Bass. He's the key to our success."

"Okay, do not worry. I got him in my back pocket, and he will do whatever I say. I am about to call him right now," N. O. says emphasizing his clout.

N. O and Theo hang up, and Theo dials another familiar telephone number.

"Hello Tommy, I need you again to help me handle some business!"

"What do you need me to do?" Tommy asks. He has a prevailing feeling that Theo is about to ask him to do something that might get him locked up or even killed.

"You okay, Tommy?"

"Yeah, I'm all right. What's up?"

"Well, I need you to bring some of your boys to the church meeting at New Harvest in a couple of hours."

"I don't understand, Theo. I know you don't want me to take somebody out in front of a church full of witnesses."

"Naw, Tommy. What I need is for you and your boys to stop these guys before they even enter the church."

"But how do I, in a couple of hours, take these guys out when I don't even know them?"

"Tommy, I only want you to keep them from coming to the meeting. I don't want you to go beyond that if you know what I mean!"

"So how do I know who they are?" Tommy asks, puzzled.

"Simple! Go to the New Harvest website and click on the link for the church's leadership. Then look for the Deacons tab and for pictures of Deacons Fellowes and Haran. I'll send you their addresses, and if you can get to them before the meeting, great, but if not, I just need you to stop them before they can attend the meeting this evening."

"But what happens if we don't find them before the meeting?"

"Then I'll need for you to create a diversion during the church meeting this evening before they get a chance to speak. If you or any of your boys get arrested, I'll take care of your bond and attorney's fees, but I'm thinking that with about a thousand people there you could start a ruckus, even break an arm or two on these guys and get out of the church before the cops come," Theo says with a smirk in his voice.

Continuing, Theo says, "The meeting ought to be heated cause we're gonna be talking about money, so if a scuffle broke out, most folks would be surprised, so surprised they probably wouldn't recognize you or your boys after you do your work and leave."

"Okay Theo, I'll bring some of my best men, just two or three to handle this, but you know I don't like doing this type of job in a church. It just don't seem right to me!"

"With what I'm gonna pay you, you'll get over it."

"They hang up with Tommy doing as he was told looking up the Deacons on the New Harvest website.

Meanwhile, N. O. Decides To Call Trustee Bass

"Hello Pastor, I was just thinking about calling you," Trustee Bass says.

"Oh really," N. O. says with concern dripping off each word.

"Yes Pastor, I'm concerned about the meeting tonight. You see Deacon Fellowes and Deacon Haran called me, and they are on their way to the church to do some Xeroxing of their little audit of the church accounts,..."

"So why would that concern you, MY BROTHER?" N. O. says, interrupting Trustee Bass.

"Well Pastor, you know I did not fuss when you made me make your cousin Co-Chair of the Board. I always looked the other way when he'd take a few dollars here and there during the count. But now he's gone too far! Way too far because he's now doing some big time stealing and altering of the books. He said he had your permission to do the investments for the church, and now the deacons have discovered that more than a quarter of a million dollars is unaccounted for from the church's investment accounts. Theo said he gave you all but twenty thousand dollars and I needed to keep quiet or I'd get all the blame since I'm the person on the Board that most people would blame for any wrongdoing."

"Did you say he only got twenty thousand dollars and I GOT THE REST?" N. O. yells, livid and pacing in his room.

"He said he only got twenty thousand dollars, why that dirty,"

"Pastor, I don't believe what he said about you, but here's the problem. Deacons Fellowes and Haran have what they say is proof positive that the two of you have been stealing, big time! They are going to ask the church to vote you out and ask the church to press fraud charges on both you and Theo."

"So, my brother, what are you going to do this evening?" N. O. asks in a threatening tone.

"Well, I was thinking about not even going to the meeting and let the chips fall where they may," Trustee Bass says, his voice trembling.

"Oh, hell no! You will be there and you will accuse those two troublemakers of being behind what has happened and that they are just trying to cover their tracks by blaming these financial shortcomings on my family. You Got It?"

"But Pastor,"

"Do not but Pastor me! Be at the meeting, or else!"

CLICK

N. O. hangs up on Trustee Bass and paces back and forth saying to himself, "That damn cousin of mine. Always telling me he had my back when all the time he was stealing larger sums of money from the church than he let on. Now I am thoroughly convinced that he was behind the blackmail scheme. My own flesh and blood! I feel like killing him, but I am going to get my money back, then I will crush him, even if I have to pay someone to hurt him."

N. O. paces back and forth. Then he remembers a chance meeting right after he had gotten out of jail some months ago.

"I know what to do! I will call Deacon Crooke and ask him about the big guy who was attracted to his attorney at the club that night I got out of jail. I will ask the big guy to be security for me at the business meeting, but I better get moving on that because I only have a couple of hours."

N. O. dials Deacon Isa Crooke's number.

"Hello Pastor, what can I do for you?" Deacon Isa Crooke asks. He is suspicious of N. O. calling him on the day everyone expects a contentious church business meeting.

"Deacon, you know there are many unfounded rumors floating around the church, and I think I might be attacked physically, so I was thinking, remember the big guy at the club you took me to the night I got out of jail?"

"You mean, Tommy?"

"Yes, him! I was wondering if you could contact him, I know this is last minute, but I was wondering if you could ask him to be my bodyguard for tonight's church meeting,..."

"But Pastor, we have security at New Harvest, so why would you want someone like Tommy to come in to protect you?"

"Well, all the members of our security force are members, so I do not know where their sympathies lie," N. O. says thinking fast on his feet.

"Ah Pastor, I'm not so sure things are going to get that serious to require a bodyguard."

"Well, I would feel more comfortable if the guy, Tommy, or someone like him were there just in case things get out of hand!" N. O. says.

"Okay Pastor, I'll call Tommy, and if he can't make it, I know he knows someone who can handle the situation. But Pastor, let me handle this. We can't allow your name being brought up in any situations where things do get out of hand and people find out you hired a known felon to handle your business. I'll make the arrangements. Okay?"

"Okay Deacon. I appreciate it. Hopefully, Tommy will remember me since it has been a while since he saw me."

"It won't be a problem, Pastor. Like I said, let me handle it."

N. O. and Deacon Crooke hang up and Deacon Crooke laments, "This is just a lot of foolishness! The Pastor is about to get booted out if he don't listen to me. And his stupid and greedy cousin, that fool is just too selfish! I told him long ago that he should cut Pastor in for a bigger slice, but he's hard-headed and selfish. Now I gotta go in there tonight and get everything straight and keep Theo from exposing me as the ring leader of the scam at New Harvest. We had a sweetheart's deal, but Theo thinks he's smarter than everybody. I may have to have Tommy take him out because he's messing with my money now!"

Deacon Isa Crooke sits in his huge recliner and thinks for a moment, then calls Tommy.

"Hello Tommy. It's Isa, Isa Crooke. What are you doing in the next couple of hours?"

"Well, I'm supposed to do a job for Theo, why, what's up?"

"A job for Theo, like what?"

"Oh, he wants me to stop two dudes from attending some church meeting at y'alls church this evening. So Isa, what's up?"

"So what's Theo paying you, Tommy? You know you met him through me! We go way back!"

"Ya know he never told me, but I assume around five grand."

"Well Tommy, I'll pay you ten grand if you take Theo out, but not at the church. As long as he doesn't have you kill anybody tonight, you'll get your money, but after tonight I don't want to ever hear from or see Theo Lane again.

I know you can handle that, can't you?"

"For sure!"

"Okay, and by the way, the Pastor will need a bodyguard tonight, and truthfully, I'm sick of him, too, so if he should come up missing, there'll be another ten grand waiting for you. And you know I'm good for the dough, right?"

"Oh yeah! Like you said, we go way back."

"Well, tonight make sure that my Pastor gets out of the church without being mobbed,..."

"But what about my deal with Theo?" Tommy asks, excited by the turn of events that will put a lot of money in his pocket.

"Don't worry about Theo. I'll handle him and tell him you are there to protect our interests."

"Okay Isa. Look, I gotta go and round up my boys and see if we can take out these two guys Theo wants out of the way."

"Okay, but be extra careful Tommy because I'll need you at the church if things get as rowdy as I think they're going to get tonight."

"I got your back, Isa. You've always looked out for me, so I owe you big time!"

"Thanks, Tommy. See you later at New Harvest."

"Right!" Tommy says, hanging up his cellphone.

"Lord, what have I gotten myself into? All I was trying to do was to get back a little of what I put into the church when I used my lottery winnings to help build the church. Now I got an arrogant, greedy and lustful Pastor and his conniving, crazy cousin trying to bring down all that I've built. It ain't gonna happen! Not now, not ever, never!" Isa Crooke says as he gets his satchel with his nine millimeter hidden at the bottom.

"Guess I'd better get over to New Harvest and see what's going on."

4:13PM New Harvest Missionary Baptist Church – Deacons' Office

"Hey Deac, how many copies do you think we will need of our report?" Deacon Fellowes asks Deacon Haran.

"Well, typically we only have about two hundred people attend the Quarterly Business Meetings, but since we will be talking about the church's financial condition, I think we will need at least a thousand handouts," Deacon Haran responds as he staples the four page front-to-back Xeroxed handouts.

"Okay then, my brother, that means I need to do about four hundred more copies." Deacon Fellowes says.

Both men are totally unaware that Tommy has his thugs maintaining surveillance in front of their homes. Theo forgot to tell Tommy what kind of cars they drive, so the fact that there are cars in both men's driveways, the plan to temporarily waylay them is foiled. Deacon Fellowes, who has a personal grudge against N. O., and Deacon Haran who has repeatedly chastised N. O. for his false teachings, especially of the prosperity Gospel, are safe and secure in the Deacons Office of New Harvest, or one would think they were safe. The two men finish copying and stapling the handouts and look at one another, fearful on one hand that what they will share with the church might ultimately destroy the church but mutually content that what they will share with the congregation must be brought to light before N. O. and Theo drive the church into bankruptcy. It is a difficult decision but one they are determined to live with!

Both men who are secreted in the Deacons' Office hear the hustle and bustle and boisterous conversations of people arriving early for the business meeting. People in too many churches don't regularly attend their quarterly business meetings, but if there is some major controversy and or the potential for a good verbal fight, well that is another story. People will arrive early almost like the people who tailgate before an NFL or MLB game! Tonight's meeting is expected to be a gladiatorial contest. Many people want to figuratively and literally see BLOOD!

So many people are arriving early to ensure they get a good seat upfront in the Fellowship Hall that Deacons Haran and Fellowes overhear them, most of whom sound angry, make comments such as, "We're going to get this money situation straight tonight!"

"We'd better or I'm going to call the State Attorney General. I hope the rumors about us being broke aren't true, but if they are, well, I gotta do what I gotta do!" said yet another member.

Yet another said, "Well I knows that Pastor ain't got nothing to do with no money missing. That's all I can tell you!"

Throngs of people dressed very casually virtually rush into the Crooke Fellowship Hall. Since Deacon Isa Cooke had made a large donation to the church's building fund from his lottery winnings years ago, the members agreed he and his wife should be honored by having the Fellowship Hall in the new sanctuary named after them. The conversations seem to get louder and louder as the members pass by the Deacons' Office where the two men have stacked all the reports. They continue to hear comments from the members, some very positive and others overwhelmingly negative about how the pastor and trustees, especially Theo, have squandered the church's surplus funds.

"Well Deac, it's almost showtime. It's time to face our folks and let the chips fall where they may!" Deacon Fellowes says, sighing deeply.

"I'm ready to get this over with," Deacon Haran, the youngest and definitely the most intelligent and honest member of New Harvest's Deacon Board says with authority.

New Harvest's Fellowship Hall is large enough to accommodate about five thousand people. It is about seventy percent full and its only 5:25PM, when the Business Meeting is not scheduled to start until 6PM. There are four long banquet tables aligned in a straight line on the portable dais. There are two microphones to each table and tent cards that designate where the principles, Pastor Goode, Trustee Bass, Trustee Lane, and the deacons are to sit.

On the main floor there are circular banquet tables each with twelve chairs for the congregation. There are several microphones on mike stands evenly distributed throughout the main floor so members with questions and comments may go to one of the strategically placed microphones without venturing too far from their table. Most of the people who have arrived have taken seats at the tables closest to the dais. There are at least four thousand members in attendance, the largest group ever, and the noise from their conversations is deafening.

Theo is frantically pacing down the corridor near the Pastor's Office leading to the Fellowship Hall. The door to N. O.'s office is open, but it appears he is not there. Suddenly, Theo hears the flushing of a toilet and now knows where N. O. has been. N. O. exits his private bathroom and is stunned to see Theo standing in front of his desk.

"Hey Theo, you scared me! How long have you been standing there?" N. O. says, adjusting his belt and making sure the creases in his pants are straight.

"Not long. Hey, I thought we said we'd meet here at 5PM, and where is Trustee Bass?"

"He's supposed to be here, and he'd better be here. He has a tough job of convincing the members that everything is financially in order!"

"He'd better be here, or we both go down *TOGETHER!* You know what I mean?" Theo says, about to light a cigarette, then realizing its inappropriateness.

"Theo, calm down. The Lord is not going to let what I have built here crumble over a few measly dollars. Right?"

"Look Cuz, we ain't talking about a few measly dollars; we're talking about big bucks and,..."

"Hold on, Theo, you told me we were only skimming a few thousand dollars a month from the church, so why are you upset about this meeting. Was there more money being skimmed, and more importantly, if there was more money misappropriated, why was my cut so small?"

Before Theo could answer, there is a knock on N. O.'s office door. They both realize they have been having their discussion with the door wide open. They turn around and see Deacon Isa Crooke and Trustee Bass standing in the doorway. Deacon Crooke has a look of disgust on his face while Trustee Bass's expression readily indicates he is very scared.

"What the hell are y'all doing? Ya got your door wide open and you're talking about stealing money from the church when any member could've walked by! What the hell was ya thinking?" Deacon Crooke says, whispering sternly, stepping inside the Pastor's office with Trustee Bass in tow. He slowly closes the door behind them.

"Watch the way you talk to me old man, Theo says, menacingly stepping toward Deacon Isa Crooke.

"Before you even think about stepping to me, you'd better ask somebody! I'm old school, and you'll come up missing if you even think about harming me," Deacon Isa Crooke says, matching Theo's menacing and threatening posture.

"Gentlemen! Gentlemen!" N. O. says, stepping between the two men to defuse the situation.

"Look, we all have something to lose tonight if we do not stand unified against Deacons Fellowes and Haran. Brother Bass, your credibility here will be destroyed! Deacon Crooke, the church you worked so hard to establish and build will be destroyed. Theo, well, you are going to lose either way it goes because you will not be able to steal from the church anymore after tonight and,..."

"You mean *WE* won't be able to steal from the church, don't cha, Cuz?" Theo says, showing his obvious anger.

"Point made, *COUSIN!*" N. O. responds sarcastically.

"And I will lose my stature in the local and national religious community should we not handle this situation tonight. So Deacon, I need your support, and Brother Bass we really need your support. We need for you to shove the blame for the financial discrepancies onto Deacons Haran and Fellowes tonight! You have to sell the congregation on the lie that they are the thieves and are only trying to cover their tracks. That will give us time to buy an unscrupulous auditor who we will instruct to make the books look good. Now that may cost us a little money, but I know people who we can trust to show we are not in bad shape. We have been scamming the people this long, even though some of us have benefited more than others,..."

N. O. says, as he looks over at Theo with contempt.

N. O. further states, "So we can do this if we get through tonight's meeting. Are we agreed? Are we in concert?"

Well, if it goes bad for us, I'm outta here. I have my passport and a suitcase full of cash in my car, and I'll head to the Cayman's if things go wrong tonight, Theo thinks to himself as he calms down knowing he always has a plan B.

"Pastor, I'm not feeling well, and I believe that the stress from this whole situation that is not my fault is making me sick, so I want to leave before,..."

"Oh you're staying, MY BROTHER!" Theo says as he opens his sports coat jacket showing his small ten shot Kel Tec PF 9MM pistol."

"Ain't nobody going home until the fat lady sings tonight, nobody!" Theo says re-buttoning his sports jacket, knowing he has made his point crystal clear.

"Okay, okay Theo," Trustee Bass says with tears welling up in his eyes. "I'll do my best, but if things don't go right,..."

"They will go right if we all just keep our heads," N. O. says, placing his right hand on Trustee Bass's left shoulder to reassure him.

"Okay, let's line up and walk confidently and in single file into the Fellowship Hall. Brother Bass, did you make copies of OUR report that contradicts the Deacons' report?" N. O. asks, rolling his neck and shoulders like Mike Tyson in a boxing ring before a championship fight.

"Yes, Pastor. I got them under the tables on the dais," Trustee Bass says barely above a whisper.

"Buck up man. You can't go in there acting like this," Theo crudely and menacingly blurts.

Trustee Bass then nervously takes a seat, his body shaking violently.

"He's right Brother Bass. We are all counting on you, so please get yourself together before we enter the Fellowship Hall," N. O says, realizing Trustee Bass is scared beyond belief.

Trustee Bass finds the strength from N. O.'s encouragement and stands erect like a soldier and says, "Okay, I'm ready!"

They march single file into the Fellowship Hall with N. O. in the lead followed by Deacon Crooke, then Trustee Bass and Theo bringing up the rear. The formerly boisterous crowd suddenly goes silent. Everyone seems to be in awe of how confidently these men, who many suspect of being crooks, walk to the elevated dais. The church members stay mute until everyone is seated, and they only start to whisper when Deacons Haran and Fellowes enter the Fellowship Hall with a hand truck with three Xerox boxes full of their documents. Instead of joining the others on the dais, they motion to a few of the young men of the church to help them pass out their documents.

"Wait one minute! A point of order," Deacon Isa Crooke shouts into one of the microphones on the table where he and Pastor and their crew are sitting.

"We have rules, and we use Roberts Rules of Order for *ALL* our meetings here at New Harvest. So before anyone passes out any documents, we have to go through the agenda, and Pastor and I both must see and approve whatever you are passing out before we determine if they are relevant to our business meeting."

"Oh they are relevant, all right!" Deacon Fellowes says emphatically.

"Well, we will be the judge of that," N. O. says, politely trying to curry the favor of the members.

"By the way, my Brother, why have you fought against me ever since I was led to this Church by the Lord? You have always treated me with contempt. So, my brother, what have I ever done to you for you to despise me so much?"

N. O asks, using a polite tone in thinking he can start turning the tide against the two malcontent deacons with this question.

"Oh, don't play dumb! You know why I don't like you, *PASTOR!*"

Deacon Fellowes says, leaning into and grabbing the microphone.

N. O. simply shrugs his shoulders to indicate he is totally confused.

"Okay, maybe you don't remember my face because it was drenched with blood, but we met at the intersection of 16th and George Washington Carver one night several years ago."

N. O. leaps from his seat astonished, in a move that surprises not only himself but everyone else in attendance. There is a hush over the Fellowship Hall.

"I see you remember, Pastor. Yeah, it's me, the man whose wife and unborn son you killed because you ran a red light and broadsided my car."

Slowly returning to his seat, N. O. says, "But someone else, I believe a guy named Richard Turner was convicted and sent to prison for that crime, so how could you think it was me?"

"And why do you have so much information on who did the deed? Why would that particular story stay in your mind after all these years unless you felt guilty for both the crime and that another man went to prison for a crime you committed?"

"Ooooohhh!" the New Harvest members say in a unified tone to indicate that Pastor had no real come back for Deacon Fellowes's tirade.

"From his body language and the look on his face, it looks like Pastor must've had something to do with the accident Deacon Fellowes is talking about," one member said to neighbors at the table.

"Yeah, he lookeded shook!" said another member at that same table.

Realizing that N. O. is struggling to regain his composure, Deacon Isa Crooke intervenes by saying, "Gentlemen, we are here this evening to discuss the church's financial standing, and again I ask that you two deacons stop passing out whatever those documents are until,..."

"With all due respect, Deacon Crooke," Deacon Haran interrupts,

"We feel that the church has every right to know where we stand in terms of our financial viability. I also know that New Harvest's congregation has labored under a veil of suspicion and innuendo about our financial status for far too long. It is time that we alert the members who have invested so much into this House of God, a house of God that is obviously favored by the Lord, and make everyone aware of just where we stand financially,..."

Deacon Haran says, receiving a thunderous approval from the clapping and amens that permeate throughout the Fellowship Hall.

"But Deacon Haran, you know the word better than most, and the word says we should do God's business decent and in order," Deacon Crooke fires back.

"Well, again, with all due respect, Deacon Crooke, we are doing just that. Deacon Fellowes and I have irrefutable proof that someone has been misappropriating funds from the church. Most of these misappropriated funds were taken from the church investment fund handled by Trustees Bass and Lane."

"Wait one damn minute! Are you accusing me of stealing the church's money, you nerd?" Theo says angrily, standing and pointing at Deacon Haran with an accusatory finger.

"We've got proof that you and Deacon Fellowes are the ones stealing the money and trying to say that me and Pastor are the thieves."

"We never said anything about the Pastor stealing. Was that a Freudian slip?" Deacon Haran says, laughing.

"WHOA!" The crowd says in unison, realizing that its two gotcha's in a row against the Pastor.

"Look, we've got our paperwork too and we're gonna have Trustee Bass explain it to y'all first," Theo shouts loudly to get everyone's attention. He looks over at N. O. who has not recovered from Deacon Fellowes accusation regarding the hit and run accident. He sits on the dais as if he is heavily medicated.

"Okay Trustee Bass, come on and tell them who is stealing the money from the church!" Theo says, still shouting into the microphone. N. O. is still silent and Deacon Crooke just sits in his seat watching Theo's feeble attempt to control what the members believe and what they are thinking.

"Trustee Bass! We're waiting," Theo says, feigning sincerity and honesty.

Rising from his seat as if his entire body is racked with pain, Trustee Bass asks some of the Deacons on the dais to look under the tables and retrieve the reports, the fake reports, and ask that they be distributed among the congregation assembled in the Fellowship Hall. Once this feat is accomplished, he taps the microphone in front of him and slightly above a whisper says, "Sisters and Brothers, like Theo said, we discovered," he pauses and looks in the direction of N. O. for support but gets none. He then looks at Theo who has an expression on his face that says, "go on, go on!"

"Sisters and Brothers, I can't lie! There has been funds taken illegally from the church's funds, and it was taken mostly by Deacon Lane and Pastor. They made me come here tonight to tell you and,..."

"Hey, wait a minute, Bass, why you going against the plan?" Theo shouts at Trustee Bass as Theo who now has the microphone in his hand shouts angrily...

"The plan?" Deacon Haran says loud enough for all in attendance to hear.

"What plan Brother Lane? We are listening," Deacon Haran continues.

"Yeah, what plan?" Deacon Fellowes chimes in.

The atmosphere in the Fellowship Hall is reaching its boiling point. The masses assembled are all trying to talk at once, and the various conversations are very distracting. The majority of the folks are opposed to Theo and the pastor, but a few still support the pastor. The noise is so deafening and distracting that Deacon Haran goes on the dais and asks for order. Getting almost everyone's attention he says, "Sisters and Brothers, we are asking that you wait patiently until all the handouts have been distributed, and then take a few minutes and look them over. I am talking about the handouts that Deacon Fellowes and I created that are being passed out, not those created by Trustees Bass and Lane. After everyone gets our handout, then we want each of you to take about ten minutes to review what is on the handouts. Then we will go over the church's finances line by line."

Theo is pacing back and forth on the dais. He is fuming. He is not getting any support from N. O. or Deacon Crooke, who are letting him hang himself. Theo suddenly feels much better because he sees Tommy enter the Fellowship Hall with a few of his men.

Theo signals Tommy, but N. O. and Deacon Crooke are completely oblivious of Tommy's entrance.

Theo sneaks off the dais and roughly grabs Tommy by his left arm. Tommy recoils and gives Theo a look that says, "Back up off me!"

"Hey man, I'm sorry! Where you been? And why didn't you take care of business like I told you?" Theo whispers in a raspy voice.

"Look, we were out in front of both dudes' houses and found out through a neighbor that they both had left home earlier today headed to the church. You still owe me for my time spent sitting in front of their houses."

"Okay. Not a problem, but what I need for you to do now is grab all these reports being passed out and say that you are representing the pastor and that the handouts are all lies. Can you do that?"

Tommy looks at his men and they look at him and he responds with little hesitation, "Not a problem!"

Tommy and his men's physical size are so imposing that as they go table to table politely asking for and taking the reports from the New Harvest members, they meet little if any resistance. Like most Baptist churches, there are more women members than men, and even the men are intimidated by these huge men taking the handouts right out of their hands.

"Hey, what's going on?" Deacon Fellowes asks, as one of Tommy's men grabs the stack of reports out of his arms while he was counting out the twelve for each table.

"Pastor's orders," Tommy's man says tersely.

Theo has repositioned himself on the dais and appears happy with the turn of events. He grabs the microphone again and says, "Ladies and gentlemen, we will now pass out the correct financial reports, so please give these men the fake reports, so we can dispose of them. They are nothing but trash."

Deacon Haran is joined by Deacon Fellowes on the dais and shouts, "Pastor, by what authority do you have theses thugs come into the house of God and snatch our truthful reports out of members' hands?"

Before N. O. can speak, Theo says, fuming, "I'm about *REAL TIRED* of you and all your interference! I'm about to knock you out if you open your mouth one more time. Ya feel me?"

N. O. finally says, "This is getting out of hand! The meeting is over. We will reschedule for sometime next month. I will have an independent auditor come in and look at our finances and make a report to the entire congregation. Good night everyone."

"Oh no, it's not over," Deacon Fellowes says as he lunges across the dais at N. O. like a bull charging a matador full of rage.

Tommy, who is triple dipping, getting paid by Theo, Deacon Isa Crooke, and N. O., jumps on the stage to separate Deacon Fellowes from N. O. But Theo has already drawn his pistol. He has completely lost it. He looks like he is crazed and intent on taking out anybody and everybody! He pulls his pistol and aims it at Deacon Fellowes.

Deacon Haran, standing at the left end of the dais, sees Theo's drawn pistol and rushes toward Theo in an attempt to grab him before he shoots Deacon Fellowes or someone else.

One of Tommy's guys, seeing that Tommy is in Theo's line of fire, and not realizing that they are working for the Big Three: Theo, N. O., and Deacon Isa Crooke, pulls his 9mm and aims it at Theo, who pulls the trigger just as he is grabbed by Deacon Haran. The first shot is misguided and hits the ceiling of the Fellowship Hall. Theo and Deacon Haran wrestle over the pistol that gets lodged between them pointing toward the floor.

Blam!" the 9mm blasts as Theo and Deacon Haran look at each other nose to nose. Deacon Haran's lips quiver. His brow wrinkles. His eyes bulge, and his knees buckle. He then slowly loosens his grip on Theo and slumps to the floor with a bullet wound in his abdomen. The bullet also passes through him, striking Tommy in the back of his right calf. Ed, one of Tommy's guys, seeing that Tommy is hit and bleeding, fires a shot and hits Theo in his chest just above his heart. Staggering, Theo tries to **shoot** N.O., thinking he is the cause of his downfall.

"If I ain't gonna make it, neither are you," Theo struggles to say, walking like the Frankenstein monster dragging his left leg as he takes a couple of steps forward pointing his 9mm at N. O.

Theo fires another round, but his shot misses its mark and hits Ms. Jenkins in the fleshy part of her right shoulder just above her collar bone.

"Big Momma! Big Momma!" Chastity shrieks as she leans over her grandmother who is writhing in pain on the floor.

"Somebody help us. My grandmother has been shot," Chastity shouts over and over with tears streaming down her face.

There is complete pandemonium in the Fellowship Hall. People are scrambling over each other like ants on an ant hill trying to get out of the Fellowship Hall and avoid being shot. Total chaos! People are screaming and hollering as they run out of the church with no regard for age or gender as they push one another aside heading for the nearest exit. Many people grab their cell phones and call the police. Others call their loved ones, and some call the local TV stations Tip Line, thinking about their opportunity to cash in and get their fifteen minutes of fame.

Deacon Fellowes lunges again at N. O., who picks up Theo's gun and attempts to shoot him. In the desperate struggle for control of the pistol, a random shot is fired striking Deacon Isa Crooke in the buttocks.

Blam! Blam! Two more shots are fired while N. O. and Deacon Fellowes struggle for the gun. They both look at each other wrestling over the gun. There is a look of abject horror on both their faces. Then suddenly, Deacon Fellowes slowly loosens his grip on N. O. and falls abruptly to the floor. He lays in a fetal position seriously wounded. Blood is cascading from his left shoulder. He is unconscious. N. O. stands over him with the smoking pistol in his hand and shouts,

"My God, what have I done?"

He drops the 9mm to the floor. It discharges, and a bullet strikes Bob, another one of Tommy's guys dead center in his back.

Like a scene from a cop and robbers movie, the SWAT team arrives in full SWAT regalia. They shout orders for everyone to lie on their stomachs on the floor. They check Tommy's guy, Bob, who was accidentally shot when N. O. dropped Theo's gun and it discharged. They determine he is still alive and call for an ambulance. The officers check everyone on the dais, then the rest of the people in the Fellowship Hall. Theo dead! Deacon Haran dead! Deacon Crooke slightly wounded and unable to sit down to be treated! Deacon Fellowes seriously wounded! Tommy slightly wounded! N. O. not wounded but covered with blood, the blood of Deacon Fellowes! An officer checks Ms. Jenkins and determines she is slightly wounded. He motions toward the triple double doors of the Fellowship Hall and gives the all clear sign so the paramedics may enter. The chaos that existed during the shooting is replaced with the order of the EMS personnel who have set up a triage to determine the priority of who should be treated first. Some people are still hysterically crying and screaming in shock. Some are lying on their stomachs complaining about the bruises from almost being trampled to death. Still others are lying in pools of their own urine, traumatized from the turn of events at what was thought to be a civil New Harvest Quarterly Business Meeting.

The EMS workers are shortly joined by the Crime Scene Investigation unit personnel who have already taped off the front of the church and all the exits doors. They are taking photographs and searching for shell casings. They are trying to distinguish the blood splatters of those who were shot, or splattered or injured from the force of the fall.

The coroner's staff also arrives and goes about their analysis of the crime scene. They perform their preliminary duties to determine the cause of death. One morgue attendant brings in a bunch of body bags, not knowing how many will be required. The lights from the camera flash bulbs are ever present in the Fellowship Hall. Outside, both the police and the press are frantically trying to interview witnesses who were in the Fellowship Hall during the shooting.

"Stay behind the yellow tape!" one police officer shouts.

"Ma'am! Sir! Can I ask you just what happened in there?" say members of the press who are trying desperately to get to some of the New Harvest members, to speak to them on camera.

It's a scene reminiscent of a recent shooting where a deranged man went off and shot thirteen of his co-workers to death in a glass factory. People in the neighborhood have arrived enmass and stand behind the yellow tape with morbid curiosity hoping to see a dead body come out on a gurney. The reason for their wait will shortly be fulfilled.

N. O. sits on the stage floor trying as best he can to tell the police officers surrounding him his version of the events at New Harvest's Quarterly Business meeting. For the first time in many years, he is unable to properly arrange his words. He is totally inarticulate. His pulpit eloquence is like a faint memory. He talks like a blithering idiot as he attempts to respond to the questions directed at him from the police officers.

Those men who were not able to get out of the church before the police arrived were searched for weapons, and when it was discovered they did not have any, they were taken outside and interviewed by the police in a portable precinct station in a semi. All of Tommy's guys had weapons, so they were handcuffed and detained. It was a pure mess at New Harvest. It was unimaginable, a shooting in the House of God!

Back At Ms. Jenkins's House

"Wow, Ms. Jenkins, so that is how you were wounded?" Reggie asks, startled by the events of that fateful night at New Harvest.

"Were you scared?"

"Reggie, please! You done seent the neighborhood I live in. Ain't nothing gonna make me scared after living here for over thirty years. There's two places I don't get scared and you can't run me outta, my church and my neighborhood!" Ms. Jenkins says in pain.

"Are you okay Ms. Jenkins?" Reggie asks with the concern of a grandson who is crazy about Big Momma.

"Yeah Baby, I'm okay. Just a little pain from my close friend, Arthur!"

"Arthur?" Reggie asks, puzzled.

"Yes, Arthur Rithus!" Ms. Jenkins responds, smiling through her obvious pain.

"Well I am going to get out of here, Ms. Jenkins. I am going to take all my notes and the recordings and start writing the book. Since I have already started working on the book, it should only take me two or three weeks to get my first draft ready for your review, I mean Chastity's and your review. This has been a great experience for me, and I promise that whatever I get from this book, I am going to generously share with you."

"Now Reggie, I done told you I ain't worried bout you taking care of me. Just see to it that my grandbaby gets whatever is coming to me. You promised, member?"

"Yes ma'am, and I will keep my word. But Ms. Jenkins, you sound like you do not plan to be around much longer, and you need to stop thinking like that!"

"Baby, I lived my life and ain't got no regrets. I also knows tomorrow ain't promised to nobody. My grandbaby is gonna need some help in this thing called life. That's why I want you to take care of her, and I knows y'all likes each other. Y'all need to stop fussing and cussing and just get married!" Ms. Jenkins says, bursting into uproarious laughter.

"I will give it some thought!" Reggie jokingly says, smiling and planting a tender kiss on Ms. Jenkins's forehead.

"Goodnight, Ms. Jenkins. I will call you in a couple of weeks and stop by and start reading the story back to you. Okay?"

"Okay, Baby!"

Reggie leaves, and on his way home he reflects on how blessed he has been to have spent time with Ms. Jenkins. He never had that kind of relationship with his grandmother and now realizes just how important and wonderful the experience is to have a "Big Momma" in your life!

3:34AM TWO DAYS LATER

Ring! Ring! Ring!
Reggie struggles to find his cordless telephone and almost knocks it out of its cradle. He rubs his eyes and asks himself, "Who could be calling me at this time of night? Must be someone at the station!" he says to himself.

"Hello," he says in a slightly hoarse and gruff voice.

"Hello Reggie. This is Chastity! Big Momma is in the hospital. They say she don't have much time left and she wants to see you," Chastity says rapid-fire and tearfully over the telephone.

"What?" Reggie says, abruptly sitting up, rubbing his eyes.

"Chastity, are you saying she's about to die?" Reggie asks, his eyes tearing from the thought he is about to lose a very dear friend.

"Yes, Reggie. They says she had a severe heart attack and she is so weak from it and her other health problems that she probably won't be around much longer!"

"Chastity, are you at the hospital?"

"Yes!"

"I am on my way."

Reggie dresses without taking a shower or washing up. He has got to make it to the hospital before his beloved Ms. Jenkins expires. It's early in the morning, so he virtually runs every red light from his house to the hospital. He pulls up to valet parking and almost leaves his car in gear while he tosses his keys to the valet attendant.

Sir, you'll need a ticket to retrieve your car," the valet attendant says, tearing a ticket stub in half and rushing to the hospital's revolving door to give Reggie his part of the stub.

Reggie stops at the reception desk and asks for Ms. Jenkins's room number. He is asked if he is a relative. He lies and says confidently and sincerely, "Yes, I am her grandson."

"She's in room N404."

Reggie rushes from the reception desk to the elevators.

"Come on! Come on! Why is it taking so long for an elevator to come? Damn, these elevators are slow!" Reggie says, pacing back and forth.

Finally, an elevator arrives, and Reggie impolitely rushes in without any regard to the hospital employees who are exiting the elevator.

"Slow down, brother," a youthful looking male orderly about to go on break says as Reggie brushes past him almost knocking him off balance.

When the elevator door opens on the North Wing, he checks the directional signage to see which direction room N404 is located. He walks briskly to Ms. Jenkins's room. He slows his pace, and as he enters the room he sees Chastity and a forty-something couple standing around her bed. Chastity is holding her grandmother's hand. The other two people stand silently, weeping and praying.

Ms. Jenkins's eyes are closed, but somehow she must have felt Reggie's presence because as he approaches her bed she opens her eyes.

"I knew you'd come, Baby," Ms. Jenkins says as she motions for him to come closer.

Trying to make both himself and Ms. Jenkins feel better, Reggie jokingly says, "Come on now, Ms. Jenkins, what are you doing here? You know you promised to cook me a thousand more of those wonderful meals. Look at me, I gained ten pounds since I have known you. Come on now, get up and put your clothes on so I can take you home."

Chastity looks at Reggie lovingly and smiles in appreciation.

"Not this time, Baby! I'm going to meet the Lord, and I'm not afraid! I'm at peace and I know I am leaving my great grandbaby in good hands."

Chastity suddenly falls to her knees and with both hands resting on her grandmothers arm begins to cry. She is inconsolable!

"Big Momma, you can't go! **PLEASE!** You can't leave me! Big Momma, please don't leave me, I need you."

The couple rushes over to console Chastity. They make a feeble attempt to lift her off her knees. She is dead weight and distraught.

"Now now, Baby, you've got to stop that crying. I'm okay, and I'm going to a better place. You just gotta let Big Momma go."

Reggie moves in closer to Ms. Jenkins. He helps the couple lift Chastity up off her knees, and they place her in the big visitor's chair next to Ms. Jenkins's bed. Chastity continues to be inconsolable. Ms. Jenkins motions for Reggie to come closer. He leans closer to her so she can whisper in his ear, and she says, "Don't forget your promise. You'll take care of my grandbaby for me, right?"

"Yes ma'am," Reggie says tearfully.

Ms. Jenkins smiles and looks at everyone around her bed. She looks over at Chastity with an expression of pride. She looks at Reggie with a smile that says she will miss him. She looks at the couple and winks at them. She looks toward the door as if someone were standing there. Reggie turns to see who she was looking at, but there is no one there. She then says, "I'm ready!"

She takes one last long glance at Chastity then Reggie.

"Aaaaaaaahhhhhhhh" is the sound she makes as all the air in her lungs is expelled. She then smiles with the most peaceful look on her face. Her eyes blink rapidly for a few seconds, then close as if she were drifting off peacefully to sleep. The audible alarm on the Life-line monitor goes off and the indicators all flat line. The nursing staff immediately appear in the room, pushing everyone aside to get to Ms. Jenkins. They try feverishly to resuscitate her, to no avail.

"I'm terribly sorry, she's gone. She was the sweetest little lady," the nurse says as she pulls the sheet over Ms. Jenkins's face.

Reggie grabs Chastity who has jumped out of the chair and is fighting to hold her great grandmother. He holds her tenderly in his arms, her head buried in his chest. While he restrains her, he tearfully whispers over and over, "It's going to be okay! It is going to be okay!" He kisses her on her forehead over and over again.

1:20PM The Next Saturday

Ms. Jenkins Going Home Service was held with the Family Hour at 10:30AM and the Going Home Services starting at precisely 11:00AM. New Harvest's sanctuary was packed. It was standing room only. The floral arrangements were so plentiful that an outside observer would have thought that a dignitary was being laid to rest. Reggie had arranged for her remains to be driven to the cemetery in a horse drawn hearse. She had always wanted that because she remembered seeing such a scene in an old movie. She had often stated, "When my time comes, I want to go to the cemetery in one of them horse drawn hearses like the character, Delilah Johnson, played by Louise Beavers in the movie, *Imitation of Life*." Reggie saw to it that she got her wish.

At the repast, Chastity is still taking the loss of her grandmother very hard. She had invited Reggie to ride in the family limousine with her and the couple from the hospital. Reggie then learned that they were Ms. Jenkins's nephew from San Antonio and his wife. The members of New Harvest over-extended themselves expressing their sympathy to Chastity. She made an attempt to respond in a gracious manner, but she was still in the throes of tremendous grief. When the repast was over, the funeral director had the limousine driver take Chastity back to Ms. Jenkins's house. Since Reggie was invited to ride in the limo, he left his car at Ms. Jenkins's house. When Chastity and Reggie entered the limousine, Chastity waved at all the people who were standing in front of the church. As soon as the limo was out of sight, Chastity collapsed. Her head landed in Reggie's lap. She was totally exhausted, so Reggie maneuvered her body so she would lie in his arms. She lay there asleep until they reached Ms. Jenkins's house.

"Chastity, Chastity, wake up, we're here. We are home," Reggie says. As she slowly sits up, he casts a lustful look at her well-proportioned legs because the skirt of her suit has moved up well above her knees. Her black textured stockings only enhance the view. When she gets out of the limo he takes another look at her frame. He says to himself, Whew! This girl is built."

Chastity looks through her purse to find her keys. Locating them, she turns to Reggie and kisses him on the cheek.

"Thanks, Reggie, for all you've done. Big Momma really loved you. She loved you like a son."

"Thanks. Do you want me to come in and sit with you for a while?" Reggie asks, hoping she will say yes, his desire to make love to her just barely suppressed.

"No, I'm really tired. I got a lot to do tomorrow about taking over the house."

"Chastity, I have already taken care of that for you. Your grandmother had executed a quit claim deed giving the house to you. She also had set aside some money in an account to pay the taxes on the house for the next twenty years or more. So you are good!"

"Thanks Reggie, Big Momma told me you would look after me. I appreciate it."

"Are you sure you do not want me to come in for a little while?"

Reggie asks again, this time with more pronounced begging in his voice.

"Yes Reggie, I'm sure," she says, this time kissing him softly on his lips.

"If you come in, then we might do something I'll regret. I promised Big Momma I would save myself for my husband, and I know you don't want marriage from me, to be your wife I mean! So I guess this is goodnight. I hope you'll call me sometime, though. I still have strong feelings for you, and I'd like to stay in touch."

With a serious tone of dejection in his voice, Reggie responds by saying, "I understand! And I "will" keep in touch. I promised your grandmother I would always look after you, and that is what I plan to do!" Reggie says as he tenderly pulls her close to him with both hands and kisses her passionately.

Stunned, Chastity says, "Wow, Reggie, I know I'd better say goodnight before I change my mind about the promise I made to Big Momma! Goodnight."

"Good night, Chastity," Reggie says, watching her open the door to what is now her house.

Back to the Present Day

A month earlier N. O. had recovered sufficiently from his heart attack that he was taken to the federal maximum security prison. He was processed and spent the first fourteen days in solitary confinement. He reflected on his sudden fall from grace but was content with the fact that he would serve his time and one day be released to restore himself with the community. He was given two, twenty-five years to life sentences, to run concurrently. He was counting on getting out early for good behavior. He had at the very least a promising future because his son Jabez and daughter Delilah had started a church that attracted a growing number of young people their age. N. O. dreamed about being released from prison then joining his children in their ministry. After all, if they had not been tainted by the scandal of his ministry, maybe people would forgive and restore him after he was released from prison.

He thought about getting a divorce from Marie Antoinette but decided to let her make the first move in that vein. He daydreamed constantly about the future. But today he is being released into the prison's general population. Coming to prison was the most frightening event in his life because he thought he was going to a country club prison, based upon the plea deal his attorney made on his behalf. However, the judge rejected that part of the plea deal, and now, here he sits among some of the most hardened criminals in the state. With his obvious fear showing, he walks slowly across the prison yard. He is always looking around and over his shoulder in the recreational area of the prison, the area known as the yard. It is obvious to the other inmates that he is new because he is carrying the unmistakable expression of fear and discomfort on his face. Suddenly, he hears a familiar voice.

"Reverend Goode, right?" the too tall, and hefty prison guard asks.

N. O. recognizes the guard as one of two brothers who had finished his basement.

"Hey, it's Michael Stevens, right?" N. O. says, extending his right hand to shake Michael's. N. O. has a feeling, a sense of relief, albeit temporary.

"Yeah, that's right. I'm one of the Stevens brothers. We did work on your basement, oh, about six years ago."

"Well, am I glad to see you! How long have you been working as a prison guard?" N. O. asks, still tentative about being on the yard.

"Oh, about six years. Why?" Michael responds, tersely.

"Oh, I was just wondering how experienced you were at this institution and if you had any tips for me to stay safe in here," N. O. says nervously.

"Tips, yeah I got two for you. One, snitches get stitches! And two, don't bend over for the soap!"

"But aren't you and the other guards supposed to look after people like me to see that we do not come to any harm? You know I am not supposed to be placed in a maximum security prison! I was supposed to be incarcerated in a minimum security prison as part of a plea deal," N. O. says, choking up from his nervousness.

"Well, you gotta take your chances like everybody else because you won't make many friends in here."

"But can't we make a deal so you can protect me and let the other guards know to protect me? I am willing to pay you and whomever!"

"Reverend, you must have me confused with someone who has a faulty memory. One of the reasons I had to take this job is because people like you wouldn't pay me and my brother after we did work for you. We made the mistake of trusting you because you were a so-called-man-of-God. But we had to learn the hard way that even preachers can sometimes be crooked."

"But I promise I will pay you if,..."

"Not interested dude! You burnt me once after my brother and I got your basement straight. You refused to pay us and then told us if we wanted to get our money we'd have to sue you. And when my brother's wife was diagnosed with breast cancer and he asked you to pray for them, all you did was try to sell them on some pyramid scheme selling some Caribbean health drink!

So, naw, you're on your own in here, and *GOOD LUCK,*" Michael Stevens says sarcastically as he abruptly walks away.

N. O. looks around, scans the yard, and sees other prisoners in groups based upon race. There is a heavily tattooed white supremacist group in one area of the yard, what appears to be the African Americans militants in another, and the Latinos in yet another. These groups all look at N. O. menacingly.

Finally, he sees the men who are all dressed in tight shirts tied in a knot, exposing their navel to resemble a bra. They are all also wearing extremely tight jeans and lipstick. Their mannerisms suggest an exaggerated, overstated degree of femininity. N. O. turns to get back into the main area of the prison yard when he hears one of the men from the latter group yell, "*HHHHEEEEYYVY! HHHHEEEEYVYY,* Handsome! Us girls just drew strays, and I won YOU!"

He was a tall slender and extremely feminine acting man who was sitting in the midst of this particular group. He sits poised like a woman in a tight mini-skirt in his too tight jeans.

"Oh GGGOOODDD!" N. O. says.

"Hold up, Honey, we need to talk. Don't you recognize me? I am Brother Newt Swisher! I used to be the Director of the Pastor's Choir at New Harvest years ago."

"No," N. O. shouts, looking around fearfully to see what the other prisoners must be thinking.

"Oh, you remember me! I was the best choir director New Harvest ever had, but you and that no-music-training Minister of Music, Sister Beverly Jeruson, conspired to fire me because you said that you'd never have a choir director switching around in *YOUR* choir stand." The man continues by saying, "I was one of the highest paid choir directors in the city, but because of you, I lost everything. EVERYTHING! So I sold a little drugs to make ends meet, and here I am! But LOOKA HERE! LOOKA HERE! Now you're in here with me and my girls, and we run things in this corner of the yard. So I guess the tables have sho nuff turned on you, huh, Handsome?" The man continues in a shrill, high-pitched voice dripping with anger.

N. O.'s body quivers and he quickens his pace so much to where he is almost running. He is attempting to get back into the main facility and off the yard. He looks over his shoulder, and sure enough, his new friend is right behind him. Newt has his right hand gently laid across his chest like an ultra feminine Southern Belle suffering from the intense August heat. His gait is laced with switching.

"HHHHEEEEYYYY!" Newt shouts again and again as he walks just as fast to catch up to N.O.

"Hold up!" Newt screams to the obvious delight of most of the men on the yard, no matter their affiliation.

"Oh God, please help me," N.O screams loudly, still walking at a very fast pace.

The seasoned prisoners who witness this event all laugh uproariously, and they are joined by guard Michael Stevens. Among all the observers of N.O.'s hasty retreat, he seems to be the most pleased.

The Lounge in the King Roderick Hotel. 6:02PM Tuesday Six Months Later

Marie Antoinette has gone on with her life. She sits in this small, quaint, blue collar lounge, which has minimal business, on a Tuesday night. Even if there were a major convention in town, this would be the last place any travel coordinator would recommend to out-of-towners! It is in a part of town Marie Antoinette rarely frequents. She sits at the bar waiting on Salome, who has returned home permanently from California. Marie Antoinette refuses to divorce N. O., but they do not communicate much with each other. For visits, N. O. relies totally on his children, Jabez and Delilah because Salome has yet to forgive him. Their visits are becoming less frequent because they observe an unusual change in their father's demeanor. He is no longer the powerful, forceful, and strong man they grew up knowing as their father. Marie Antoinette is waiting on Salome, who has come home, had an abortion, and been cleared of any semblance of HIV/AIDS.

"May I help you, Miss?" the tall, slender bearded bartender asks.

"Well, I was waiting on someone, but I guess I will have a glass of your best Moscato."

"Okay, Miss. Coming right up."

"May I run a tab?" Marie Antoinette asks as she goes into her purse and pulls out a fifty dollar bill.

"Sure!" the bartender quickly responds, thinking he will get a big tip.

She again reaches into her purse and pulls out a platinum cigar case that holds four cigars but only has three inside. She then finds her platinum cigarette lighter and lights the cigar.

"Oh, I'm sorry Miss, but this is a smoke free establishment. You'll have to put that cigar out."

Marie Antoinette looks around and notices that most of the few patrons are in their own worlds off in the corners of the lounge, so she turns around facing the bartender and says, "Are you sure this is a smoke free establishment?" as she slides a fifty dollar bill across the bar's counter to the bartender.

"Well, I guess as long as you finish it before my manager comes in or a customer complains, I guess you're good. Hey are those Cuban? How'd you get them?"

"I have a connection, and there is an old saying, 'them that knows don't tell,'"

Marie Antoinette says, smiling.

Laughing, the bartender shrugs his shoulder and returns to placing wine glasses in the overhead glass rack.

"Oh, I forgot; you ordered a glass of Moscato," he says, reaching into the beer and wine cooler behind him and retrieving a liter bottle of the bar's best Moscato. He then grabs one of the large water glasses from the tray of just washed glasses and fills it to the brim. The bartender is mindful of the generous fifty dollar tip.

"Thanks," Marie Antoinette says, lifting the unexpected portion of wine and leaning it slightly toward the bartender as if she were both saluting and thanking him.

Where is that girl? Salome is the most punctual of my children, Marie Antoinette thinks to herself.

While she waits for Salome, her mind begins to wander and she reminisces about the trials and tribulations of her family.

Back to the Year Salome enrolled in College in California

During Salome's first semester in college she frequently called home complaining to her mother about being homesick. She wanted to come home, but the Goodes had spent a lot of money enrolling her in this prestigious Art School because she had begged them relentlessly while a senior in High School. Marie Antoinette encouraged her to stick it out for at least the first full year. She also hatched a plan to ensure her that her baby girl was safe and content.

Marie Antoinette dials one of her best friends and fellow Delta Soros, Lisa Trenton, in California.

"Hello Lisa, this is Marie. How have you been?"

"Well! Very well," Lisa responds, surprised to hear from her old sorority sister.

"Girl, everything back here is going great. I know you saw N. O.'s national commercials about the church! You need to come home and see the house we bought. It is really nice, and we got plenty of room if you want to come and stay for a while!"

"Girl, I just might do that. I could use a break from this fast-paced city. We grew up in a big city, but it is nowhere as fast as life is out here in California."

"Lisa, I need a big favor."

"Sure girl. We are Soros, and you know you can count on me. What do you need?"

"Well, you know my baby girl, Salome, is going to school out there."

"Yes, she called me once, and I told her she was always welcome for dinner or to stay the weekend at my house if she wanted to," Lisa responds.

"Yes, I know, she told me, but you know she is fiercely independent and will not take help from anyone, so I was wondering," Marie Antoinette says.

"What do you need, Marie?"

"Well, if she thought I had someone watching her, she would reject the help, so I was thinking that we could figure a way for her to meet that nice and handsome nephew of yours, Dwayne, and,..."

"Oh, Marie, not a problem. But how would they meet without it seeming like we fixed them up?" Lisa asks.

"Well, I have an idea! I will send you her picture and address. Dwayne could frequent all the local hot spots for people their age in the vicinity of her apartment and the Art School out there until he ran into her. He could then use his considerable charm to get to know her acting, like he just wants to be a friend. He could make her feel real comfortable because she is a very friendly girl, too friendly sometimes to suit me. But I really think this plan will work. He must not let her know he is related to you, and who knows what could happen? We might be related through more than our sorority!"

"Sounds like a plan! And Marie, I never knew you were this devious," Lisa says jubilantly.

"Oh girl, no one ever gave me credit for having any street smarts. Everyone looked at me as this sheltered, prissy, little, sweet and innocent child, and that has always worked to my advantage. I know how to scheme when I need to. After all, I am married, and how do you get your husband to do your bidding without being a little devious?" Marie Antoinette says, laughing robustly over the telephone.

"Miss, are you ready for another Moscato?" the bartender asks, interrupting Marie Antoinette's reminiscing of her call of over a year ago with her Soro, Lisa.

Before she responds, Marie Antoinette looks at her watch and says, "Where is that girl? It's 6:26PM, and we agreed we would meet here at 6PM!"

Sighing, she says, "Yes, I guess I might as well have another one. And my name is Marie. What's your name?"

With the both of them smiling at each other, they politely shake hands.

Marie then starts to reminiscence again about her telephone call with Lisa.

"Lisa, I'll let you go. We'll talk later. I love you!" They both hang up.

At this moment Salome calls her.

"Hey Momma, I am so sorry that I have not called you sooner," Salome says, out of breath.

"Girl, why didn't you call me and tell me you were going to be late?"

Marie Antoinette says in an irritated tone.

"Momma, I met this publisher at the bookstore and we started talking about social issues. He was telling me how he had just come from California where one of his clients did research about teenage runaways who get trapped into pornography. I felt so comfortable with him that I mentioned I knew a little about the pornographic industry and would be willing to help him do research from the perspective of an adult in the adult entertainment industry."

"You did what?" Marie Antoinette asks, stunned by what she perceives to be her daughter's stupidity.

"Momma, I did not tell him I was in that business. I just told him I lived in the area where they did a lot of filming for pornos. Momma, he wants me to write a book about women being in the porno industry since I seemed to know a lot about California and the adult entertainment industry!"

"So you met a publisher and he wants you to write a book about how those filthy moves are made? Girl, are you crazy? Haven't you learned from your past experiences? Why would you even talk to someone here in your own home town about that filth?"

Their conversation is interrupted as the bartender approaches and says, "Okay Marie, my name is Devaughn. Pleased to meet you."

He pours her another hefty glass of Moscato and walks away.

"Look Salome, just get here so we can talk about this, okay?"

"Okay Momma. Bye!"

Returning to her drink, Marie begins to reminisce again.

I never thought my good intentions would end up with my baby being taken advantage of by Dwayne. Neither Lisa nor I knew he was a sleazy player, one involved in prostitution, gambling and drugs. Thank you Jesus, my baby had the strength to resist his attempts to get her strung out on that dope. But she did let him get her into making those dirty movies. He was slick, real slick! First, he had her posing nude for some low scale magazines. Then he had her dancing in a strip club, and that was followed by pornographic movies.

RING! RING! RING!

Marie Antoinette's thoughts are interrupted once again. She looks at her cellphone's caller-id and sees Salome's number.

"Momma, please hear me out! He wants me to write a book where I place myself in the lifestyle of a porno star. I told him I had neighbors who were in those movies and we talked frequently about their lives. That is what sold this publisher on me, and of course, I would use a pseudonym."

"But Salome, remember how you were led into that business in the first place. You met some nice guy, what was his name again, oh yes, Dwayne, and he set you up for failure. Baby, think about what you have to lose if you go through with this book deal! This publisher who says he has good intentions could have the same intentions as Dwayne."

"But Momma, he is a wonderful and understanding man, a man who is in the church,..."

"In the church? What would a man in the church be doing promoting a book about pornography?" Marie Antoinette asks, shaking her head and wondering if her daughter has lost her mind."

"Momma, he is the publisher of many books dealing with the ills of this society, like teenage pregnancy, drugs and prostitution, the unemployment and underemployment of minorities. He wants me to write the book not to promote pornography but to show its evil impact on young vulnerable women like me."

There is dead silence on Marie Antoinette's end of the telephone.

"Okay Baby, but I want to meet this man before you sign any contracts. I want to have him checked out to ensure he is who and what he says he is!"

"Oh thank you, Momma! Thank you! I really want to do this. I feel I can help some other innocent and naive young women who might fall under the sway of a smooth talking PIMP! I believe that my ministry at Jabez and Delilah's church will be to asset at-risk young women," Salome says, happy that her mother has been convinced that she has matured and is on the right track.

"Girl, hurry up and get here so we can talk and have dinner! I've had two drinks already," Marie Antoinette says.

"Okay, Momma. I am on my way."

I never thought that things would work out like this, Marie Antoinette thinks to herself as he continues to reminisce.

While my primary plan backfired because Salome got into the pornography business because of my setting her up with Dwayne, everything still worked out for the best. My baby is home! I would have never in a million years thought that Dwayne was such a gangster. However, God worked everything out on my behalf, and he is now serving a lengthy sentence in federal prison for drug possession, forgery, operating a pornography ring, and tax evasion. I guess he was not as smart as he thought he was! My baby's home now and that is all that matters. I pray that the Lord will forgive me for my deceitful methods, but I had to get her to come home.

When Salome received the letter from the California Department of health, little did she know it was a fake! I had orchestrated that whole situation. I must admit is was a big gamble because when she received the phony letter saying she had HIV/AIDS, she could have become so distraught that she could have committed suicide. But I know my children, and Salome is the strongest-willed of them all. I just pray she never discovers that I was responsible for Dwayne entering her life or that I was responsible for the letter from the California Department of Health saying she was HIV/AIDS positive. Now that was a feat in itself. I had this teenage computer geek create the fake letterhead for me from the Health Department's website, thinking that I was going to use it as part of a practical joke. The letter head was so authentic looking I had no doubt that Salome would see it as the real thing. I then expressed the letter in a sealed envelope to Lisa, who mailed it for me so it would have a California bulk mail postage stamp on it. She had no idea what the contents of the letter were and she never was a nosey sister, so I was not worried about her opening it and checking the contents. I tried to think of everything. I knew that when Salome received the letter she would call me and not tell her father because she has never forgiven him for hitting me and his unfaithfulness. I also knew that because we are so close I could convince Salome to come home for treatment. But when she came home, a miracle happened! No HIV/AIDS. She then thought she had been misdiagnosed in California! So I was covered on that aspect of my plan. I just hope that as time passes she will get her mind right and join her sister and brother in their ministry. Lord, please forgive me for going to such extremes to get my baby to come home.

     She seems happy now and has come to grips with her past. I also pray that she never finds out that while on a trip to California to visit her and Lisa, I was approached by Dwayne about the DVD's she was in. He had just completed compiling and editing the DVD's from tapes, so I knew what he had and they had not been distributed. I learned this from being a member of the Communications Ministry at New Harvest who made the copies of N. O.'s sermons each week. I knew how the process worked. That fool only wanted five thousand dollars for the originals. The deal I made was that he would give me all the tapes used to make the DVD's and the DVD masters. I had a friend in the movie industry, who did not know Salome was my daughter, validate I had the original copies, just in case. Satisfied that I had everything, I told Dwayne that the only way I could pay his blackmail money was for me to send the DVD's to my house so my husband would pay the blackmail. At first he was resistant and distrustful, but when I told him he could accompany me to the post office and watch me package and mail the DVD's to my house, he was okay with my offer. He did, however, ask to see my driver's license, to make sure they were mailed to my house. He obviously thought that by sending the DVD's to my house, and given who I was married to, he was in a win - win situation. While on my way to the bathroom in his make-shift studio, I noticed he had a glass top coffee table in an area that was set up like a living room. I noticed a baggie with white powder in it on the sofa behind the coffee table. I assumed it was cocaine!

     "Marie, how are you doing on your drink? Do you want me to top it off for you?" Devaughn asks, causing Marie Antoinette to stop reflecting on what she had done to get her daughter to come home.

     "No Thanks. My daughter should be here in a few minutes,"
     "Is she as beautiful as you?"
     "More so," Marie Antoinette says proudly.
     She begins to reminisce again.

Well I had no intention of paying him, so I bought a disposable cell phone out there and called both the DEA and FBI and led them to believe I was a teenage girl and he was my pimp and that not only was he dealing drugs but he was also using under-aged girls and boys in his dirty movies. If either federal agency traced my call, I would simply tell them, I had bought the disposable phone for Salome but lost it before giving it to her. I had no idea that in all actuality Dwayne was deeply involved in the drug, pimping and child pornography scene. I thought they would just raid his place and find the drugs, but he got a lengthy sentence when they found the drugs and the pornographic movies with the children in them. He was trapped! He could not tell them about our deal because he would only be adding another crime (blackmail) to his other criminal activities. Anyway, I do not think he ever figured out it was I who called the authorities. And even if he did, he will be incarcerated so long he would be too old to even think about retaliating against me."

Inhaling too deeply on her Cuban cigar, Marie Antoinette starts coughing incessantly.

Devaughn gives her a glass of water.

"Thank you," she says, still choking and lightly pounding her chest.

Poor N. O.! What an idiot he was to think that his little, innocent, passive wife did not know about his infidelities and his scheming with Theo to steal from the church. He never suspected that I knew about all his affairs with the sluts at New Harvest who would sleep with him just because of his being the Pastor. They were like the misguided women that follow athletes around the country and sleep with them for a few dollars. The sad commentary is that some of them do not realize they are nothing more than prostitutes. N. O. used them, and they used him. He wound up getting tricked by his own flesh and blood. Theo was stealing large amounts of money from New Harvest and only giving N. O. a small percentage. What a fool my husband was! I bet if Theo were alive right now, he would be upset if he knew that I was the one behind taking his and N. O.'s money at the homeless shelter.

RING! RING!

"Momma I will be there in ten minutes. Okay?" Salome says excitedly while she still talks to the publisher at a coffee house.

"Okay, Baby," her mother responds.

Where was I? Marie Antoinette asks herself as she remembers how she dealt both N. O. and Theo a serious financial blow!

Oh yes, when I found out that Theo and N. O. were stealing church funds, I approached Deacons Haran and Fellowes and told them my plan. I told them that N. O. was being blackmailed because he had a record for statutory rape and his record was expunged. Somehow someone got a copy of his old criminal records and was about to expose him. I told them I planned to divorce him and that if they would help me, I would be willing to go for a fifty-fifty split with their half going back into the church's treasury. Being honorable men, they took the deal. I drove the car. Deacon Haran posed as the old homeless man, and Deacon Fellowes drove the car that blocked Theo's car in. It was truly a work of art. I am so pleased with myself that I could scream. When I think about that money, most of it Theo's, plus the money N. O. had in his safe, plus the twenty-five thousand I got from Dr. Clark Hudson, I should have been a criminal mastermind! But I thank God that he just let me fly under the radar, and other than Deacons Haran and Fellowes, no one has any idea that any of this happened or that I was behind it ALL!

At that moment Salome comes through the door. "Momma, I finally made it. Thanks for waiting. I have so much to tell you about my meeting with the publisher."

Salome and her mother greet each other warmly, and Devaughn checks out Salome from head to toe.

Marie was right, she is a beautiful woman, he says to himself.

"Momma, what has come over you? Is this my mother drinking wine and smoking cigars outside our house? What happened to the lady I knew who was so protective of her public image?" Salome asks teasingly.

The big screen TV over the bar is on. Marie Antoinette and Devaughn had been halfway paying attention to a local reality talent show on Channel Eight. Suddenly, there is a "Breaking News" flash on the TV screen.

"Hello, this is Juanita Sanchez for Channel Eight news. This has been a big news day in our city. Dr. Clark Hudson, noted local physician, was arrested at his home this evening as a result of a year long police investigation into his trafficking human organs. It is alleged that Dr. Hudson assisted in the death of at least twelve people who were not in jeopardy of expiring, to supply wealthy clients who needed specific organs. He has denied all charges."

News 8 reporter, Juanita Sanchez continues by saying "In other breaking news, prominent local attorney, Imma Shyster, was arrested earlier today at the state penitentiary in New Raleigh. She is being accused of trying to secret two small caliber polymer, a form of plastic, Glock pistols and plastic ammunition into the prison. Her obvious intent was to give these weapons to her client and alleged boyfriend, Tommy Bryant. Prison officials report that she brought the dissembled pistols into their facility thinking they would avoid detection by the metal detector. This appears to be a well-orchestrated plan because using the guise of attorney client privilege, she was to meet Mr. Bryant in the prison's conference room used by the DA's, prisoners, and the prisoner's attorneys. A corrections officer alleged to be part of this elaborate scheme was questioned, and he denied involvement. It is believed that once Ms. Shyster was alone with Mr. Bryant, he would reassemble the weapons and the two would make a John Dillinger-like prison break, taking the corrections officer alleged to be an accomplice hostage. This corrections officer's usual post, coincidentally, was right outside the conference room in question. Warden Sylvester Trent said that he was not at liberty at this time to share with me what evidence they have, but a reliable source did say that they found a large amount of cash, forged passports, changes of clothes, and disguises in her car. Warden Trent did share with me Ms. Shyster obviously fell victim to the urban myth about undetectable plastic and porcelain firearms and explosive devices used to avoid metal detectors, as portrayed in the movies: *In the Line of Fire*, starring John Malkovich and *Die Hard 2: Die Harder*, starring Bruce Willis, and the recent attempts to smuggle plastic explosives on international flights. Mr. Bryant is a noted hit man who has been suspected for years of operating a murder-for-hire organization. He is serving ten to twenty-five years for his involvement in the recent shootout at New Harvest Missionary Baptist Church. This shootout led to the death of three people, including Theo Lane, the alleged master-mind of the embezzlement scheme at New Harvest. This shootout also led to the fall from grace and imprisonment of New Harvest's Pastor, Nathan Obadiah Goode. Reverend Goode was one of the most prominent mega church Pastors in this state. Warden Trent said the weapons might not have been detected had it not been for the corrections officer operating the metal detector being a former employee of the Bureau of Alcohol Tobacco and Firearms. This corrections officer, while an employee of ATF, was specially trained to detect these types of plastic weapons. The corrections officer alleged to be involved in this plot is being held on charges of criminal conspiracy to facilitate a prison break. It looks like Ms. Shyster will need some excellent legal counsel herself because my sources suggest she is facing twenty years or more in prison if found guilty of the gun and attempted prison break charges. How she could consider throwing her prominent career away for a man like Tommy Bryant is beyond me! I guess this plot suggests we can't believe everything we see in a movie!" This is Juanita Sanchez reporting live outside the state prison at New Raleigh, for Channel Eight News."

"Wow!" Salome says, thinking about the fact that her father was mentioned on the News.

"Yeah, wow!" Marie Antoinette says, realizing that only by the grace of God she wasn't featured on that same breaking news account.

"Thank you, Jesus!" Marie Antoinette says as she turns her attention to her daughter. She is at this moment the happiest she has been in many years.

- THE END -

Epilogue:
One year later, Salome released her book using a **pseudoym** about the fallacies of the pornographic industry. It was entitled: *From Preachers Kid to Porno Star: How the Pressure of Being Raised as a PK Ruined My Life*. Her book wound up being on the Best Sellers List.

Oh, by the way, two years later Reggie did complete his book: *The Rise And Fall of Pastor NO Goode,* and it was met with critical acclaim. He was promoted at Channel Eight to the early afternoon anchor desk. He also took a year long sabbatical for his book's promotional tour. He is married and has an eighteen month old son named Reggie Jr. His lovely wife is the noted local fashion designer, Chastity.

-The End For Real!-

About the Author

"Brother James" (a.k.a. Henry James) was born and reared in Louisville, Kentucky. He is the second eldest of eight children of the late Reverend Robert W. and Juanita Mae Alexander James. He was educated in the Louisville Public School System. He is an avid reader of history (African and African American, US , and World history), Religion, Political Science, Philosophy, Behavioral Science, and Psychology. He also enjoys various genres of music and has a massive book and music collection.

Credits
Cover Design Concept: Brother James
Cover Artwork and Illustration: Tim James
Cover Photography: Deborah Brown
Cover Design Layout: Maderia Long